Choose Your Weapon

The Duel in California, 1847–1861

Christopher Burchfield

Fresno, California

Choose Your Weapon
Copyright © 2016 by Christopher Burchfield. All rights reserved.

Published by Craven Street Books
An imprint of Linden Publishing
2006 South Mary Street, Fresno, California 93721
(559) 233-6633 / (800) 345-4447
CravenStreetBooks.com

Craven Street Books and Colophon are trademarks of
Linden Publishing, Inc.

ISBN 978-1-61035-277-2

135798642

Printed in the United States of America
on acid-free paper.

Library of Congress Cataloging-in-Publication Data

Names: Burchfield, Christopher, author.
Title: Choose your weapon : the duel in California, 1847-1861 / Christopher
  Burchfield.
Other titles: Duel in California, 1847-1861
Description: Fresno, California : Craven Street Books, [2016] | Includes
  bibliographical references and index.
Identifiers: LCCN 2016036447 | ISBN 9781610352772 (pbk. : alk. paper)
Subjects: LCSH: Dueling–California–History–19th century. |
  California–Social life and customs–19th century. | California–Politics
  and government–1846-1850 | California–Politics and govern-
ment–1850-1950
  | Politicians–California–Biography. | Newspaper
  editors–California–Biography.
Classification: LCC CR4595.C2 B87 2016 | DDC 394/.809794–dc23
LC record available at https://lccn.loc.gov/2016036447

For Genedal, to whom I owe very much

Contents

Men blown from every border land
Men desperate and red of hand
Of men in love and men in debt
Of men who lived but to forget
And men whose very hearts had died
Who only sought these wilds to hide
Their wretchedness

—Outaw, judge, poet, star member of the dueling fraternity,
Ned McGowan, 1879

Acknowledgments

I would like to thank very much my wife, Genendal Lea Burchfield, for her support over the many years of this endeavor. I would also like to thank Sylvia Ann Sheafer of Glendale, Al and Marne Wilkins of Weaverville, and Margaret Bauer of Los Molinos, for their encouragement in undertaking the research and writing of this history of early California. Special thanks also for the technical help provided by Christopher Harper of Chico, Larry Jackson of Heidelberg Graphics of Chico, and Ada Golden of Forbestown.

Also, many sincere thanks to Sybil Zemitis and John R. Gonzales of the California Section of the California State Library in Sacramento, Annie R. Mitchell of the Tulare County Historical Society, Lorrayne Kennedy of the Calaveras County Archives, John Bettencourt of the Sacramento County Historical Society, Betsy Cammack of Sierra City, Michael and Jean Sherrell of The Californians: The Magazine of California History, Daryl Morrison of the University of the Pacific Library, Tod Ruhstaller of the Haggin Museum in Stockton, Robert J. Chandler of the Wells Fargo Bank History Department in San Francisco, Edwin L. Tyson of the Searls Historical Library in Nevada City, and the staffs at the Society of California Pioneers in San Francisco, the California Historical Society Library in San Francisco, the University of California at Berkeley, and the Huntington Library in San Marino for their help in researching this book.

Preface

Ifirst came across the subject of dueling in California while researching the state's newspapers for a book about its Gold Rush editors. Over the years this led my wife and me into many a county historical society museum and library. Prior to our work I had never considered California a Wild West state in the tradition of Texas, Oklahoma, or Arizona. Yet the following fact began to emerge from the journals we reviewed: even during those state's most turbulent times, they never came close to matching the turmoil that engulfed California during what was then known as its "Golden Era," 1849 to 1861.

The disorder was such that it reached far beyond mining claim disputes and barroom brawls, right into the state legislature, the state supreme court, and of course the governor's mansion. Several members of its delegation to Congress became involved in some of the most outrageous acts in our nation's history. At the time I wondered why so few people seemed aware of California's past. Since then several well researched books about its desperadoes and lawmen have come forth. They portray several figures from the 1850s and many more in the years following the Civil War. Still, no single volume focused on the 1850s, when so many desperadoes entered journalism, politics and the professions.

Almost immediately it became apparent that part of the reason for this dearth of information was the newspapers of that period were but single sheets of paper folded over once, presenting the reader with four pages of information only. This quite obviously limited the amount of space the editors could devote to any given incident. The public's slight knowledge of California's more colorful early characters was deepened by the fact that on the heels of the Golden Era arose the Civil War. It was during this period that a "reform" minded press took hold in the state, while at the same time its history fell into the hands of several like minded historians.

Some of these writers were quite frankly embarrassed by the state's ante-bellum past. They tended to marginalize, and where they could, eliminate many of its early newspaper editors and politicians from discourse. When comparing one of these "certified" post–Civil War histories with the incidents described in the newspapers of the 1850s, it was often difficult to believe we were reading about the same state.

The volume on California frontier editors has not yet been completed, but the research did lead to the subject at hand—the fact that so many of its leading journalists were so willing to shed their blood on the dueling ground—very often in shootouts with leading political figures, businessmen, doctors and lawyers. The number of these formal gunfights reached past seventy, far more than any other of the thirty states over the same period. Because so many of these duels did involve politics *Choose Your Weapon* also presents a sketch of the state's political scene, a sketch that is almost as startling in its variance with the official record as the number of duels.

Toward the end of the research I came across a large number of articles in certain 1880s and 1890s newspapers written by those who had survived that long ago Golden Era. In addition to providing a fresh reminder of how much the culture of California has evolved between 1854 and the present, these columns furnished a reminder of how much the culture had evolved even between the years, 1854 and 1894.

Dueling as an institution left much to be desired. It cost the lives of too many fairly worthy individuals. They were not always fought honorably, and the reasons for which they were fought were often trivial, regarded as such even by the standards of the time. But overall the *code duello*, and the culture the *code duello* embodied, presents a projection of the human spirit that reflects rather favorably against the soft, indulgent portrait we see of ourselves today.

1

Golden Era California

One of the most gifted and quarrelsome of California newspaper editors in the 1850s was Andrew C. Russell, a native of North Carolina who came west with the first wave of gold seekers. But like many Southern gentlemen types, he never intended to support himself by mining. Instead he took a seat on the editor's tripod and began penning editorials for the *San Francisco Picayune*, the fourth newspaper to be established in that town. Impeccably honest and perhaps overly earnest, Russell's editorial style ruffled many feathers.

One of his early editorials caught the eye of Captain Joseph Folsom, a New Yorker who had come west with Jonathan Stevenson's regiment. Folsom had just inherited the Leidesdorff estate and had also recently assumed part ownership of the *San Francisco Herald*, edited by John Nugent. Angered by Russell's charges relating to the Leidesdorff claim, Folsom challenged him to a duel. Russell accepted and chose dueling pistols at ten paces. On September 11, 1851, the two exchanged shots in downtown San Francisco without effect and the affair ended.

Folsom was only the first of three major figures Russell, over the course of time, sought to bring down by gunfire. Even then, as the editor only too well knew, California was reeling from more corruption than any ten other states put together. Much of the blame for this predicament lay upon the shoulders of Democratic Governor John McDougal.

McDougal was raised in Indiana, where he earned a law degree before going off to fight in the Black Hawk Indian War. After that campaign he joined an Indiana regiment and went off to serve in the Mexican War as well. In 1849 he arrived in California by ship, accompanied by his wife, Jane, and a daughter named Susan. He attended the first Constitutional Convention in Monterey, and was one of the original signers of the Constitution of California. During the convention, upon being nominated for lieutenant governor, he quipped, "I reckon I'll take that. I don't believe anyone else will have it."

He served under the state's first governor, Peter Burnett, for thirteen months, at which point Burnett resigned because of numerous disagreements with the state legislature, and because he felt he was being under paid. Bold, handsome, clever and witty, when McDougal assumed the governor's chair in 1851 much was expected of him. But when he inexplicably began pardoning well known desperadoes the state's reservoir of good will toward him dried up. "The Pardoning Governor," as he was sometimes called, was not known to associate with any of those he cut loose, but it was widely believed that he was selling pardons. This was particularly so with regard to his release of Charles P. Duane, a San Francisco saloon owner who had beaten an actor nearly to death. Worse was his pardon of Hamilton McCaughly who had shot and killed a judge in Napa County, before a large crowd.

"I, John McDougal," another nickname he earned through his vociferous pronouncements, saw his stock plummet further when he announced his opposition to the San Francisco Vigilance Committee of 1851. In July of that year, with the aid of Sheriff Jack Hays and Undersheriff John Capperton, he made a spectacular rescue of three men sentenced to be hanged by the committee. Though the three were later retrieved by the vigilantes and hanged, McDougal's bold stroke made quite an impression on the settlers. However widely he was disliked as a governor, he was not a man to be trifled with.

Andrew Russell was just one of several editors fuming over McDougal's erratic behavior; but as usual his pen was just a bit sharper than the others. In September 1851, on the heels of his duel with Folsom, the editor was roughed up at the Union Hotel by the governor's brother, George McDougal, angry over one of his editorials. When Russell challenged McDougal to a face-off, he chose dueling pistols at twelve paces.

About forty spectators gathered in a lot to the rear of the Red House on the old El Camino Real as the pair took their positions. While the pistols were being loaded, Russell noticed a figure in the crowd he did not wish to be on the ground (The governor himself?). Protesting to his second that if he shot McDougal, he would only have another fight on his hands, Russell refused to commence shooting until the phantom left. McDougal's seconds pleaded with the unknown, but he refused to leave and Russell's seconds called the duel off. While opposing partisans taunted the editor for what was perceived as cowardice, most of San Francisco defended him.

George McDougal departed San Francisco shortly after. A frontiersman to the core, he was found some years later living with the Arapaho Indians in Wyoming. In 1859 he returned to San Francisco, denounced civilization in harsh terms, and left for remote Patagonia where last heard from he was living with another Indian tribe.

Russell was still smarting from charges of cowardice when in January 1852 he took Governor McDougal to task for his failure to respond to an alleged outbreak of Indian hostilities in the Mariposa region. McDougal was so furious over the editorial he decided to challenge him immediately. His aides however cautioned that dueling was against the law; and as a courtesy to the office he should wait for his term to expire—three days, January 11—before sending the challenge.

McDougal resolved his impasse by resigning immediately.

Russell accepted and chose dueling pistols at twelve paces. The site was the south side of a creek separating San Francisco from Santa Clara (now San Mateo) County where about fifty followers gathered to watch. At the first call of "Fire—one, two, three—stop!" both McDougal and Russell fired at two. While Russell's ball rushed harmlessly by his antagonist, McDougal's struck him in the right hand, tearing the flesh from three fingers and blowing the handle off his pistol. The ball continued on into his chest, where partially spent it cracked one rib.

Russell's second pronounced the duel ended, while the editor, still on his feet, acknowledged that McDougal was "an honorable gentleman." In response the governor strode over and failing to note where Russell had been hit, clasped his mangled hand. In the ornate style of his time Russell called out, "Do not shake my hand, Governor, for you have wounded me severely!"

Realizing his error, McDougal dropped the injured hand, seized the other, and shook it firmly.

Despite his triumph on the field of honor, McDougal left office in some disgrace. He may not have been a governor for all seasons, nor even a governor for one season. But a more exciting, two-fisted, pistol-packing chief executive cannot be found in California annals.

Two years later he played a star role in sparking the riot that broke out at the Democratic Convention in Sacramento. In 1856, when the second Vigilance Committee took over San Francisco, then Governor Neeley Johnson, in attempting to suppress the vigilantes, appointed none other than John McDougal to head the "Law and Order Party." Later in the same year he was arrested for voter fraud. After casting a vote in San Francisco, he affected a change of clothing and took a ferry to the East Bay where he voted yet again. Thereafter his personal and public life went into a tailspin from which he never recovered. He died in 1866 from drinking to excess.

Andrew Russell meanwhile moved to Sacramento, where toning down his editorials, he wrote for the *Sacramento Union*. He edited a number of other

3

newspapers through the 1850s, closing out the decade with the *Stockton Daily Argus*. With the outbreak of the Civil War he picked up his thorny quill of old and attacked the Union war effort against his native South. His editorials proved so nettlesome that in September 1862 the West Coast censor, Major General George Wright, closed down the *Argus*.

2

In the Beginning

The nineteenth-century French writer Jules Janin once wrote, "A duel . . . grasps the sword of justice which the laws have dropped, punishing what no code can chastise—contempt and insult. . . . Those who oppose dueling are either fools or cowards."

At the time this quote appeared the "code of honor" ruled in California. The reign of the duel in fact had begun in 1847, even before the province became a state and by 1852 had taken a vise like hold. In April 1854 the editor of the *Sacramento Union* wrote that he had counted more duels in his three short years in California than in all his previous life in Alabama, a state where dueling had long been in practice. The "Code of the West," as it became known, maintained its grip until the onset of the Civil War. During this period so many duels were fought, it was then a common topic of dinner conversation throughout the eastern United States and England.

The tradition of antagonists meeting in cold-blooded combat before a throng of spectators reaches far beyond even David and Goliath. But around 590 AD these contests took a more formal turn when Gundebald, king of the Burgundians, established the judicial duel. Hoping to abolish perjury in his courts, Gundebald decided to throw the question of guilt or innocence into the hands of God. Through mortal combat the Almighty would surely see the guilty punished. Thus, a Burgundian accused of a crime could plead not guilty, and defend his plea with his life. His accuser would stand by, ready to make good his accusation with his own life. Each then chose one or more advisers, later known as seconds, to prepare for their day of reckoning. For obvious reasons women, children, priests, invalids, and men over sixty years of age were exempt from accepting these challenges.

Through the Dark Ages the judicial duel spread from Burgundy to northern and southern Europe. Generally fought with staves and pole axes in an arena with seating for judges and spectators, proxies were sometimes employed by those less skilled, and who could afford to pay their alternates. In such cases the principal sat in an adjacent room, a rope slung around his neck. The instant his proxy went down on the field he was hoisted aloft. But by 1400 it had become obvious, even to the judicial duel's most stubborn defenders, that too many desperadoes, having proven their worth with a pole ax only, were still terrorizing the countryside. After 800 long years the judicial duel became a relic of the past.

Well before the judicial duel disappeared, the tournament or chivalric duel arose. Fought by sword wielding knights on horseback, tournament duels became the rage during Western Europe's High Middle Ages, and by 1200 was the most popular form of public entertainment. Over time pressure from the church restricted these duels to Mondays, Tuesdays, and Wednesdays, with no dueling on holidays. By 1600, largely owing to pressure from the church, the tournament duel also disappeared.

But before the demise of either the judicial or tournament duel the "duel of honor" had established itself, having appeared around 1000, at a time when men of status were finding it increasingly difficult to win reparations for insults. Barred from seeking justice in court, "gentlemen" now sought justice on the dueling ground. By 1350 the duel of honor had become such a measure of English custom, that Edward III convened a court of chivalry to devise a code of standards. The second by then had emerged as more than just a bodyguard; he was an adviser on weaponry and a skilled negotiator of terms.

As the character of the duel of honor evolved so did the weaponry. From pole axe, to horseback and sword, to bows and arrows, by 1600 the light Hispano-Italian rapier had become the preferred weapon. Just one hundred years later the dueling pistol emerged as the most popular instrument in England and Ireland. From there the duel made its way to America.

The causes of the duel of honor evolved at approximately the same pace as the weaponry. From the Middle Ages to the Renaissance they were often fought over women. Reflecting on the tempo of the times, one defender of the code wrote, "A man seducing a wife or daughter; for this and such like offenses the law can make no adequate restitution." Dueling over women declined after the Reformation, but over the centuries remained a significant factor.

By the seventeenth century "giving the lie" had become the major point of contention between gentlemen. So sensitive had men of means waxed over the matter of prevarication that entire treatises on falsehoods were written. These booklets tended to divide the lie into three categories: "the vain lie," "the conditional lie," and "the certain lie." These in turn were divided into subcategories.

As the eighteenth century advanced giving the lie was joined by other provocations: among them, all thoroughly reviewed in various manuals, were "the retort courteous," "the quip modest," "the reply churlish," "the reproof valiant" and "the counter check quarrelsome." Because the duel of honor was practiced in many countries, with various weapons, quite naturally diverse dueling codes evolved. The most significant for the United States was the *code duello*, formally adopted in England and Ireland in 1777.

Even though there were variations to the *code duello*, it was generally accepted that the challenged party dictated the choice of weapons, the distance and dueling site. The challenger might win the choice of site if he could demonstrate that the locale chosen by his opponent was harmful to his chances. The challenger also had the right to shorten, but not lengthen the distance set by the challenged party, and he alone had the option of ending the duel before the agreed upon number of shots were fired. Any challenger winning the choice of weapons owed his good fortune to either the magnanimity of his opponent, or the vastly superior negotiating skills of his second.

Other important points of the code—position on the ground, and which second was to sound the call, were decided upon by one or more coin tosses, or by drawing lots. The second who won the right to sound the call got to pose the preliminary question, "Gentlemen, are you ready?" In response the duelists, from their positions would call out "Ready." The second then began the count: "Fire—one, two, three—stop!" The duelists could begin shooting at "Fire" but were compelled to cease at "Stop." Any duelist risking a shot before "Fire" could be gunned down by his opponent's second. Left open to negotiation was the question of whether the duelists faced each other, or stood with their backs to one another, then whirled at the call.

The *code duello* also required that the affair of honor be conducted politely from beginning to end. The challenge was to be expressed clearly, the affront named, the reason defined, the appointment and site all determined in an amicable manner. Very often disputes were settled by the seconds before the combatants ever reached the dueling ground; just as often the seconds arranged an "adjustment" on the ground before a shot was fired. A good second knew weaponry, possessed a genuine sense of justice, and was above all, urbane.

In 1836 a treatise titled *The Art of Dueling*, written by A Traveler, appeared in England and the United States and was quite popular. The booklet dealt with weapon choice, weapon care, and shooting practice. It also offered the duelist a primer on how to conduct himself before, during, and after the duel. Among the points A Traveler made:

> The duelist must not indulge in gloomy thoughts the night before.
> Should declare war against nervous apprehension.

If possible laugh away the evening over a bottle of Port.

If sleep fails, take some amusing book to bed—one of Sir Walter's novels. If a lover of the romantic, Byron's *Childe Harold* will do.

Have your second awake you at five with a strong cup of coffee and a biscuit.

Be sure you have secured the services of a medical attendant, who will provide all the necessary apparatus for tying up wounds or arteries and extracting balls.

Wash your eyes very clearly.

Leave the house without awaking the wife and children and head for the dueling ground. Make sure the pistols are in the case in the chaise. Pistols left behind subject the party to much inconvenience and ridicule.

Arrive at the site first, dismount, walk about, puff on a cigar and observe that the second is marking off the ground correctly.

When your opponent arrives, cast your eyes closely and mark him if there is any nervous tremulation in his movements, while yourself remaining firm and stiff as a statue.

Among other points made by the author: the seconds were to retire eight yards from the line of fire before sounding the call; the surgeons and observers were to stand at least two yards behind the seconds. The duelists, attired in formal dress, attempted to offer the smallest possible target by presenting their sides to their opponent with shoulders thrust back, stomach sucked in, and feet placed together. The pistol, held in hand, was most often, but not always pointed toward the ground. After the exchange of shots, A Traveler concludes with the following:

I cannot impress upon an individual too strongly the propriety of remaining perfectly calm and collected when hit; you must not allow yourself to be alarmed and confused. But summoning up all resolution, treat the matter coolly, and if you die, go off with as good a grace as possible.

3

The Duel in America

The duel arrived in America with the first Europeans, but was not commonly practiced before the Revolution. Strangely enough, America's first duel was not fought in the South, but in New England not long after the Pilgrims landed. In 1621 two Plymouth Bay colonists, Edward Doty and Edward Leicester squared off against one another with sword and dagger. Both were wounded.

With one or two other exceptions, dueling remained almost unknown in New England where the church and a generally sober, well-ordered population strongly condemned it. By contrast the duel became, relatively speaking, fairly common in neighboring New York, New Jersey and Pennsylvania, particularly in the years after the Revolution. Alexis de Tocqueville noted that while dueling was not as prevalent in America as in France, those duels that were fought were deadly by European standards.

Dueling was even more widely practiced in the Southern states. Around the turn of the nineteenth century it became so popular in South Carolina a dueling club was formed. But shortly after its establishment, the club president was killed in a shootout with an Englishman. His death led to the club's disbandment, and for several years after dueling went into a decline in that state. A similar incident for a time discouraged dueling in Virginia. Richmond was then home to a famous duelist named Powell. When a visiting Englishman remarked that "Virginia was of no use to America because it took fully one half its population to keep the other half in order," Powell challenged him. In the exchange that followed he was killed by the Englishman's first shot.

Whereas dueling in Europe was largely restricted to gentleman of the professions, in America with its spirit of egalitarianism, many who simply aspired to be gentlemen issued challenges. And while in America "the direct lie" might provoke a duel, more often than not it was the "retort churlish," or the thwarted outcome of a tavern brawl.

America also made an original contribution to dueling in the realm of posting. A potential duelist would place a notice or "card" on a bill board, denouncing the target of his anger in hopes of drawing a challenge. One of the first instances of posting was by the notorious General James Wilkinson. Hoping to provoke Senator John Randolph of Virginia into issuing a challenge, Wilkinson posted the following notice about the taverns of Washington, D.C.: "Hector unmasked. In justice to my character, I denounce to the world, John Randolph as a prevaricating, base, calumniating scoundrel, poltroon and coward."

He failed to draw a challenge from Randolph.

Most of America's duels involved long forgotten lawyers, army officers and newspaper editors. Some involved famous figures, among them Alexander Hamilton and Andrew Jackson whose "affairs of honor" are so well known they need no treatment here. One of the country's most bizarre, little-known duels was between De Witt Clinton (later governor of New York) and a political opponent, John Swartwout. Prompted by remarks Clinton had made about Swartwout's character, it was fought in 1802.

Though Clinton offered to apologize to Swartwout, he refused to place his apology in writing as his challenger demanded. Thus the two and their seconds met with dueling pistols on the ground outside of New York City. Both missed on the first three calls to fire. On the fourth call Clinton shot Swartwout in the right leg below the knee. While the governor moved off the ground to await a settlement, Swartwout had his surgeon extract the ball, then demanded another shot.

Clinton reluctantly resumed his position and at the next call sent a ball into Swartwout's other leg just above the ankle.

"Are you satisfied?" he shouted.

"No sir, proceed!" cried Swartwout, barely able to stand.

Clinton turned and strode off the field without apologizing. Watching him go, Swartwout turned to his second and said, "What should I do, my friend?"

"There is nothing further for you to do but have your wounds dressed and go home!"

The *code duello* might have been continued practice in the Northern states until the Civil War, had it had not been for a duel between Congressmen Jonathan Cilley of Maine, and William J. Graves of Kentucky. The affair was sparked by some angry comments Cilley made about James Watson Webb, editor of the *New York Enquirer*. Webb responded by asking his friend Graves to deliver a note to Cilley, demanding a public apology or satisfaction on the dueling ground. At the Cilley-Graves meeting Cilley refused to admit that he had slandered Webb and made additional comments about him. Offended by Cilley's "breach of etiquette," Graves challenged him on the spot. Cilley accepted.

As the challenged party he chose rifles—distance, eighty yards. The rifle duel, while not quite an American innovation, was already far more common in the United States than anywhere else in the world.

The parties met on February 24, 1838, near Marlborough, Maryland. Both missed the first two calls to fire. On the third call Graves shot Cilley in the chest. As he collapsed Cilley turned to his second and said of Graves, "I entertain the highest respect and most kind feelings."

Graves started in Cilley's direction in hopes of rendering aid, but was stopped by his second who said, "My friend is dead, sir." The congressman left behind a wife and three young children. His death brought on such a storm of protest that dueling all but disappeared north of the Mason-Dixon Line.

America's dueling epicenter by then was Louisiana. Nearby Mississippi and Tennessee also tallied an impressive number of duels between public functionaries. In the old Southwest, unhampered by scolding clerics and crusading journalists, even doctors took the field of honor. Quarrels between doctors very often arose out of methods of treatment, then a good deal less certain than today. One of the most notorious doctor duels was fought between Samuel Chopin and John Foster, both of New Orleans.

The two squabbled bitterly over the treatment of an ailing law student. What one would prescribe in the morning, the other would throw out that evening. At a chance meeting in the student's room, Chopin and Foster engaged in a violent brawl that resulted in a challenge, with pistols the choice of weapons. The next morning Foster shot Chopin in the jugular vein, killing him instantly. In an apt postscript, a few days later the law student died of Foster's undivided attentions.

Another famous Southern duel was fought outside of Natchez, Mississippi. On September 19, 1827, Dr. Thomas Maddox, supported by Major Norris Wright, Robert Crain and the Blanchard family—took the field (a sand bar in the Mississippi River) against Samuel Wells, backed by his brother Thomas Wells, the Cuny brothers, and the legendary Jim Bowie. After an exchange of shots without injury, Maddox and Wells announced their mutual satisfaction and turned to greet their advancing supporters.

The Cuny Brothers and Bowie were strolling toward Wells when they noticed that Maddox's men, on the other side of the bar, seemed to be racing toward him. They too broke into a run toward Maddox. In the melee that followed, General Cuny, who had long harbored a grudge against Colonel Crain, said, "This is a good time to settle our difficulty," and drew his pistol. Bowie drew his in support of the general.

Crain pulled his pistol and waited for Cuny to fire, but seconds later it was Crain and Bowie who exchanged shots, the colonel's ball striking Bowie in the chest. The blond giant (some say his hair was red) tossed his empty pistol aside, and lunged at Crain, who with his pistol also empty retreated. Cuny too advanced on Crain, as the latter leaped across a gulch, turned, pulled a second pistol and fired at the general, mortally wounding him.

By now Bowie, despite his wound, had also leaped the gully. With no more loads, Crain dodged his attack. Moments later Major Wright, who had rushed to Crain's aid, pulled his sword cane and slashed at Bowie. Bowie drew his knife and fending off the blows, fell to the ground suffering a second shot, from another party, this one in the thigh. Prostrate, he suffered yet a third wound when Wright took a whack at him with his sword. With the blow glancing off his ribs, Bowie reached up, seized Wright's coat hem, and yanked him downward on top of himself. He then muttered, "Now, Major, you die" as he plunged his knife through Wright's back, into his heart.

Though Bowie's life was despaired of, he of course survived. The knife he used to kill Major Wright had been forged by his brother, Rezin P. Bowie, of Avoyelles Parish, Louisiana. The first Bowie knife in existence, it was 9¼ inches long, 1½ inches wide and single edged. Later variations of the Bowie knife, forged by various sutlers across the frontier played a role in several California duels and became so common in that state they were re-christened the "California Bowie knife."

4

The Duel Comes to California

The duel appeared in California in 1847, one year before the commencement of the Gold Rush. Until then, most the seven hundred or so American settlers present were mountain men types who tended to settle their differences with guns and Bowie knives without a formal challenge. Only with the arrival of American army officers, lawyers and businessmen did the "Code of the West" gradually take hold. California, an unsettled land, without a reform minded press, or an organized clergy, was indeed fertile ground to sow the seeds of chivalry.

The first known challenge was issued in Los Angeles by its first American governor, John Charles Fremont. The target of Fremont's ire was his successor, Colonel Richard B. Mason, the great-grandson of George Mason, one of America's founders. The trouble stemmed from Lieutenant Colonel Fremont's larger problems with General Stephen Watts Kearny. In April 1847, Kearny, having assumed full charge of American forces in California, ordered Fremont to muster out his 350-man battalion. He then sent Mason to Los Angeles with orders to replace him as governor. Upon arriving Mason sent Fremont a note, ordering him to discharge his battalion and convey his horses to headquarters. When Fremont ignored him, Mason issued a second order, which was also ignored. He repeated the order for yet a third time, and in addition demanded that Fremont bring all his official papers with him.

After some delay the Pathfinder appeared in Mason's office with but a small portion of his paperwork. On being asked for the balance, he replied that he had sent most of his papers to Washington, then added in prickly fashion that he had not brought the horses either. He then asked why Lieutenant Colonel St. George Cooke was present. In Fremont's words, "Did you bring him to spy on me?"

Completely out of patience Mason shouted, "Any more of your insolence and I will put you in irons!"

Fremont left the room in a huff and the next day sent his paymaster, Pierson B. Reading, into Mason's office with a challenge. Mason accepted and chose shotguns with slugs. When Reading reported back Mason's choice of weapons, he also informed Fremont that he did not know of anyone in the U.S. Army more deadly with a shotgun than Colonel Mason.

The impending duel was soon the talk of Los Angeles, overshadowed only by talk of Fremont's repeated instances of insubordination against Kearny. The specter of the state's first two governors taking the field against one another made quite an impression on the American settlers and *Californios* alike.

Fortunately for Fremont, Mason insisted that the duel must wait until their scheduled meeting with Kearny in Monterey. Later in Monterey, when informed of the affair, the general immediately forbade it and the matter ended.

Almost. In 1850 Mason returned to St. Louis after a tour of duty in Mexico, and on learning that the Pathfinder was in town sent him a note, expressing his immediate readiness to meet with shotguns. Fremont never responded.

The first actual duel in California took place in early 1848, and was fought between Lieutenant Bonneycastle of Jonathan Stevenson's New York Regiment, and Henry F. Teschemacher, an Englishman who had been living in San Pedro since 1842. Few details of the duel are known, other than it involved the affections of a woman.

Teschemacher was then working for the firm of Howard and Mellus, pioneer exporters in hides and tallow. At that time Henry Mellus was engaged to a young women residing in San Pedro. At a ball that winter in nearby Los Angeles, his bride-to-be complained that Bonneycastle was flirting with her, and making a general nuisance of himself.

Mellus promptly sent Teschemacher over to Bonneycastle with a challenge. Though the lieutenant protested that the woman was mistaken, he nonetheless accepted the challenge. It was then that Teschemacher, who was immensely fond of his employer, took matters into his own hands. With Mellus's marriage just two weeks off, and his possible death hanging in the air, he decided to stand in for his employer. Bonneycastle—who could have, but did not object to the change of targets—chose rifles at forty paces.

In the firing that followed, outside of San Pedro, Teschemacher's first shot snapped off Bonneycastle's small finger and ripped up the length of his arm, leaving it so badly mangled it was later amputated. Teschemacher, who emerged from the duel unscathed, was later to became mayor of San Francisco.

The feud between Fremont and Mason and the Bonneycastle-Teschemacher duel not withstanding, the code had yet to really take hold in California. Through 1849 the mass westward movement of Americans brought no recorded duels. Significantly however a duel almost took place at the state Constitutional Convention which gathered that year in Monterey. In September delegates from each of the mining districts, representing all the twenty-nine Eastern states, gathered at Colton Hall. Despite the sectional antagonism that might have been expected between delegates from Northern and Southern states, in a spirit of accommodation most worked hard to forge the Constitution. Matters threatened to get out of hand just once.

The incident arose out of an argument between James McHall Jones, a Kentuckian, and Henry A. Tefft of Illinois. It was sparked when Jones complained to a friend about several of the convention's time wasting procedures. Tefft, a member of the committee on procedures, overheard Jones and objected, with a quote from Junius: "There are men who never aspire to hatred—who never rise above contempt."

Jones insisted that he had the protection of the house from such a gross insult, and demanded Tefft apologize. Tefft refused and word soon spread that Jones would challenge him. At this point another delegate, Benjamin Moore, entered the fray. A tall dark Southerner, Moore had extreme views on the Southern way of life. While the other delegates had signed the convention roster, appending their occupations accordingly, Moore had listed himself as a man of "elegant leisure." Rising to speak before the convention, he informed the delegates that they should not be troubled by the personal differences between Jones and Tefft. "Let it be settled outdoors," he argued, meaning a duel was in order.

At this point William Gwin, another Southerner, rose and demanded Jones and Tefft be forced to settle their dispute indoors, and without bloodshed. "The majesty and power of the house should be brought to bear upon this case, and it should be settled before these gentlemen are permitted to leave their seats!"

Gwin's plea bore fruit. Jones and Tefft settled their argument inside the convention without resort to arms. In the coming days as the convention proceeded Gwin tried to attach an anti-dueling clause to California's Constitution, one that would forbid any duelist from holding public office. A Mississippian whose brother had been killed in one of the bloodiest duels in that state's history (both duelists died lingering deaths), he spoke of the bloody carnage the code had brought to neighboring Louisiana.

> If you go through the cemetery of New Orleans you will see the whole earth covered with the tombstones of the victims of honor. It is a wonderful and melancholy sight. . . . The practice of dueling has not sprung up here in California yet, and it is to be hoped that it never will. If by our action here,

15

we can have any influence on preventing it we should certainly exercise that influence.

The delegates, a majority of whom were from Northern states, voted Gwin's proposal down. Thus, on the heels of the Fremont-Mason and Jones-Tefft affairs, and the Bonneycastle-Techemacher duel, the Constitution's framers had implied to the settlers that the practice of dueling would not be frowned upon in California.

5

The Year 1850

Eighteen fifty began as peacefully as '49, but four months into the year an omen of bad times to come appeared in the San Joaquin Valley town of Stockton. Stockton, named after Commodore Robert Stockton, was established by Charles M. Weber who arrived in 1847 with a small band of settlers, two hundred horses and four thousand head of cattle. Until the discovery of gold in 1848 the locale had been a large camp, centered by a thatched roofed general store–saloon, owned by trapper Joseph Buzzell. After the Gold Rush it became a jumping off point for the Southern Mines and grew rapidly, by 1852 claiming 2,800 citizens. At any one time however, the number of horse, mule and ox driven teams, pausing for the night assured that the town had a population several times that size.

Stockton claimed many settlers from New York, among the most prominent being Henry Marshall, a gambler and close friend of Stockton's first *alcalde*, George Belt. Another of the town's first settlers was a Canadian named Duncan Perley who in early 1850, in partnership with another attorney, David Terry, set up a law practice.

In April of that year Perley was representing a client who had brought charges against a saloon owner for absconding with his money. The coins in question had been placed before a presiding judge named Reynolds when Henry Marshall, testifying for the saloon owner, burst into a tirade, denouncing Perley in harsh terms. Perley reacted by drawing a pistol and pointing it at Marshall. In a move nearly as climactic, while a constable disarmed Perley, Judge Reynolds rose, swept the coins off the table into his hat and announced, "The court must take care of itself!"

The trial was adjourned and later that day Perley was fined $50. While Judge Reynold's injudicious conduct caused little stir among those present, that same afternoon Marshall sent George Belt over to Perley's office with a challenge. He accepted and chose dueling pistols at ten paces. During the night however he appears to have had second thoughts. Prodded by his chosen second, David Terry, he nonetheless decided to meet Marshall.

Here Terry, rather than working to settle Perley's troubles, as the ideal second might have done, only inflamed his principal, making a settlement next to impossible.

On May 11, Perley and Marshall, accompanied by Belt and Terry, and a crowd of spectators met in a field adjacent downtown Stockton. In the first exchange of fire Marshall's ball plowed into the dirt just in front of Perley, while Perley's whizzed over his head. On the second call Marshall's ball again plowed into the earth in front of Perley. This time the Canadian's shot whipped Marshall's hat off, tearing a hole in it. Marshall, using his prerogative as challenger, declared himself satisfied and the duel ended.

Perley continued practicing law in Stockton for many years after. Not by coincidence he served as Terry's second in his 1852 face-off with George Belt; nor was it a coincidence that Marshall stood in for Belt in the very same duel. Perley also played a key role in sparking the infamous Broderick-Terry duel of 1859.

The year 1850 also saw the first duel fought in San Francisco. The affair was between Judge Alexander Wells and A. Jackson McDuffie, a lieutenant in Jonathan Stevenson's New York Regiment.

For better or worse, Alec Wells, as he was known, was typical of the many scandalous figures who made their way to California in search of fame and fortune. He was a slightly built, handsome fellow who had obtained a law degree before joining the ranks of New York City's storied Tammany Democrats. He arrived in San Francisco in 1849 and the following year was appointed to fill a recently vacated seat in the state assembly. At the capital, then in San Jose, Wells's talent as an orator soon earned him the nickname "Little Thunderer."

Nonetheless, his reputation as a drinker soon surpassed that of orator. On one of his many benders he stopped by the California Guard armory and forced an argument on Lieutenant McDuffie, breaking off the row by shouting "pickles!" a popular retort in those days. This brought a challenge and on a Sunday morning in March 1850, Wells and McDuffie fought with pistols at ten paces. Two shots were exchanged without effect and the affair ended.

This was not the last of Wells's brushes with the code of honor. The following year, while drunk he burst uninvited into a house party attended by what was then termed San Francisco's intelligentsia—Dr. Augustus Bowie, Charles Fairfax, John Nugent, and Archibald Peachy among others. Coolly greeted, Wells strode around the table, toasting each guest with a thorny pun. Informed that his remarks were extremely offensive, he left. The following morning Hamilton Bowie, brother of Augustus, carried a challenge to his room. The letter cited the profane nature of his insults, and asked for satisfaction from Bowie, Fairfax, Nugent, or Peachy—his choice. Learning of his obnoxious statements the night before, Wells was so horrified he sent an apology and the challenge was withdrawn.

Wells died suddenly in San Jose in October of 1854. His passing was deeply mourned by his wife, children, and scores of saloon associates. The funeral, held under a full moon, was a long, somber, torch light procession. Alexander Wells's duel was inconsequential, but his short, tumultuous life exemplified that led by so many other recent West Coast arrivals.

Elsewhere in 1850, the only duel of note was the Tellotson-Kenny affair of June 9. Kenny shot Tellotson just above the knee at the Yerba Buena Cemetery in San Francisco (where City Hall now sits).

But even before the Tellotson-Kenny and Perley-Marshall duels, and perhaps prompted by the Wells-McDuffie affair, in April 1850 an anti-dueling statute was introduced in the state legislature. Crafted by San Francisco Assemblyman George Penn Johnston, section one called for a one- to seven-year prison sentence for anyone convicted of dueling; section two required the convicted to pay the dead duelist's debts, while section three ordered him to pay the dead duelist's family a sum of $10,000. On April 18, 1850, Johnston's entire bill passed both the State Assembly, and Senate.

The *code duello* thus appeared to have been stopped in its tracks by legislative code.

Interestingly enough, George Penn Johnston, like William Gwin who earlier sought to insert an anti-dueling clause into the state Constitution, was from Mississippi, renowned for its duels.

6

The Keystone Fire-Eater

Despite passage of the Johnston anti-dueling statute the following year the Code of the West truly took hold. By then the co-mingling of adventurers from different parts of America, and the world, had become a singular event in itself. Prior to the Gold Rush relatively few Americans had traveled more than two or three counties from their home town, let alone to another state.

Well before the Gold Rush, members of Jonathan Stevenson's New York Regiment had arrived. Accounts reveal them to have been a clannish bunch who felt they had certain vested rights in the state the '49ers and other late comers were not entitled to. Other arrivals also had opinions of new neighbors from strange places. The pioneers of Ohio, Indiana, Illinois, and Missouri held a good-natured contempt toward anyone hailing from east of the Appalachian Mountains. The Southerners in turn took an amiably contemptuous view of anyone north of the Mason-Dixon Line.

Only a short time passed before the Southerners and Westerners learned that the New Yorkers and their Pennsylvania brethren were a match for them in the rip roaring free-for-alls and shootouts that were such a hallmark of life in California during the '50s. One of the most striking of these eastern "gentlemen" was a frail Pennsylvania attorney named William Hicks Graham. Will Hicks, as he was known, was the son of a successful Philadelphia merchant. His mother, oddly enough, was a Quaker.

Shortly after arriving in San Francisco in 1850, he took a position with Roderick N. Morrison, the city's probate court judge. There, he became fast friends with city attorney Frank Pixley, Morrison's nephew and a native of New York State. Though Pixley later atoned himself through gallantry during the Civil War, he was at the time one of those much hated criminal defense lawyers who would become such a fixture on the California legal landscape.

Less is known of Judge Morrison, other than he was known to be wildly extravagant with his court expense account, which understandably made him very popular with his staff. At the time Graham was working for Morrison there was much bickering in San Francisco over whether the judge should preside over the Leidesdorff Case. Captain Joseph Folsom had recently laid claim to the Leidesdorff estate and opposed Morrison sitting in judgment of his suit. Backing Folsom was the *San Francisco Daily Herald*, published by John Nugent, and then edited by the famous filibusterer, William Walker.

In early January 1851, an editorial appeared in the *Herald*, blasting Morrison's credentials relating to the Folsom case. The attack angered his aides, Graham and Pixley, even more than the judge himself, and the pair, with Morrison's consent, decided to silence the *Herald*—no easy task. Walker was a Tennessean, reputed to be one of the best marksmen in the West, while Nugent had an equally fearsome reputation. Nonetheless, Graham and Pixley decided to singe the two grizzly bears in their den. Still uncertain as to whom the author of the editorial was, Pixley sent the *Herald* a letter, denouncing the writer as a "poltroon, liar and coward."

The next day Edmund Randolph, a friend of Nugent's and Walker's, and a major figure in his own right, appeared in Morrison's office and informed all present that Walker had penned the editorial. He then complained that the wording of Pixley's letter was so taut it left no room for Walker to explain himself. When Pixley replied that he, Morrison and Graham were not interested in any "explaining," Randolph left and returned a half hour later with Walker's challenge.

In the negotiations that followed Walker readily agreed to Graham and Pixley's choice of weapons—Colt revolvers, distance ten paces (thirty feet), and the date of the duel, January 12, 1851. The duelists were to stand with their backs to one another and at the word, wheel and fire. But Randolph felt that one of the conditions was too brutal—namely, the duelists upon whirling were to advance on each other while continuing to fire. This made it almost certain that one of them would be killed. In the end, despite Randolph's objections, Walker agreed to this condition too.

While Walker immediately chose John Nugent and Joseph Folsom as his seconds, over at Morrison's office, who would face Walker, let alone be his second, had not been determined. Quite a row broke out between Graham and Pixley for honors; a coin toss finally decided the point. Not surprisingly Graham, winner of the toss, chose the loser, Frank Pixley, as his second.

In the days leading up to the duel Graham exercised his pivot and fired his revolver at targets all day long. He had always been a pretty fair shot and by the morning of the duel was in top form. In all about seventy spectators gathered on the corner of Ninth and Market Streets. No attempt by authorities was made to stop the duel. Among the crowd of watchers was

Sheriff Jack Hays, State Supreme Court Justice Hugh Murray, city judges Ned McGowan and Alexander Wells, and most of the town council.

Thus, before a good portion of California officialdom Graham and Walker took their positions at ten paces, backs to one another. A few wags in the crowd then suggested that Graham might have the advantage: "He's so thin Walker might as well be shooting at a bamboo stake."

Moments later as the call to "Fire!" echoed down Market Street, Walker and Graham spun around and shot at each other. To the astonishment of everyone Walker missed Graham by a country mile, while Graham's bullet passed through the calf of his leg, inflicting a painful wound.

Firing ceased as a good deal of chatter erupted from the crowd, some of it focused on Walker's bad marksmanship, some of it on ending the duel immediately. But Walker, though in pain, insisted on continuing the duel. As a concession to his wound, Pixley and Graham agreed that on the next call the antagonists would face each another, thus eliminating for Walker what would have been a very painful whirl.

With his wound well bound in a rag, Walker took his position and waited. At the word "Fire" he stepped forward and once more snapped off a bad shot. A second later he embarrassed his partisans further by crumpling onto the street with a ball lodged in the thigh of his other leg. In the pandemonium that followed, chagrin gave way to anguish as Walker's physician announced that his second wound "might be fatal."

The doctor's pronouncement proved as wide of the mark as Walker's shooting. His patient recuperated and went on to survive yet another duel with newspaper editor William H. Carter, prior to leading a filibustering expedition into Nicaragua.

The shooting of Walker of course did not silence the *Herald*, as Nugent immediately replaced him on the editor's tripod; nor did the Folsom case ever make its way to Judge Morrison's docket. But basking in the glow of San Francisco's newly found respect, Graham, Morrison, and Pixley found the *Herald*'s editorials too picayunish for notice.

A few months after Judge Morrison vacated his bench to try his luck in the mines. At the mining camp of Carson Creek, Calaveras County, while on a drunken bender he engaged a Dr. Friend in a wild brawl. In the midst of the brawl Dr. Friend drew his revolver and shot Morrison to death. Frank Pixley led a much longer and more successful life. Through the 1850s his jury packing talents and quick attention to legal detail continued to wheel many a desperado out of the state's jails, into its courtrooms, and then back out again onto its lonely, dangerous roads.

Will Hicks Graham was never heard to say anything good about William Walker, but his dislike of the editor paled when compared to his hatred for

San Francisco tax assessor George Frank Lemon, a tall, square-shouldered associate of California's most powerful legislator, State Senator David Broderick.

Lemon had arrived in California in 1850 with a mistress, a Mormon woman named Anna Hughes. His relationship with Anna had always been rather casual and when he introduced her to Graham he did not seem to mind when the two began seeing each other. Will Hicks fell deeply in love with Anna and in the summer of 1851 married her.

Within weeks of his marriage however, Graham discovered that Lemon and Anna were still bedding down together, as though his wedding had never occurred. His wife it seemed had done a reversal on an old Mormon institution. Outraged, he stormed inside the Oriental Hotel where Lemon was having a drink, strode over to his table, seized a glass of water and shouted, "I suppose you consider yourself a gentleman?"

"Yes."

"You would then resent an insult if one was offered you."

"Yes."

Whereupon Graham threw the glass of water in his face. Several at the table broke up the brawl before it got underway, thus allowing Lemon an opportunity to later send a challenge.

The next day Graham waited in vain. Learning that the challenge would not be forthcoming, following an old American tradition, he posted the following notice at Portsmouth Square, in the middle of downtown San Francisco. "July 1, 1851: I hereby post and publish George Frank Lemon as a scoundrel, villain, liar and poltroon and declare him to be out of the pale of gentlemen's society. William Hicks Graham."

Unable to ignore him any longer, Lemon passed word that he would appear at Portsmouth Square at ten o'clock Wednesday morning, armed with a five shooter. At the hour he gathered with his followers in front of the office of the *Alta California*, while Graham and his supporters took a position across the plaza. After an hour of eye balling his adversary and jawing with companions, Lemon strolled off toward the courthouse at the lower end of the square, prompting Graham to set off in the same direction. Reaching the lower end first, as Lemon approached Graham shouted, "Draw and defend yourself!"

Both men drew their Colts and within seconds flicked off three shots. Graham missed all his, while one of Lemon's balls struck him in the arm, spinning him to the courthouse steps. As Graham lay on his backside trying to steady his revolver for a shot, Lemon leaned over and at point blank range fired into his face. The ball passed through the left side of Graham's chin, blasting four incisors to bits. Lemon was about to discharge the finishing shot when several bystanders disarmed him.

Graham was carried to a room in the California Exchange Building where he was attended by a doctor who extracted the ball from the back of his mouth. Despite the loss of his teeth, a tear in his tongue, and a hole to the back of his mouth, within ten minutes he was on his feet. He nonetheless spent the next several months subsisting on a spoon diet, his jaw cloaked in a sling.

When Graham was sufficiently recovered he sent Lemon the inevitable challenge. Among his demands, at the word "Fire" the two would advance on each other from twelve paces, firing their revolvers until one or both went down. Lemon, then editing *The Commercial Advertiser* in Benicia, insisted Graham's conditions were too barbaric. But because of the barbarous nature of his own earlier assault, his peers pressed him to accept.

On September 14, 1851, opposite the state armory in Benicia the two met, Graham, flanked by his second, Judge Levi Parson, and Lemon flanked by his second (unknown). Before a large crowd, at the call to fire they began advancing on one another, furiously working their revolvers. Amidst a staccato of barking explosions Lemon collapsed in the dirt, a ball lodged in his shoulder. Rushing over with his bag of instruments was Lemon's surgeon, who knelt, examined his wound and pronounced it fatal.

It proved another faulty prognosis. Despite its seriousness, Lemon, like Walker before him, recovered from his wound. He later returned to New York, and when the Civil War broke out was commissioned a colonel. He was killed in the Battle of Balls Bluff while fighting alongside the renowned U.S. senator, Edward Baker.

Will Hicks Graham once again had emerged victorious on the field of honor. Recognized wherever he went, California chivalry approached him with caution and respect. Two years later he became secretary to James Estill, director of the state prison at San Quentin. Estill's prison contract was to later explode into one of the great scandals of the 1850s, but Graham remained with him until 1857, when both were removed from office. Amazingly, he was afterward appointed state inspector of weights and measures by Governor John B. Weller.

Equally surprising, his marriage to Anna lasted nine more years, and brought him three children. In 1860 he divorced Anna and left for the boom towns of Nevada. There he burnished his reputation as a gunfighter further by shooting down two more men in separate gun battles. One of them was the noted outlaw, Jack McBride. He thereafter came down with tuberculosis, and moved to Los Angeles where under the care of the "Sisters of Charity," he died in 1868.

7

The Duel at Coyote Hill

At first reading one wonders whether the duel at Coyote Hill is worthy of historical notice. But given the notorious reputation one of the duelists was to later gain, and the presence on the ground of the most powerful politician in California at the time, it becomes a story worth telling. It also presents a good composition of what life was like in the mining towns, both with regard to the casual manner in which the inhabitants faced death, and their quaint, yet profane manner of speech.

Referred to by one writer as the "most dung hill duel" ever fought, it took place in Calaveras County in the early fall of 1851. On that sultry September afternoon crowds of miners and others were loafing about Main Street, Mokelumne Hill, when Billy Mulligan, a native of New York, made some sneering remarks about Southerners. Offended was Alabama-born Jimmy Douglas, another loafer, who retorted that Mulligan was "not a gentleman."

Douglas had a point. Despite all his airs, Billy Mulligan was more a varmint than a gentleman; but then, so too was Jimmy Douglas. One unhappy word led to another and the two decided to settle their argument on the field of honor. Neither was familiar with the code, but hell bent on using each other for target practice, they decided to make the best of it.

Very little is known about Jimmy Douglas. Prior to his arrival in Calaveras County he had spent a year in Stockton where he gained some renown for gunning down a horse thief in full flight. Since settling in Calaveras he had collected quite a circle of friends, few of whom would have privately described him as a gentleman.

More is known of Mulligan. At the age of twenty he departed New York for Texas where he joined the Texas Rangers. According to Jack Hays (later San Francisco's first sheriff), leader of the Rangers, Mulligan's courage was much admired among those with whom he served. During the Mexican War he repeatedly volunteered for missions behind enemy lines, on each occasion returning with a hair-raising tale to tell. Mulligan was five feet six inches tall and at 130 pounds was as wiry as he was profane. A good shot with revolver and rifle, he was an even better shot with his fists, regularly thrashing men half again his size.

After agreeing to fight their duel at nearby Coyote Hill, Mulligan and Douglas chose their seconds (unknown) and agreed to use five shooters at a distance of twelve paces. Should both miss on the first shot, they were to advance one step toward each other before the next exchange. The two set out for the dueling ground on foot, followed by a raucous crowd of over one hundred. There, beneath Coyote Hill's lengthening shadow, the event took on all the trappings of a carnival as Mulligan and Douglas strutted about the ground, exchanging ribald banter and dirty jokes with the crowd.

The jesting became so long winded that some wondered if the duel would come off before dark. Finally one of the spectators, none other than U.S. Senator William Gwin, then on one of his visits to the hinterlands, wielded his presence. Quieting the crowd, he announced that he opposed dueling, and had even attempted to insert a clause into the state Constitution that would have prohibited a duelist from holding public office. But inasmuch as the duel was going to take place regardless, it should be fought "in a manner befitting gentlemen."

Heeding the senator's advice, Mulligan and Douglas muffled themselves and with five shooters in hand took their positions. A coin was tossed to determine which second would win the right to call "Fire." Douglas's man won.

Moments later Mulligan, forgetting Gwin's counsel, pulled a $50 octagonal "adobe" gold piece from his pocket and tossed it onto the ground midway between himself and Douglas. "Bet you can't hit me Jimmy!" The crowd erupted into chatter as Douglas sifted through his pockets, pulled out $50 in coin, and tossed it in Mulligan's direction. Seconds later at the word "Fire!" they cocked their triggers, fired and missed.

As earlier agreed on, in preparing for the next shot each man advanced one pace toward the other. Mulligan then plumped another adobe onto the ground and shouted, "Bet you can't hit me Jimmy!" Douglas's second immediately canvassed the crowd for enough coin to counter Mulligan's octagonal. The fans eagerly obliged, marveling at how the duelists bore themselves with such easygoing valor. Seconds later, at the word Mulligan and Douglas leveled their five shooters, fired and missed.

Within a smokey haze Mulligan again plumped a $50 adobe onto the ground while Douglas's second tossed out $50 more in coin. On the third call their five shooters again cracked without effect. The crowd watched in animation as Mulligan tossed yet one more octagonal onto the ground, and Douglas's second reciprocated. On the fourth call they again fired and missed.

For the fifth and last time Mulligan flipped out an adobe while Douglas's man tossed out $50 more in assorted coin. At the word Mulligan aimed, fired and missed. A half second later Douglas's bullet sliced through the fleshy portion of his shoulder.

"Just a scratch!" shouted Mulligan, turning toward the crowd, baring his arm.

Within moments the two paladins were engulfed in a sea of prattling humanity. The shooting had been atrocious, but Mokelumne Hill had seen more excitement over the past two hours than in the past two weeks. Never had two duelists shown such swagger in the face of what should have been certain death. Senator Gwin, who was also a doctor, pushed his way through the crowd, examined Mulligan's wound and called for a bandage. A member of the crowd shed his boiled shirt and handed it to Gwin who bound Mulligan's shoulder.

A short distance away Douglas, the victor, and winner of $500 called for quiet. He then announced that Mulligan had borne himself with such gallantry that he was indeed "a regular gentleman." He then called for all present to follow him to "Moke Hill" for a grand blow out. All the drinks were on him. Both duelists were hoisted aloft and carried into town on the shoulders of their cheering partisans—the jaunty Billy who had thrown out the $50 octagonals, drawing the loudest "huzzahs."

Inside one of Mokelumne Hill's several saloons the pair and their partisans sidled up to the bar. Calls were then made for a speech. Always as eager to talk as to fight, Mulligan rose and in the language of his day addressed the crowd:

> Boys, listen to what I've got to say. There ain't no dirty son of a bitch that dare say my friend Jimmy Douglas shot a man all the way up. You mustn't think he can't shoot good because he shot so poor today, and I did too; but he can't beat me shooting anyway. We both like to a done better, but somehow we couldn't, I'm sorry to say; but we'll do better another time, when we're in a better fix. Don't you think we will Jimmy?

Jimmy rose, seized and rocked Mulligan's hand, then said, "We will that, Billy."

Mulligan and Douglas never shot at each other again. But while Jimmy Douglas drifted out of the public eye, Charming Billy went on to much "bigger and badder" things. During his stint as jailer of San Francisco, he himself was arrested on several occasions for assault and battery. At a time the city could ill afford uniforms for its officials, it was often difficult to tell whether he was an inmate or the jailer.

By then an ardent Broderick Democrat, and an associate of Judge Edward McGowan, he was San Francisco's most notorious "shoulder striker." From 1852 through 1855 he and his gang, which included such worthies as Yankee Sullivan, James Casey, and Charles P. Duane repeatedly showed up at polling sites on election day. There, armed with knives, revolvers, and "slung shot" (chunks of lead loaded into stockings), they invariably sent members of the more effete Whig Party fleeing for hearth and home. During the famous 1854 senatorial battle he was a point man in the attempt to kidnap State Senator Jacob Grewell just before a key legislative vote. His banishment from San Francisco by the Vigilance Committee of 1856 and various gunfights afterward are grist for many more stories.

8

Murder at Industry Bar

The Douglas-Mulligan shootout provided high-grade entertainment for the denizens of Mokelumne Hill, but as 1851 began to fade California's field of honor received a jolt without parallel in its annals. In October of that year a party of Chinese miners struck it rich at Industry Bar on the Main Fork of the Yuba River, Nevada County. As was so often the case in those times they were run off their claim by a gang of Americans. Shortly after, the Chinese appeared in Nevada City so distraught they offered half of their claim to anyone willing to help them drive the claim jumpers out.

U.S. Navy Midshipman George Dibble responded by organizing a posse. A powerfully built Mississippian, well-liked by most of those who knew him, Dibble and his posse proceeded to Industry Bar, drove the claim jumpers off and reinstated the rightful owners. He and his posse afterward remained on site to work their share of the claim. Among those present was a gambler named Edward "Jim" Lundy, a Canadian by birth, considered one of the best shots in Nevada County.

A flashy dresser with a superiority complex, Lundy was nonetheless not pleasing to look at. Sometime after arriving in California he took up dealing faro in Sacramento. There, in a quarrel with the proprietor of his table, he attempted to knock him out with the blunt end of his revolver. The owner managed to dodge his blow, and applying a drawn Bowie knife laid Lundy out onto the ground—minus one eye.

Late on the afternoon of October 30, Dibble, Lundy, and the others were sitting around a table spinning yarns and cracking jokes when Dibble asked, "When was it that fruit first swore?" Several unsuccessful attempts to answer were made.

"When the apple damned the pair of course," said Dibble.

Everyone laughed except Lundy, who from across the table said, "It's no such thing."

The color drained from Dibble's face as he rose and glowered at Lundy. This was not the first time the gambler had insulted him in front of others, and for a moment it appeared that he might actually reach across the table and pound the life out of him. Restrained by friends, Dibble warned, "You must not contradict me in such a way. You have done it too often already."

"You are a lying, thieving son of a bitch, and I am a bigger mark to shoot at than you."

"Very well, sir," said Dibble, brushing his coat sleeve, barely under control, "we will try it on when General Moorehead comes over from Nevada City."

"I am responsible for what I say," replied Lundy, obliquely accepting the challenge. He picked Colt revolvers at ten paces and named Charles Morse, one of the few friends he had in camp, as his second.

As expected General J.C. Moorehead appeared the next morning and agreed to serve as Dibble's second. He nonetheless tried to persuade the midshipman to make a settlement, first arguing that Lundy, a gambler, was too far beneath Dibble's station in life to duel with. Failing in this tactic, he argued that Lundy was such a good marksman he himself stood a good chance of being killed. Despite these pleas the midshipman refused to withdraw his challenge.

That night as Dibble lay next to a companion in camp he wrote several letters to friends back east, one of them to a sweetheart awaiting his return from what he had once termed, "the land of gold." Lundy took his blankets and camped alone on a nearby hillside.

The following morning, November 1, Moorehead and Morse measured off the ten paces and Dibble and Lundy took their positions. There then followed a heated argument over the call. Instead of the customary "Fire— one, two, three—stop!" at which the duelists would begin shooting at "Fire," Lundy insisted the shooting begin with "One." At his insistence Dibble and Moorehead agreed to this odd change of practice. Here, Lundy turned to Morse and pointing to the left side of his chest quietly said, "I will shoot his heart out!"

Moments later just as the sun peered over the pine fringed hills to the east, Moorehead, who had won the toss to make the call, asked, "Gentleman, are you ready?"

"Yes," shouted Dibble and Lundy.

Moorehead began the call, "Fire—"

Without waiting for the agreed upon "One," Lundy raised his revolver and fired a bullet into the left side of Dibble's chest. With a profound look of amazement, Dibble cried, "You son of a bitch, you fired before the word. You have nearly killed me!"

Moorehead, unaware that Dibble had been hit turned and asked, "Are you satisfied?" Dibble opened his coat and shirt, baring a wound pumping blood from his chest. Several friends rushed to his support, but Dibble shoved them away and stumbled off by himself. One hundred fifty feet away he wheeled twice and dropped in his tracks, dead. Lundy's bullet had pierced his heart.

In disbelief Moorehead pulled his revolver and made a rush for Lundy. As he attempted to shoot him, his wrist was seized and he was disarmed. Several miners cordoned Lundy off as an argument broke out over whether to hang him on the spot or rush him to Nevada City for trial. In the end the latter argument prevailed.

He was tried, found guilty of murder and sentenced to hang. An appeal was made however, and the proceedings found to be irregular. Lundy was granted a new trial. He remained in jail for over a year as his case dragged on, during which time many of the witnesses drifted away. Late in 1852 the judge finally entered a *nolle prosequi* into the books and set him free.

Lundy may have escaped legal justice, but he did not escape justice altogether. Two years later, while laying over in the southern mining town of Sonora, he staggered into his hotel room drunk, and fell asleep. That night the hotel caught fire. In their flight from the flaming structure, none of the other guests thought of waking him, and in the morning all that was found was a heap of charred bones.

Among several lesser known duels of 1851, on September 21, F.R. Bright exchanged shots with H.D. Evans at the *Sans Souci* House in San Francisco. Both missed and with the urging of seconds ended the duel.

Late in November a duel took place in San Francisco between two black men, George Johnson and Scipio Jackson. The affair was prompted by Jackson's courtship of Johnson's niece (name not known), and was fought with revolvers in the woman's presence. In the exchange Jackson shot Johnson in the shoulder, inflicting a serious, but not deadly wound.

Thus did the code of honor take hold. Despite Assemblyman Johnston's 1850 statute providing reasonably severe punishment for the offense, in a land where juries were reluctant to convict red handed killers, empaneling a jury that would convict a duelist was impossible.

9

Judge Terry's First Duel

California boasted many hard towns in the 1850s, not all located in the mining counties. Some such as San Francisco, lay by the coast, while Marysville, Sacramento, and Stockton were planted within the fertile Central Valley. Among Stockton's early settlers one of the most prominent was George Gordon Belt, a former quartermaster sergeant for Jonathan Stevenson's New York Regiment. Belt stood six foot three and possessed the kind of powerful build early settlers admired. He was also a dead shot with either pistol or rifle. After being mustered out of Stevenson's regiment in 1847, at the age of 22, he left San Francisco for Stockton.

Not surprisingly, despite his youth, Belt was chosen the town's first *alcalde*. He continued to preside as judge even after the alcalde system was dropped. Two years later, with a partner named Nelson Taylor he set up a tent store at the corner of Center Street and Webster Avenue. Later, with his brother Upton Belt, he bought a trading post and ferry on the Merced River. The post was located just above the bridge at present day Merced Falls and was then known as Belt's Ferry. For a time in 1852 and 1853 the Belt brothers hired Sam Ward, the celebrated Washington lobbyist and chef, to operate their ferry.

From 1849 through 1851, Stockton, like San Francisco, was plagued by a loosely organized band of desperadoes. On several occasions Alcalde Belt, determined to bring law and order to the town, hanged not only murderers but common thieves. His vigilante tactics gained him the undying enmity of California's legal profession. Nonetheless, his measures were supported by Stockton's merchants, and when he stepped down as judge in May 1850 to tend his businesses, he was still very popular.

In 1850 a stranger, fresh from disappointment in the mines, appeared in Stockton's dusty streets. As big and powerful as Belt himself, and with a hair trigger temper to match, his name was David Terry. A lawyer by training and a Texan, he set up a law practice with also recently arrived Duncan Perley. Despite Terry's distaste for Belt's cavalier methods of dispensing justice, and the fact that he was wary of anyone hailing from north of the Mason-Dixon Line, the two became good friends.

Early in 1852, however, Belt learned that one of Terry's associates, a so-called Doctor Roberts, alias Captain Yeomans, was a horse thief and an impostor who was wanted in Mexico for highway robbery. When he complained about the company Terry was keeping, the latter insisted Roberts was "an honorable man." Belt repeated his charges, whereupon Terry called him "an unmitigated liar and a scoundrel."

Furious over the name calling, the following day Belt sent Henry Marshall into Terry's office with a demand to either apologize or accept a challenge. He refused to apologize, accepted the challenge and named as his second, Duncan Perley. It was of course no accident that Perley and Marshall lined up on opposite sides of the feud, they having fought the first duel in Stockton two years before.

Friends of both Belt and Terry tried to arrange an "adjustment" satisfactory to both. Perley's desire to settle was prompted by a fact little known to readers of Western history: while Terry possessed some knowledge of the dueling code, he was unpracticed with firearms. All of his brawls—and there had been several since arriving in California—had involved the use of either a cane, his fists, or his renowned Bowie knife.

Several of his Texas friends felt that as the challenged party he would claim his right to use the Bowie knife. Yet it appears that Terry was well aware there was no precedent for using such a weapon in a duel. Hacking at each other with knives was a common pastime among frontiersmen, but there was no written code for employing them in an affair of honor between gentlemen.

Because Terry's lack of practice with firearms was almost unknown among Stocktonians, few were surprised when he chose to meet Belt with dueling pistols. Many were nonetheless astounded to learn that he chose to meet him at a distance of just ten feet. The specter of two such large men, almost able to reach out and grasp each other from that distance, struck many as incongruous.

Both Belt and Marshall were jarred by the distance, calling it "unprecedented and barbarous." But Terry was inflexible. Finally Belt and Marshall sought out William S. Swasey, an early pioneer and authority on the code. Swasey listened to their argument, but decided that Terry, as the challenged party, had a right to "name his distance."

Belt finally agreed and early on the morning of January 15, 1852, he and his crowd, followed by Terry and his party, departed for the dueling site, Mormon Island in the San Joaquin Delta. The Reverend James Woods, one of Stockton's recent arrivals from the East, was lodging at the Dickerson

House on Center Street when he was awakened at four in the morning by loud talk in the adjoining lobby. Through the cloth walls of his room he could hear locals clamorously discussing the duel as they prepared to leave for Mormon Island. Concluded Woods, "I have surely arrived in the wild and woolly West."

The duel was to take place at sunrise, but minutes after the sun had risen Belt and Marshall were still in deep conversation. Finally Marshall turned, strode over to Perley and informed him that if Terry continued insisting on a ten foot distance, Belt reserved the right to question one more authority on the code. Terry declined to lengthen his span by a single foot, and to the disappointment of the crowd the duel was placed *en tapis*.

Marshall returned to Stockton and wrote a letter to Calhoun Benham, another authority on the code of honor. A few weeks later a letter arrived from Benham informing Marshall that Terry was within his right to name his distance, however short it might be. But by then momentous news had arrived in Stockton. Terry was astonished to learn that Dr. Roberts was indeed a highway robber. Belt's charges were proven to the letter. Terry immediately sought him out and apologized for his abusive language. Belt in turn accepted the apology.

Many years later Terry was asked why he had chosen to duel Belt at such close quarters. He replied that he had always suspected his opponent, despite his superior marksmanship, possessed a faint yellow streak. At the customary ten paces (thirty feet) he would have stood no chance against him. But by shortening the distance to ten feet, Terry felt that his superior self- confidence would ensure at least an even chance.

David Terry of course went on to later fame and infamy: most particularly his strong support of David Broderick in his running battle with the San Francisco Vigilance Committee of 1856; and by a strange twist of fate, his deadly duel with the same Broderick in 1859.

Of the other figures in the Belt-Terry feud, Henry Marshall was gunned down some years later in a shootout at Tuolumne City. Duncan Perley remained a close friend and business partner of Terry for many years. George Belt appears not to have lost his standing in Stockton after his tangle with Terry. A preponderance also suggests that he continued to recklessly apply the hangman's noose.

In October 1856 he led a posse in pursuit of the famous stagecoach robber, Tom Bell. While Bell sat astride a horse among the willows lining the San Joaquin River, Belt spotted him some distance away, climbed off his horse and quietly approached. As he emerged from behind the willow branches, shotgun cocked and leveled, he announced, "I believe that you are the man we have been looking for."

Tom Bell surrendered.

But rather than escort him to Stockton for trial, Belt and his posse held an informal inquisition on the spot and hanged him. That evening they returned to town with only his scalp.

On June 3, 1869, Belt was walking up the east side of Center Street in Stockton with two companions when he was approached by William Denis, a 70-year-old relative by marriage who had threatened him over a cattle dispute. Hoping to avoid trouble with a man of such advanced age, Belt and company turned and crossed the street. Denis pulled his revolver and steadying his sights with both hands, pulled the trigger. The bullet struck Belt just behind the ear, killing him instantly. Thus did end the life of a California pioneer almost as colorful and controversial as David Terry.

10

Senator Broderick's First Duel

California's ledger of colorful pioneers from New York is very long, but without doubt the most formidable from that particular locale, was David C. Broderick. Brought up in the rough and tumble of New York City politics, he arrived in San Francisco in the fall of 1849. With a partner named Frederick Kohler, inside an assay office on the south side of Clay Street, the two went into the minting business, forging $10 shags using $7.78 worth of gold dust. It was a mode of conducting business that would have landed them in jail almost anywhere in the world but California. Within a short time the two were wealthy men. Among other ventures, Kohler went on to establish the Blue Wing Saloon, a watering hole that quickly became a San Francisco institution.

In 1850 Broderick ran for a seat in the State Senate representing San Francisco and won. During the campaign he became a fixture not only about the Blue Wing, but the town's growing number of other saloons The saloon owners and their clientele soon learned that he cared little for drinking, gambling or women. His two overwhelming passions were power and politics. Within a year he was riding the crest of a political machine that would have been the envy of any New York Tammany Democrat.

The Chief, as he was sometimes known, was gruff and subject to violent tirades; but he was also generous, and a tried and true friend to those who delivered on their promises. For a time his back room style of controlling California's Democratic Party served him well. But it also made him many enemies among the state's newly arrived Southerners, and those who had migrated from the still remote frontier states of Ohio, Illinois, and Indiana. In response, and with the prodding of U.S. Senator William Gwin, these groups coalesced into what became known as the Chivalry Wing of the Democratic Party.

Broderick's first clash with the "Chivs," as they became known, came in early 1851 against, not surprisingly, Benjamin F. Moore; it had been Moore who had attempted to expedite the duel between James Jones and Henry

Tefft at the Constitutional Convention. In an election that had been bitterly contested by Moore, Broderick had just been chosen to lead the State Senate. On January 11 as he was passing along the walkway between the Old Adobe and the Mansion House in San Jose, from not ten feet away, Moore drew his revolver and pointed it at him.

"Go ahead and shoot!" the senator shouted, striding toward Moore. The assemblyman was so cowed by Broderick's approach he tucked his revolver back into its holster and left. For days afterward San Jose was abuzz with talk of Broderick's "true grit." Moore thereafter vanished from the California political scene.

Broderick's second clash with the Chivs occurred in March 1852 following some remarks he made about William X. Smith ("Extra Billy," as he was known), who later became the governor of Virginia. Several weeks prior Smith had played a key role in engineering the election of John B. Weller to the U.S. Senate, over Broderick. Still angry over his foiled bid, in a speech to the State Senate Broderick charged that Smith habitually associated with "gamblers and mountebanks."

Smith was offended by the charge and asked for an apology. Realizing he had strayed beyond the bounds of decorum, Broderick did. But his apology was not enough to satisfy the governor's son, Judge Caleb Smith, who several days later posted a card in the *Sacramento State Journal* calling Broderick a "liar, scoundrel and a blackguard."

Broderick and Smith were in San Francisco at the time the card appeared and coincidentally crossed paths at the corner of Sacramento and Front Streets. A crowd of five hundred gathered as the two eyed each other from that short distance. But to everyone's disappointment they turned on their heels and strode away in opposite directions.

The following day Smith offered to withdraw his card on condition that Broderick challenge him to a duel. This was a round-about way to the dueling ground, but as the challenged party Smith would have the choice of weapons, distance, and dueling site. Broderick responded by sending the challenge, thus setting the stage for one of the most bizarre duels in state history.

For his second Broderick chose Vicesimus Turner. "Vi," as he was familiarly known, was a former New Orleans sports promoter who often acted as a mediator in his boss's feuds with the Chivalry Democrats. He had already made quite a name for himself in Panama, en route to California, when he challenged Cornelius Garrison—the soon to be mayor of San Francisco—to a duel. In attempting to set the terms of the affair, an intoxicated Turner insisted the two stand toe to toe with pistols cocked and pressed against the other's forehead. At the word "Fire" they were to pull their triggers.

Garrison declined Turner's challenge without loss of face.

Smith's second was Judge Edward Fitzhugh, a fellow Virginian. For a dueling site he chose a location in what is now downtown Oakland, a quarter mile from San Francisco Bay. Weapons were to be six shooters of precisely the same make—distance twelve paces.

Both duelists agreed that at the word they would begin advancing on each other, firing their revolvers at will, until one or both went down.

Broderick assigned Judge Edward McGowan the task of finding a suitable weapon. McGowan settled on a revolver owned by Charles P. Duane, a Broderick protégé, saloon owner, and one of the most feared brawlers in San Francisco. Earlier, "Dutch Charlie," as he was known, upon purchasing the revolver, had discovered that the cartridge caps often caught in one of its cylinder chambers, preventing further rotation and fire. To correct the problem he filed the chamber. Yet it was only after the duel that Duane bothered to inform McGowan of the pistol's inherent defect. Not by coincidence, Caleb Smith, in choosing his six-shooter, discovered it had the same problem. But instead of filing the chamber, he decided to opt for another advantage.

News of the impending duel spread across San Francisco and from the evening of March 17 into the morning hours of the 18 the town's fleet of white hall boats* ferried 150 spectators across the Bay. The last of the throng sloshed ashore just as the sun was breaking through the fog. Off in the distance they could see Broderick and Smith, and their partisans clustered a quarter mile apart. As the stragglers pressed forward the two parties converged.

After Smith took his position his second, Judge Fitzhugh, threw Broderick, Turner, and McGowan a surprise by demanding that as the challenged party Smith was entitled to not only the type of weapon, but the weapon itself. Though unaware of the innate defect in the revolvers, Turner and McGowan wrangled angrily over the demand until Broderick volunteered to settle the matter with a coin toss. Smith won the toss and chose Broderick's filed weapon.

As McGowan began loading Broderick's defective six-shooter, the senator pulled a heavy cased gold watch from his vest pocket and handed it to Turner. In yet a second passage of events, even more fateful than the exchange of weapons, Turner handed it back, saying, "Keep it, its part of a gentleman's wearing apparel. If the other side does not object, wear it."

---

* Boats used to ferry passengers to ocean-going vessels were then called white hall boats.

Judge Fitzhugh, witness to the exchange, made no objection and Broderick pocketed his watch. The six shooters were handed to the duelists and moments later Fitzhugh called out, "Gentlemen, are you ready?"

"Ready!" answered both.

"Fire!"

The revolvers cracked simultaneously, but after the first shot Broderick's cap caught in the cylinder, preventing further fire. In the face of Smith's barrage, he clasped the revolver between his knees to force the trigger back. Just as he straightened himself with cocked trigger, one of Smith's rounds slammed into his stomach, staggering him and knocking his hat to the ground. He recovered his balance and returned fire, emptying his weapon without effect.

With all rounds expended, Turner rushed over and unbuttoned Broderick's coat. On examination he found that Smith's bullet had struck his gold watch, shattering it into fragments and causing a small flesh wound. A curious crowd pressed around as Turner tucked his shirt back into his pants and asked if he was ready to continue the duel.

"Certainly I am."

Turner ordered the crowd back then left to confer with Fitzhugh. A few minutes later he returned and told Broderick that Judge Smith had acknowledged him "an honorable gentleman."

"That is sufficient."

Turner escorted Broderick to the middle of the dueling ground where he and Smith shook hands, ending the duel.

Judge Smith continued practicing law until 1856. That year he joined William Walker's filibustering expedition into Nicaragua and was killed in the fighting there. Judge Fitzhugh moved to Mariposa to practice law, and was among the first to discover the giant sequoia trees. Vi Turner's trail across the California landscape fades after the duel, and beyond 1856 disappears altogether. By contrast Judge Edward "Ned" McGowan's trail grows easier to trace with every passing year.

But the easiest trail to follow of all is Broderick's: his brawl with Assemblyman James Fraenor in late 1852; his face down of Colonel Billy Peyton in 1853; his attempt to legislate himself U.S. Senator in 1854; his key role in provoking the Baptist Church riot at the Democratic Convention that same year; his stand against the Vigilance Committee of 1856; his bargain with William M. Gwin (made inside a shower stall), to make both of them U.S. Senators, and finally his duel with State Supreme Court Justice, David Terry in 1859.

11

Juanita Avenged

In the early part of 1852 near Downieville, Sierra County, an affair of honor took place between John Kelly and William S. Speare, the first duel fought in the state over a woman. Around Sierra and Nevada counties, John Kelly was known as "Kelly the Fiddler" for his skill in playing that instrument. He did his fair share of scraping the creek beds for gold, but was never so happy as when scraping a bow across his fiddle. His opponent in the duel was William Speare, a handsome young lawyer with a fine sense of humor when sober. Yet this was the same William Speare, who in July 1851, in a state of intoxication, joined a Downieville Vigilance Committee. As a member of that committee he was the prosecutor in the trial of Juanita Joseffa, who became the first woman to be hanged in California.

A writer vividly recalled how three prominent state figures were in Downieville on the day the hanging took place. The most prominent among them was U.S. Senator John B. Weller who was standing on the balcony of a hotel within view of the lynching. Later asked why he had not made a greater effort to save Juanita, Weller lamented, "The hopelessness of her plight was beyond my eloquence."

Amidst the same tumult another prominent politician, Stephen J. Field, climbed atop a barrel where he tried to harangue the crowd into turning Juanita over to the sheriff (she had killed a miner under questionable circumstances). Sensing that he was impressing no one, Field then shouted at the top of his lungs, "Walker, get Walker!" He was referring to William Walker, the third noted figure in Downieville that morning. Unfortunately Walker had left shortly before the mob assembled. Perhaps the Connecticut Yankee and Tennessee Chivalryman together could have saved Juanita's life.

But alone Field was tumbled from his barrel, and the mob led Juanita to a bridge over the North Yuba River. There she removed her panama hat and lifted her tresses high over her head to aid the hangman in slipping the noose around her neck. Minutes later she was swinging at the end of a rope over the surging waters of the North Yuba. Yet in those years the pace of life was so ferocious that within weeks of Juanita's lynching almost everybody in Sierra County, including William Speare and John Kelly had placed the event behind them.

The following year a more fortunate young woman whose name has been lost to posterity settled in Downieville and soon became an object of affection for Kelly and Speare. Their rivalry soon became intense. So intense friends of both tried to settle their claims to the charmer, but neither would budge from his position, which was—"I must have her."

The young woman only inflamed passions further by insisting that she loved both of them. As the weeks passed Kelly became so annoyed with Speare's more eloquent style of courting that he decided to challenge him to a duel in the "fist to skull" fashion. Speare would not hear of it. Rather, he insisted they settle the matter in a mode approved by gentlemen—Colt six shooters at twelve paces. The two would open fire at the word and continue firing until their revolvers were empty. The survivor would gain the woman's hand, while the other would provide a chore for the undertaker.

Kelly agreed and chose as his second an easygoing miner named Tom Coburn. Speare chose Joseph C. McKibbin, a popular figure around Downieville who would one day represent Northern California in the U.S. Congress. A Dr. Dronin agreed to act as surgeon for both.

The duel was no secret and on the day of the meeting a large crowd followed Kelly and Speare out of Downieville to Sportsman's Flat, one mile above town on the North Yuba River. The woman who sparked the duel solemnly accompanied Kelly and Speare to the flat, where after being assisted across the river, she seated herself on a rock with a commanding view of events to unfold. Like Rachel of old, she refused to be consoled and wept at the prospect of losing one, or perhaps both her lovers.

Speare's second, McKibbin, meanwhile won the right to call fire. After explaining how the call would be made, McKibbin, using a term that belied the gravity of the occasion, called out, "Are you duffers ready?"

"Yes, ready", shouted Speare.

"Me, too," cried Kelly.

"Fire!" shouted McKibbin.

The hills echoed with the report of gunfire; yet everyone, including the damsel across the way, was surprised to see Kelly and Speare both on their feet. As no more calls were to be made, Speare immediately cocked his weapon and took aim. Kelly, whose Colt had jammed, turned pale and then red as Speare carefully drew his bead and pulled the trigger. His Colt went off with a bang, but to the astonishment of everyone Kelly remained standing.

The crowd fell silent as Kelly resumed his struggle with the Colt while Speare prepared for another shot. Suddenly in desperation Kelly reared back, and with a shout that could be heard half way to Downieville, flung his revolver at him.

Speare ducked beneath the hurtling gun, turned on his heels and ran. The crowd, informed that he had violated the code of honor, rushed off in pursuit. Speare led them on a frantic chase over ridge and gulch, was knocked down and carried back to the dueling ground. There he was confronted by the triumphant Kelly and the young woman, who by this time had re-crossed the North Yuba and taken her place at his side.

That night Downieville learned that Joe McKibbin and Tom Coburn had loaded the two six shooters with blanks. That is why of the two weapons, Kelly's, as it hurtled toward Speare's forehead, was far and away the most dangerous. Thus did end California's first hoax on the field of honor.

John Kelly married the pretty young woman, and tradition has it they lived happily ever after.

Not so William Speare. As the years passed he became a heavy drinker. Late in the 1850s he moved to Washington Territory where he was arrested for selling whiskey to the Indians. Later he joined a party of settlers in pursuit of the warlike Cayuse. When he and a companion became separated from the main party, they were ambushed and scalped. Thus a young fiddler named John Kelly and the Cayuse Indians scored a revenge of sorts on the figure most responsible for the lynching of Juanita Joseffa on that July afternoon of 1851.

12

California's Dueling
Bard of Avon

Friends of *Calaveras Chronicle* founder Harry De Courcey—and among the miners and saloon owners there were hundreds—swore that he looked like William Shakespeare. In fact De Courcey was a Shakespeare aficionado, who imitated the immortal play right in the way he cropped his hair and trimmed his mustache. Through the early 1850s his pleasing voice, ringing out the stanzas of Macbeth, Henry IV, and Romeo and Juliet always brought a crowd in from the street. He was also a flashy dresser who wore a ring on each finger, and at a time when there were few women in California, was often seen in their company.

De Courcey was raised in Natchez, Mississippi, where as a young man he took up riverboat gambling and from time to time serving as a newspaper editor. On learning gold was discovered he left with the first wagon trains. Like many river boat types and journalists, he soon found mining an occupation not to his liking. Heeding the siren call of the editor's sanctum, on October 9, 1851, at Mokelumne Hill, with Henry Hamilton and J.J. Ayres as partners, he founded the *Calaveras Chronicle*.

In the realm of California politics De Courcey was one of those oddities— a Whig afloat in a sea of Democrats. Like most Whigs with political aspirations, he was soon forced to accommodate the dominant party. Over time he naturally drew close to the Chivalry Democrats, while strongly opposing the Broderick wing of the party which in 1852 had just emplaced their man, John Bigler, in the governor's chair.

Unlike De Courcey, very little is known about William H. Carter, his opponent in the duel that lay just beyond, other than that he was a close friend of Governor Bigler. A native of Pennsylvania, Carter had mined in El Dorado County before helping to establish the *Sacramento Democratic State Journal* in late 1851.

By then California newspaper editors had forged such a quarrelsome reputation for themselves, many began playfully posting signs over their doorways reading "Subscriptions accepted 9 to 4; challenges 11 to Noon."

Carter was probably among the first to hang that eye-catching notice adjacent his shingle. He was one of the best pistol and rifle shots in the state, and when not astride his tripod penning an editorial, was off hunting in the sloughs of the Sacramento Valley.

In April 1852 a highly sarcastic, unsigned column appeared in the *Calaveras Chronicle*, criticizing Governor Bigler and the newspaper it termed his "organ," the *Democratic State Journal*. The column infuriated Carter. The following month, after boarding a riverboat bound from San Francisco to Sacramento, he encountered none other than Harry De Courcey. Still fuming over the editorial, he asked who had written it. When De Courcey replied he had, and that he stood by every word of it, an argument followed during which Carter slapped him. Friends broke up the brawl that ensued.

As the boat steamed up the river De Courcey learned that Carter was a dead shot with any firearm. Yet so humiliated was he by the public slap the next day he sent him a challenge. Carter accepted. Following the acceptance De Courcey sought out an old friend, Edward Kemble, co-founder of the *Alta California* and asked him to serve as his second. Kemble had arrived in California in 1847 with Sam Brannan. It was he who had served as Henry F. Teschemaker's second in his duel with Lieutenant Bonneycastle.

Upon accepting De Courcey's request, Kemble insisted that he follow his instructions to the letter. He agreed and Kemble escorted him to a room on the second floor of the old Jones Hotel in Sacramento where he left him with orders to see no one. For the next several days, morning, noon, and night Kemble appeared in De Courcey's doorway with a jug of water, a pot of tea, and a saucer of toast. While De Courcey wolfed down his meager meal the two discussed the impending duel.

In negotiating its terms Kemble set up an intentionally long, argumentative correspondence with Carter's second, D.K. Lyle. Only after several days had passed did he agree to hold the duel on the early morning of May 9, 1852, near Washington (present day Broderick). Carter had chosen dueling pistols, distance twelve paces.

It was a bright spring morning as De Courcey, Kemble, Carter, Lyle, Dr. J. K. Pierce, acting as surgeon for both, and a small party of followers took the ferry across the Sacramento River. As they arrived on the ground Carter appeared his customary confident self, while De Courcey looked drawn and pale—not from fear, but from his confinement and fasting.

Moments later a single coin was tossed for both position and the right to call fire. Lyle won. As Carter took his place, his back to the sun, Lyle called out, "Are you ready"?

"Ready!" shouted Carter.

"Ready!" said De Courcey, squinting into the sun.

"Fire!"

Carter fired a split second before De Courcey, his ball ripping a furrow in his coat sleeve, but leaving him uninjured. De Courcey's ball landed in the dirt a few inches in front of Carter's boot.

Smiling, but looking like death warmed over, De Courcey turned to Kemble and said, "That was a close shave, Ned. Next time he'll plug me sure."

"Oh bother! But I say Harry, be careful to fire the instant the word is given. That's your best chance."

The pistols were reloaded and Carter and De Courcey resumed their positions.

"Are you ready?" called Lyle.

"Ready!"

"Fire!"

Both pistols cracked at the same instant. Standing unruffled and unharmed in the morning breeze, Carter watched as De Courcey staggered and fell to the earth. His ball had passed through De Courcey's stomach, inflicting a mortal wound. As Dr. Pierce rushed over and knelt at the stricken man's side, Carter, accompanied by Lyle, strode over, extended his hand and said, "Harry, I am sorry for you old man."

"That's all right," said De Courcey reaching up to clasp. "I've no fault to find."

Late that morning De Courcey was carried to his room at the Jones Hotel to await death. Many in Sacramento spoke gravely of his passing, but those same friends were pleasantly surprised the following morning when he awoke, not only alive but feeling better. Surprise turned to astonishment in the days to follow as he resumed his brassy manner of old.

One of his friends was Louis P. Lull, editor of the *San Francisco Whig* who was startled when De Courcey, in response to his condolences, burst out laughing. That afternoon Lull sought out Kemble and asked, "How is it Harry looks so well?"

"Harry's all right. He'll pull through."

"How can a man be shot in the stomach and still live?"

Kemble then explained that a few days target practice would not have improved De Courcey's chances. Resigned to his man to taking a hit, he told Lull that if Harry had suffered a head or chest wound, he could do nothing, but that a shot in the midsection could be countered by purging the stomach; thus the three-day diet of tea, toast, and water.

Harry De Courcey went on to a complete recovery.

Later that same year Kemble's partner at the *Alta California* was killed in a rifle duel. The editor renounced dueling as a barbarous practice, sold his share of the *Alta* and returned to New York. Three years later he returned to California, made a tour of the state's newspaper offices and published a book titled *A History of California Newspapers, 1846–1858*. Today it remains a work of great value.

Following his recovery De Courcey sold his share of the *Calaveras Chronicle* and returned to his favorite haunt—the saloon. There his convivial voice, again ringing out Shakespeare in a Southwestern twang, continued to draw the patrons. His personal life however went into a spin. Late in 1853, while helping C.W. Stiles establish the *Butte Record* in Oroville, he engaged another newspaper editor, Lovic "Long Primer" Hall, in a brawl that ended only after De Courcey plunged a Bowie knife into Hall's back. The affray resulted in several weeks confinement for both—Hall in bed, De Courcey in jail.

By then, like so many duelists before, and after, De Courcey had become a heavy drinker. He drifted back to Sacramento and then to San Francisco where in September 1854 he died alone in a rented room of what was perhaps a stroke. It had been quite a slide from the top of an editor's tripod to the bottom of a bar stool, but many turned out for the funeral of California's Dueling Bard of Avon.

13

Gentleman John

Alas how sadly times have changed! Honor pricks no editor in these degenerate days; the days of chivalry have passed away. Editors then went out on the field of honor. Kemble, Nugent, Washington, Johnston, Russell, Washburne, Rust, Stidger . . . The "Augean Stables" should be cleansed and the versatile, consistent and dignified editor appointed censor.

So wrote the "Judge of the Duel," Edward McGowan in 1878, pining away for the golden years when a fighting editor was a fighting editor. Of the many editors who fought duels during the Golden Era, the one McGowan most probably had in mind was John Nugent, publisher of the *San Francisco Daily Herald*. Over a period of sixteen months Nugent faced three duelists, a record that stands to this day.

The John Nugent story begins in 1824 on the misty coast of Galway, Ireland. His family may have been true descendants of the Emerald Isle, but were more likely Anglo imports as they arrived in New York City in 1828, already well-to-do. Devoted to their son, they sent him to Catholic College, New Jersey, where he earned a degree in the classics; he was an avid reader of Sir Walter Scott. Shortly after graduation the handsome, slightly built, meticulously dressed youth became the Washington, D.C. correspondent for the *New York Herald*.

In 1848, after the Mexican War ended Nugent, like many other young men on the East Coast, decided to go west to see what America had won for itself in the recent conflict. While laying over in San Antonio, he met the Texas Ranger Jack Hays, whose exploits during the war and on the frontier had already made him a national figure.

In May 1849, after learning that gold had been discovered, Nugent and Hays, with a party of Texas Argonauts, set out for the West Coast. Shortly after arriving in San Francisco Nugent left for Monterey to attend the Constitutional Convention. There his intellect, hard work, and graceful manners earned him the position of chief clerk for the first legislature held in California. Whether working with legislators or chatting inside a billiard saloon, Nugent was always well-mannered, but beneath his calm exterior acquaintances noted an unruffled stubbornness that some would later find maddening.

In June of 1850, with the financial backing of several recent arrivals, he founded the *San Francisco Daily Herald*, the city's second newspaper after the *Alta California*. Though a lifelong Whig, Nugent sought to keep the *Herald* independent in politics, even though he was a bitter critic of Broderick. He also gathered around him a coterie of noted Southerners. In the Southerners he found much to admire, their manners and company preferable to his fellow New Yorkers, who counted too many ruffians in the mold of Billy Mulligan, Charles P. Duane, and Yankee Sullivan. Hence the *Herald* office became a gathering place for the "rose water" crowd: Augustus and Hamilton Bowie, Charles Fairfax, Edmund Randolph, and Benjamin F. Washington.

Shortly after establishing his paper, Nugent was introduced to William Walker. He was greatly impressed by Walker's cool composed persona, in many respects a mirror image of his own. Moreover, there was his newspaper background with the *New Orleans Crescent*, and his stand on such issues as liberal divorce laws, free trade, and the rights of foreign nationals (these sympathies did not extend to freeing America's slaves). Thus did Nugent hire him to edit the *Herald*.

His distaste for corrupt politics, affecting San Francisco even at that early date, was matched only by Walker's. In February 1851 the editor involved himself in a wild exchange with municipal judge Levi Parson, whom he accused of failing to indict known criminals (Parson, you will recall, had served as Will Hicks Graham's second in his duel with George Frank Lemon). Indeed Walker had a strong point—the judge often abandoned his bench for days at a time to play the gambling tables.

Angered by the accusation, Parson closed down the *Herald*, charged Walker with libel, and ordered his arrest. At his trial, presided over by the judge himself, Walker was found guilty as charged, fined $500, and jailed. Within minutes fistfights broke out in the courtroom, amidst cries of judicial tyranny. In the days that followed Nugent reset the *Herald*'s press and applying his knowledge of the Bill of Rights, launched a series of attacks on Parson, so powerful that popular opinion forced him to free Walker and abandon the bench.

Nugent's first appearance on the field of honor occurred about a year later—March 1852—his opponent, Edward Gilbert, co-founder of the *Alta California*. Since arriving in California in 1846, Gilbert had prospered as a politician and newspaper editor. His temper, however, had led him into numerous tangles and perhaps it was inevitable that he would find Nugent's success with the upstart *Herald* annoying. Angered at having been cut out of the lucrative "San Francisco Associated Auctioneers" advertising contract, he published some malicious statements about how Nugent had closed the deal.

The *Herald* publisher demanded that Gilbert retract his claim, and when he refused challenged him. Shortly after, on the dueling ground, before a large crowd of spectators, Gilbert recanted his charge and agreed to publish the retraction in the *Alta*. The humiliation proved so great however that several issues of the *Alta* appeared without the posting. Again Nugent demanded he publish the retraction. The following day, at great personal anguish Gilbert did so. Thus did John Nugent, who had yet to fire a shot on the dueling ground, become a San Francisco celebrity of sorts.

Though Nugent's first face-off does appear innocuous, the many remarks witnesses made regarding Gilbert's cowardice made a powerful impression on the state populace, sending a clear and dire warning of the disgrace awaiting those who failed to stand tall on the "field of honor." It was a social climate that would soon lead to Gilbert's death.

Nugent's courtesy was always a hallmark of his person on the street, but not a hallmark of his newspaper columns. Just four months after his affair with Gilbert , his vehemence with the pen embroiled him in real gunfire. For some time he had been carrying on an editorial war with the Broderick Democrats, in particular with an alderman named John Cotter who had just won a seat on the city council. When Nugent charged that he had been "stuffed" into office by bogus ballots, Cotter blasted him before the Board of Aldermen. The editor read the speech and sent Cotter a challenge that he accepted.

The day before the duel, Nugent and his second, City Treasurer Hamilton Bowie, left town for present day Sausalito. Bowie, a native of Calvert, Maryland, was perhaps California's foremost authority on the "code of honor." Cotter and his second, Judge Edward McGowan, in the company of David Broderick, similarly left for Sausalito.

On the morning of the event, July 15, 1852, some two hundred followers of both parties crossed San Pablo Bay in steamers, scrambled ashore and after climbing into waiting teams of carriages raced off to the dueling ground, two miles distant at present day Rodeo. The affair had all the trappings of a Fourth of July celebration and was to have taken place at noon, but because Nugent missed the boat from Sausalito, he failed to show until 2:30 p.m. The delay caused much ugly talk about his courage that was silenced only by his appearance.

At a quarter to three, Nugent, with Colt revolver in hand, took his position ten paces opposite Cotter. Moments later as Bowie called out "Fire—one, two three—stop!" the duelists cocked their weapons, shot and missed.

On the second call Nugent fired first, and again missed. Finding that the cap had caught in his weapon's cylinder (a maddening phenomena that would continue well into the Civil War), he casually threw out his left leg and worked on it while Cotter, his revolver in hand, stood immobilized, transfixed at the sight before him. Here Broderick shouted, "Cock your pistol sir—cock your pistol!"

Recovering his faculties, Cotter cocked his revolver and fired. His shot struck Nugent in the exposed leg, inflicting a compound fracture and knocking him to the ground.

Under the rules of the code, once the word "Fire" is given no one is permitted to offer the duelists any advice, and Broderick was severely chastised for his misconduct. Several surgeons meanwhile gathered around Nugent as Cotter strode over, reached down and shook his hand. The surgeons did remove the slug, but the editor was left on crutches for eight months.

Nugent's next duel occurred in June of 1853, after the San Francisco City Council convened to draw up a new charter. Most of those at work on the charter were Broderick Democrats, among them Colonel Thomas Hayes, whose claim to a 160-acre tract of land (Hayes Valley) was quickly certified by the council. Shortly after, an editorial appeared in the *Herald*, denouncing the council members as "Dogberries." Hayes and the other members promptly published a card in the *San Francisco Whig*, denouncing the *Herald* in similar terms. The next day Nugent sent Hamilton Bowie into Hayes's office with a challenge.

Hayes accepted. A tall, imposing New Yorker of crossed eye, he had fought in the Mexican War, and served as a deputy sheriff under San Francisco Sheriff Jack Hays. Considered a better than average shot, for weapons he chose Mississippi Yagers at forty paces. Since its appearance in 1842 the Yager rifle had been made famous during the Mexican War by Jefferson Davis's First Mississippi Regiment—hence the name. This particular pair of Yagers was owned by San Francisco's most noted gun shop owner, Andrew Jackson "Natchez" Taylor.

For his second Hayes chose Judge Edward McGowan. The evening prior to the duel, McGowan nailed a shirt and a pair of pants to a board fence and Hayes began limbering up. In the ensuing practice, he shredded the garments and that section of fence with 17 of 20 shots at forty paces.

How Nugent occupied himself the evening before the duel is unknown, but in the small hours of June 13, 1853, accompanied by Bowie, he departed for the *Sans Souci* House. Hayes, accompanied by McGowan and Senator Broderick left at almost the same time. At sunrise, flanked by a large crowd of spectators, the duelists took their positions, forty paces apart, backs to one another.

Seconds later at the call to fire, Nugent and Hayes both whirled, fired and missed. At this point Broderick, revealing a gallant side to his nature, strolled over to Hayes and informed him that since Nugent was having trouble making his pivot—owing to the wound he had suffered in his duel with Cotter—the "gentlemanly" thing to do was wait until he had pivoted before firing. Hayes agreed.

On the second call Nugent turned, fired and again missed. Moments later Hayes's booming Yager sent a .54-caliber bullet into his right arm above the elbow. The shot smashed on through the editor's shoulder, staggering him and spraying himself and the turf below with blood. To the awe of spectators he again turned his back to await the next call. At the word he once more turned, fired and missed. Seconds later as Hayes drew his mark, Nugent, his right side drenched in blood, crumpled to the earth.

As he lay prone, Hayes strode over, reached down and shook his hand. The two went on to become the best of friends, in the words of Hayes's second, Ned McGowan—"How I like a man after I have fought him once!"

Hayes continued active in California politics through most of the decade. By 1858 he had fallen out with Broderick and became a Chivalry Democrat, serving as David Terry's second in the 1859 duel with his old Chief.

Nugent's duel with Hayes, which nearly cost him his arm, was the last time he resorted to gunfire to settle accounts. Though his reputation as a crack shot never lived up to billing, his mettle, described as beyond valor in the two shootouts, further bolstered his celebrity status. In the eyes of Western chivalry, it was less a matter of who got shot, than how a man bore himself on the field.

Some of Nugent's biting sarcasm disappeared from his columns after his last duel, but he never lost his courage. In 1856, alone among all San Francisco newspaper editors, he opposed the Vigilantes, offering powerful editorial support to his old nemeses, Ned McGowan, in his flight before the Vigilance Committee's numerous understrappers. His defiant stand and the persecution he suffered afterward are but two more chapters in the tumultuous life of Gentleman John Nugent.

14

The Duel at Rancho del Paso

The sun rose over the oak studded grasslands of Rancho del Paso, six miles from downtown Sacramento, California—the date August 2, 1852. Even though cooler air had drifted into the Central Valley, the birds among the adjacent trees continued sending forth their same listless notes of high summer.

In the midst of the scene a cluster of somber men in dark coats and either plug or slouched hats gathered. On the dueling ground before them, forty paces apart, facing each other with rifle butts on hips were two figures. The smaller form, sporting a goatee, vest and green surtout, was *Alta California* editor Edward Gilbert. The large, clean-shaven figure wearing a *serape* was State Senator James W. Denver. A long half hour would pass before one of them would lie dying, a victim of one of the most senseless duels in California history.

In the past James Denver's political enemies have blamed him for the tragedy; others have more correctly blamed Edward Gilbert. New evidence upholds the latter argument beyond any doubt, but also suggests that the *Alta* editor was carrying to the dueling ground an agonizing burden the senator may not have been aware of.

Gilbert was born in 1820 in Albany, New York. In 1846, with the onset of the Mexican War, he enlisted in Jonathan Stevenson's regiment and arrived in California a first lieutenant. Following the conquest of the region he rose rapidly in prominence and was elected as one of the state's first two congressmen. In 1849, the year he was elected to Congress, Gilbert co-founded the *Alta California* newspaper and soon established himself as a powerful writer. His newspaper office quickly became a gathering point for a number of San Francisco reformers, anxious to overthrow the town's political establishment. His explosive temper however embroiled him in several major disputes.

He of course was not the only crusading newspaper editor in town; aside from Andrew C. Russell of the *San Francisco Picayune*, there was John

Nugent of the *San Francisco Daily Herald*. The story of Gilbert's less than gallant conduct in his face-off with Nugent has already been told, but its devastating effect on his psyche has not.

In New York he could have easily tossed his disgrace aside, but in San Francisco he found it impossible; in the months to follow he became withdrawn. Only occasionally was he seen, shabbily dressed, walking a small dog, barely acknowledging those he encountered. Although Gilbert received solace from a number of friends, he suspected many former acquaintances of scorning his company. Some slights were doubtless genuine, but he probably imagined many more.

And as if to atone for his eclipse from the public scene, his columns in the *Alta* grew more strident. In June of 1852 he penned a column ridiculing Governor Bigler and the relief train he had organized in the Carson Valley to aid weary emigrants before their final trek over the Sierras. In charge of the governor's relief effort was State Senator James W. Denver.

Born near Winchester, Virginia in 1817, raised on a farm in Clinton County, Ohio, as a youth Denver earned a degree at Cincinnati Law School before departing for Platte City, Missouri, where he became a newspaper editor. When the Mexican War broke out he received a captain's commission, organized a company of 110 volunteers and went off to Mexico. He fought in a number of battles, including Chapultepec, and rose to the rank of brigadier-general.

After the war, Denver returned to Missouri, where he resumed publishing his old newspaper. Curiosity over California's newly discovered gold fields however soon drew him westward. He arrived in Sacramento in the fall of 1850 and shortly after departed for Trinity County where he established a pack train, transporting supplies from the Humboldt Coast into the mines.

Denver was sometimes gruff, but he was better educated than most of the miners he mingled with, and at six foot two, 220 pounds, he had a commanding presence. That year the voters of Trinity, Shasta, and Klamath Counties (Klamath was later broken up into Del Norte and Siskiyou) chose him to represent them in the State Senate. The numerous references to him in the old journals indicate the people of Northern California were not only pleased with his performance at the state capital, but proud of him.

Following the end of the 1852 session Denver accepted Governor Bigler's request to manage the Carson Valley relief train. When Gilbert's column appeared, accusing the organizers of grand standing, Denver responded in the *Sacramento Democratic Journal* with the following: "We are well satisfied that none but a personal enemy could imagine such a thing, and that enemy must be of the smallest possible caliber, who would descend so low as to pervert the facts."

Gilbert retaliated in the *Alta* with a lightly veiled challenge: "If any gentleman attached to the train, or any other friend of the governor desires to make issue upon the matter, they know where to find us."

On July 29 Denver posted a second card in the *Journal*, stating, "If the editor of the *Alta* thinks himself aggrieved by anything . . . he can rest assured he can have any issue upon the matter he may desire. Lest he shall have an excuse that he did not know where to find me, I will state during the summer I shall be engaged with the relief train [Carson Valley, Nevada], and on the first Monday in January next I expect to be in Vallejo."

When Gilbert demanded that Denver withdraw his card he refused. Gilbert then sent his close friend Henry F. Teschemacher to Carson Valley with a challenge. Denver accepted and agreed to meet on August 2, at Rancho del Paso, where the Oak Grove House had recently been erected. He then chose his second, the renowned road builder, Vincent E. Geiger. The two immediately crossed the Sierras, entering Sacramento on the night of August 1.

Denver, a good shot with any weapon and a devastating shot with a rifle, chose Wesson Rifles at forty paces. Gilbert was a good shot with a pistol, but much out of practice with rifles since his days with Stevenson's regiment. Regardless, Denver did not even own a Wesson. On the night of his arrival in Sacramento, he purchased one from a gunsmith, who was forced to hurriedly mount a sight on the disassembled weapon.

The following morning as Denver approached the dueling ground he still had not fired his new rifle. In fact the evidence suggests he thought the duel, as such, would never come off. Almost as he had accepted the challenge, he decided to end the feud without bloodshed; so had a number of Gilbert's friends who had made an overture to Denver without the editor's knowledge. Denver accepted the peace note and the news was relayed to Gilbert. But to everyone's dismay he refused to call the duel off.

Those close to Gilbert knew of his earlier humiliation and were aware of his frantic need to regain his self-esteem, a factor that could only have added to their sorrow. Denver had not been present in San Francisco earlier in the year, but probably knew of Gilbert's encounter with Nugent; still, he may not have been aware of the tremendous damage it had done to his pride. Hence his persistence in believing that even though the editor was insistent on a meeting, once on the ground, he would throw his shot away. For his part he would do the same and the dispute would end without loss of life.

Gilbert had already taken his position a quarter mile from the Oak Grove House when Denver approached on foot. Neither the strapping senator or the slightly built editor had ever seen each other before. Some sixty observers looked on grimly as the rifles were loaded and handed to each duelist. Because Vincent Geiger won the coin toss, he was to make the call.

At the word "Fire!" Denver intentionally aimed low, hoping that if Gilbert were hit the wound would not be serious. He missed. But Gilbert's shot, fired simultaneously, whirred menacingly close to his ear.

Angered by the near miss, but relieved that the duel had ended, Denver handed his weapon to Geiger and strode off toward the Oak Grove House. He was almost a hundred yards up the road when Dr. Wake Briarly, who had agreed to act as a surgeon for both duelists, overtook him. In sorrow the doctor told him that Gilbert demanded a second shot. In reply Denver said, "All I want to do is shake his hand." Briarly trudged back down the road to report his wish, only to return a few minutes later to inform him that Gilbert demanded satisfaction. Once more Denver called for a handshake; once more Gilbert demanded satisfaction.

It then occurred to the senator there was no way he could avoid another shot without losing his own honor. As he strode back down the road Briarly overheard him mutter, "Now, I must defend myself. I will not stand here all day to be shot at."

Out on the meadow he threw his *serape* aside and resumed his position. Both rifles were reloaded and handed to the duelists. Moments later as Geiger barked out "Fire . . ." the guns boomed at the same moment. With terrifying accuracy, Denver's bullet plunged into Gilbert's left vest pocket, tore through his stomach just under the rib cage, burst from his right vest pocket and whirred away. Without moving either foot, Gilbert fell full length to the ground. Despite Dr. Briarly's best efforts, he died in five minutes without uttering a word.

Uninjured by Gilbert's shot, Denver turned and slowly strode back to the Oak Grove House while the editor's friends hoisted his body into a carriage and followed. Inside they joined Denver and Geiger at the breakfast table. After exchanging regrets and condolences, all ate in relative silence. Afterward Gilbert's friends bore his body to Sacramento, and from there by river boat to San Francisco. Denver himself rode back to Sacramento, stayed the night with a friend and the following day struck out for the Carson Valley.

Gloom fell over San Francisco as more than a thousand people prepared for Gilbert's funeral. Politicians allied with him and those opposed to him praised his politics and talent as a writer. In his honor John Nugent bordered the *Herald* columns in black. Gentleman John's precise thoughts on the duel's outcome are unknown, but as perceptive as anyone in town, he must have known that Gilbert had been after blood. If he could not shed Denver's blood, he would gladly shed his own.

James W. Denver went on to become California's secretary of state, congressman for the Northern District of California and then governor of

Kansas. As governor of Kansas he assisted in forming Colorado Territory, and the city of Denver is named after him.

With the outbreak of the Civil War, he reassumed his rank of brigadier general in the Union Army. Following the war he settled in Washington, D.C., where he continued active in politics. Though he returned to California only occasionally, the settlers there never forgot the reluctant duelist who had done so much to bring their troubled young state into the American mainstream.

But if Denver hoped that long ago August morning at Rancho del Paso would fade away he was mistaken. In 1884 friends within the Democratic Party moved to nominate him as a candidate for president. Even though his chances were thought a long shot, in response opponents circulated a pamphlet blaming him for provoking the duel with Gilbert, ending his nomination prospects. He died August 9, 1892 and is buried at the family plot in Wilmington, Ohio.

15

The Captain and the Auctioneer

In early August 1852 a large throng gathered on Montgomery Street near the corner of Merchant in San Francisco. The came from all walks of life, and included Chief Justice of the California Supreme Court Hugh Murray, municipal judge Alexander Wells and such shoulder strikers as Billy Mulligan and Charles P. Duane. Familiar figures to each and all, it should be remembered that in 1852 San Francisco was still a town of less than 25,000 people.

The crowd had earlier learned that E.S. Nugent (no relation to John Nugent) was planning to administer auctioneer William H. Jones a good cow hiding. By way of notoriety, Jones the previous year had played a major role in the formation of San Francisco's first Vigilance Committee. Nugent was a blustering sea captain of Irish extraction. The captain's trouble with Jones had begun some nights before in a saloon, where deep into his cups he besmirched the auctioneer, using profane language. Jones in turn pitched into Nugent, landing several blows to the head, and knocking him to the floor where he continued to administer various and sundry kicks.

Still smarting from the blows and now cracking a bull whip, Nugent was waiting for Jones to emerge from an eating house. Shortly after, having finished a plate of beef steak and oysters, he appeared. Nugent immediately stepped over, uncoiled his whip and methodically applied eight solid strokes. Many of the watchers were unaware of the beating Jones had administered Nugent earlier in the week, and expected him to draw his revolver and at least shoot to wound him. They were thus surprised when the auctioneer, his coat now in tatters, turned and ignobly staggered off up the street. A safe distance away, he turned around, shook his fist at Nugent and shouted, "You must not attempt that again!"

The crowd was mightily amused by his hollow threat, and burst into laughter.

Hard days lay ahead for Jones as he noted many friends crossing the street to avoid meeting him. Acquaintances ignored him even after he made a special effort to greet them. Melancholy and disgusted with himself, he finally wandered into the office of tax collector, Louis Teel, and asked him to forward Nugent a challenge.

Nugent accepted with pleasure and after conferring with several San Franciscans "up on the code" decided to choose Edward McGowan as his second. McGowan in turn informed Teel that his client had chosen dueling pistols at ten paces. The pistols were to be held outward at a 45-degree angle before the word was given. At each call to "Fire . . ." the duelists were to raise their weapons, aim, and pull the triggers.

On August 12 a crowd even larger than the one that had viewed the cow hiding gathered just south of Mission Dolores. Within its midst Jones and Nugent took their places. McGowan, who had won the toss to call fire, then stepped off to the sidelines and asked the familiar question, "Gentleman, are you ready?"

Jones, holding his pistol at 45 degrees, answered "Ready."

Ten paces away, without a word, Nugent raised his pistol and fired at Jones. Miraculously he missed.

According to the code Nugent had waived his life. Many in the crowd were therefore surprised when Jones's second, Louis Teel, failed to draw his pistol and gun him down. But in the haste of assembling his tax lists that morning, the assessor had somehow left his revolver in the top desk drawer.

Deeply embarrassed by Nugent's gaffe, McGowan strode over and informed him that if he had killed Jones he would have been considered by everyone "a cold-blooded murderer." Completely oblivious of the rebuke, Nugent replied,

"I'll get him this time."

The judge contemplated abandoning the field, but in the end decided to give his principle one more chance. On this round, Nugent did wait for McGowan's word before raising his weapon. He also got off the first and most accurate shot, sending a ball through the underside of Jones's arm.

With blood streaming down his side and soaking his clothing, Jones demanded another shot. Nugent agreed. But while the pistols were being loaded his arm suddenly went numb. Urged on by a sympathetic crowd, he pronounced himself satisfied and the duel was ended. Jones, who later recovered from his wound, was helped to his carriage by, among others, Ned McGowan.

Minutes after he was driven off, Nugent, McGowan, and Hamilton Bowie, the latter having viewed the duel from the sidelines, climbed into another carriage. On their way into town the captain began bragging about his Irish ancestors whose lineage, he claimed, ran all the way back to Brian

Borothme. Irritated by his braying, McGowan told Nugent that he had acted like "a perfect blackguard" on the dueling ground.

Angered by the dressing down, Nugent told McGowan that shortly after reaching San Francisco he would receive a challenge. McGowan retorted that he would gladly "try it on" if Nugent could find anyone willing to serve as his second.

The challenge never came. A few nights later while McGowan was target practicing at a shooting gallery, he encountered the captain who acted as if nothing had passed. McGowan noted that in that night's shooting Nugent cleaned up, ringing the bull's eye more times than anyone else in the house. But while McGowan went on to become a bigger than life figure in California lore, Nugent, an increasingly heavy drinker, became a rare sight around San Francisco. He died some years later at the Stockton Insane Asylum.

16

The Leggett-Morrison Duel

At first glance there appears little reason to devote space to a duel between two miners. After all, miners had been blasting away at each other over claim disputes ever since 1849. But the fact remains that these two miners—gentlemen or not—did decide to settle their differences on the dueling ground. In addition, by dint of irony they were both Englishmen, natives of a country where the institution of dueling with firearms had originated, but was now in decline. Worse, it was aided and abetted by American miners, all of whom had emigrated from either Southern states where dueling was in decline, or Northern states where it had died out altogether. Only on the raw borderlands of California, where chivalry's grasp seemed to expand with each passing month, could William Leggett and John Morrison have ever met under such circumstances.

In the year 1851, in remote Plumas County, where the Sierra Nevada does not range so high as further south, but where the canyons are still deep, dark, and filled with gold, William Leggett and John Morrison arrived and staked their claims. Even though the two had been raised in the very same town in England, by coincidence they had never known each other. Their claims adjoined at the head of Missouri Bar on the East Branch of the North Fork of the Feather River, and proved to be among the richest in the area.

Leggett was an easy-going fellow who was quickly befriended by the American miners. A good mimic who possessed a fine baritone, he was always ready to sound his voice at the various miner dances. Morrison was also well liked and often accompanied Leggett's strains with some fine fiddling.

Over the first year the two worked their claims tirelessly, each dreaming of the day he could pull up stakes and return to Merry Old England. At the rate they were piling up the gold dust that day seemed not far off. Unhappily a boundary dispute arose between the two, Morrison insisting an extra few feet of Leggett's claim actually belonged to him. After failing to settle their dispute they each hired a lawyer, Horace Buckland, who represented

Leggett, and Washington Justice, who represented Morrison. Both lawyers carefully examined the deeds, but like their clients before them, could reach no agreement. Buckland strongly upheld Leggett's argument, while Justice similarly insisted Morrison had a right to extend his claim by several feet.

Finally the two attorneys decided that their clients should hire a third, non-interested attorney, to look into the matter: his decision would carry the day. Morrison accepted the proposal, but Leggett refused to consider it. Their hostility to one another grew to such an extent that both hired scouts to patrol their respective claims in their absence. At this point some of Morrison's American friends began urging him to settle his dispute on "the field of honor."

At first he was reluctant, but Leggett's continued refusal to submit their dispute to further arbitration so enraged him that one August morning in 1852, after another night of drinking with the Americans, Morrison sent him a challenge. He promptly accepted and chose his attorney, Horace Buckland as his second. Morrison chose Washington Justice. Despite the popularity of both men, those were rough times in Plumas County and there were many about Missouri Bar who eagerly looked forward to the duel. That both antagonists were Englishmen only added to their excitement.

The chosen dueling site was a quarter of a mile from Missouri Bar, in a ravine where two ridges joined to form a natural amphitheater. Weapons were Colt revolvers, distance fifteen paces, the duelists standing with their backs to one another. The call would be made three times, with one shot to follow each. As no physician was available a young fellow named "Doc" Logan, who had read several medical texts was chosen as surgeon for both duelists. The time was seven o'clock on the evening of August 15; the hour was chosen so the duel would not shorten the work day, while at the same time allowing enough light for good shooting.

At seven o'clock, Washington Justice on behalf of John Morrison won the coin toss for both position and giving the call. As Leggett and Morrison took their places a profound silence fell over the wooded amphitheater as the crowd of over one hundred appeared almost awed as. Justice's voice rang loud and clear, "Are you ready?!"

"I am," responded both in their clipped accents. At the call to "Fire," Leggett and Morrison spun around and pulled their triggers at the same time. Both missed.

The two resumed their positions and waited for the second call. Again at the word both whirled, fired and missed, Leggett snapping off the first shot.

By now the crowd had suddenly remembered what fine young men Morrison and Leggett were. A profound sense of guilt engulfed many as in the fast fading light Buckland and Justice reloaded the revolvers. Some murmured hopefully that with dusk at hand both would miss the last shot. The weapons were quickly passed back and for the last time Justice gave the call. As in the previous exchange, Leggett swung round first, fired, and missed. A half second later Morrison's bullet slammed into the center of his forehead.

Leggett sank to the earth, body shuttering and died before "Doc" Logan could reach him. With the sun having disappeared beyond the canopy of trees, the crowd closed in around Leggett, the dusky woodland floor having brought his pale face into strong relief. Morrison's and Leggett's friends quietly parleyed and at length decided to bury him on the spot. A pick and shovel were brought to the fore and within the leaf covered amphitheater several miners went to work. Sometime after dark they returned to Missouri Bar by lantern light.

As the months passed most of the miners, in their mad pursuit of gold, put Leggett's death behind them. Not so Morrison who sold his claim shortly after and moved to San Francisco. From there he left not for England, but for the Sandwich (Hawaiian) Islands, where some years later he died of too much drink.

17

Groveling in Los Angeles

Through the 1850s and for many years after Los Angeles was a small dusty cow town with a lawless reputation. Despite the mayhem, with some exceptions, such as the shootout between Lieutenant Bonneycastle and Henry Teschamacher, few duels were fought in Los Angeles. Horace Bell, in his *Reminiscences of a Ranger* writes that the reason so few duels were fought in town was because of the disgraceful Magruder-Osborne affair of October 1852.

This singular event took place inside Harry Monroe's restaurant on Commerce Street. The Duff Gordon Sherry was flowing that rainy evening and the men were raising their glasses to toast the greatest Americans in history. Among those present was John Bankhead Magruder, colonel of the Third Artillery Regiment, stationed in San Diego. A Virginian and Mexican War veteran, Prince John, as he was known, was a tall handsome chevalier renowned for his courage and his gifts as a dramatist. During the war with Mexico he had often entertained the troops at remote outposts by staging well reenacted plays of Shakespeare and other playwrights.

Magruder commenced the toasting by raising his glass to Andrew Jackson, the greatest man ever to "trod in shoe leather"; all raised their glasses and drank to Jackson. Another raised his glass to Henry Clay, the greatest American ever to trod in shoe leather; all raised their glasses and drank to Clay. Another raised his glass to Daniel Webster, the greatest American ever to trod in shoe leather; all raised their glasses and drank to Webster.

It finally came the turn of a Dr. William Osborne. Standing and swaying from the effects of too much sherry, Osborne raised his glass and proposed a drink "To my father—Sheriff of Cayuga County, New York, the greatest American ever to trod in shoe leather."

An embarrassed silence fell over the dining room, broken some moments later when Magruder looked up and said, "Doctor, you are a damned fool!"

Without hesitation or thought Osborne challenged Magruder to a duel. The colonel accepted and chose derringers, distance table end to table end—twelve feet. Time, posthaste.

Osborne picked Wilson Jones, a fellow diner as his second. In the coin toss that followed Jones won both the position and right to make the call. Despite this advantage the slightly built Osborne paled as he gazed across the table at the towering Magruder. The other revelers drew back against the wall and the tension in the room mounted as Jones asked, "Gentleman, are you ready?"

At that moment the doctor nervously pulled his trigger. A deafening pop rent the room as a cloud of smoke burst from his derringer. His shot went well to the side of Magruder standing little more than twelve feet away. Through the smoke he watched as the glowering Prince John took aim and began advancing around the table toward him. Turning, he scurried toward the door, a move that according to the code is not permissible. He was seized by several guests and flung back into the center of the room.

Toppling chairs left and right, Osborne stumbled around the table while Magruder continued his stalk. As he made a feint, Osborne dove under the table, scrambled across the floor, grasped Magruder by the shins and cried out, "Colonel Magruder, for the love of God, spare me for my family!"

Magruder broke free of his embrace, gave him a solid kick to the ribs and shouted, "Damn you! I'll save you for the hangman!" Thus ended the duel that Horace Bell alleges heaped so much shame on Los Angeles that no one residing in the area ever again thought of issuing a challenge.

Surprisingly, with the passage of time Doctor Osborne recovered from his disgrace. He established a drug store, became the first settler to import ornamental shrubs into Los Angeles and the first to export Los Angeles grapes to New York.

Prince John later returned to Texas. With the outbreak of the Civil War he joined the Confederacy and was commissioned a general. During the Seven Days Battle he again put his talents as a dramatist to use. In command of a badly outnumbered force, he repeatedly wheeled the same brigade into and out of view of a Union general, leading that general to believe he was commanding an entire division. Magruder's ruse forced a delay in the attack, allowing Confederate reinforcements to arrive and drive the Union Army back. Prince John later ran up a string of victories along the Gulf Coast of Texas.

18

Honorable Mention: 1852

Several lesser known duels were fought in 1852. Among those of which a good account exists was a mid-June Marysville shootout between Charles J. Blackburn and William Woodcock. The antagonists were both Southerners, Blackburn from Virginia, Woodcock from Alabama. Following a bitter quarrel over a business transaction, Blackburn sent a challenge through his second, Colonel Tom Redd.

Sometime passed before Woodcock decided to accept, choosing Judge McDaniel as his second. For weapons he selected 12-gauge double barreled shotguns with eight pieces of buckshot to the load—distance fifty paces. Strange as it may seem, Blackburn's friends discovered that the only two 12-gauge shotguns of any worth in Marysville belonged to friends of Woodcock, neither of whom would loan them out. He was thus forced to purchase one at a hardware store.

At 5 a.m., Blackburn, Woodcock, Redd, McDaniel, and a small crowd gathered one mile from downtown Marysville, adjacent the cemetery. The call was most unusual with the count running to six after the word "fire," giving the duelists more than ample time to unload both barrels into each other. Many observers were unhappy the two had not made an adjustment, principally because Woodcock was much the better shot, and because Blackburn was unfamiliar with his shotgun. James McDuffie, later U.S Marshal for Northern California, a friend of both, tried to arrange a last-minute settlement, but Blackburn turned him away, saying, "I have come to fight."

As McDuffie turned and left for the sidelines, he said "You will be killed."

His pronouncement proved almost correct. On his first fire Woodcock nearly took Blackburn's left arm off at the shoulder. With the remnants of his arm dangling, Blackburn received Woodcock's second load in the groin, ending the duel. Despite his ghastly wounds, Blackburn recovered and, partially disabled, led the remainder of his life working inside an assessor's office. Several years later Woodcock left for the Fraser River diggings, where he opened a general store.

Another duel of note in 1852 was fought on July 9 between James Wethered and Clinton Winters at the Pioneer Race Track in San Francisco. Weapons were Colt six shooters at ten paces. A crowd of forty saw both miss the first three shots. On the fourth call Winter's pistol jammed. While he was trying to force the barrel with both hands, Wethered shot him in the side. Winters recovered from what appears to have been a serious wound.

Yet another duel, this one involving none other than Roy Bean, was fought in February 1852 in San Diego. Bean was then in California visiting his brother, General Josh Bean (known to the *Californios* as General *Frijole*), commander of the state militia. Roy Bean's opponent was a Scotsman named Collins, the cause of the duel a young woman whose name has not been left to posterity. Neither Bean or Collins was familiar with the code, but determined to put on a knightly show for the lady, as well as San Diego residents in general they decided to "do it up" on horseback.

Just outside of town, on the morning of February 24, at the word, before a highly excited and eclectically dressed crowd, from one hundred yards distance Bean and Collins put the spurs to their mounts, and with Colt revolvers raised, bore down on each other. As they closed within thirty feet, Collins fired two shots at Bean. Both missed. A split second later, their mounts within fifteen feet of each other, Bean, taking deliberate aim, shot Collins in the leg. His second fire caught Collins's horse in midstride, tumbling it to the ground.

The downed horse notwithstanding, the affair was wildly applauded by the many women in the crowd. While Collins thereafter disappears from California annals, Bean later made it big in Texas where he became known as "Judge Roy Bean; the Law West of the Pecos."

Just the month before (January 10), a lesser known San Diego duel was fought between Crosswaite and Watkins. On the fifth fire Crosswaite was mortally wounded. And in San Francisco, on February 4, a pistol duel took place at the Presidio between J.W. Hunter and Judge A. Gorham; Gorham was shot in the hip.

On June 16, in Washington, Yolo County, William Chappell and R. Ross fired once at each other without effect. Finally, in San Francisco, Archibald Peachy and James Blair exchanged shots at fifteen paces. Peachy discharged his load into the air, while Blair held his fire, ending the duel.

The Chappell-Ross and Blair-Peachy duels in some respects resembled the show duels formerly fought in the eastern United States and Europe. It was common then for duelists to throw their shots away, to the ignorance of many viewers, thus preserving the life and honor of both gentlemen. After 1852 the show duel disappeared in California, where frontier mores made it almost impossible for seconds to work out the sort of face-saving, life-saving devices still accessible to the rest of the world.

19

The Senate Challenges the House

One of the most harrowing duels ever fought on the frontier was that between U.S. Senator William Gwin, and Congressman Joseph Walker McCorkle. Of the two combatants Gwin has since been recognized by friendly and hostile historians alike as one of the most influential politicians of his time.

He grew up in Tennessee where his father, a close friend of Andrew Jackson, often brought the younger Gwin to the president's house for dinner. William became a great admirer of Jackson, and there is little doubt that the great bearing he later displayed as a senator resulted from his close observance of Old Hickory's manner.

After earning a degree in medicine at the University of Nashville, Gwin departed for Mississippi, where thrusting aside his education he engaged in land speculation. He later became a U.S. Marshal before moving on to Texas, where he was elected to Congress. It was also in Texas that he married Mary Hampton Bell, a charming woman whose gifts as a Washington hostess many claim rivaled that of Dolley Madison.

In 1849, after learning that gold had been discovered in California, he departed for the West Coast by steamer. On board he informed his fellow passengers that unlike most of them, he would not be heading for the gold fields. Instead he was planning to remain behind on the coast, working to establish statehood for California. His listeners thought the idea of California becoming a state was half-baked, and reacted with lots of back slaps and friendly derision.

Yet within the year Gwin's dream became a reality. Under his stewardship a convention gathered in Monterey and drew up a state Constitution. The courtly, persuasive Gwin saw many of his suggestions pass muster. And despite his Southern roots he voted against establishing slavery. One of the provisions he was most insistent on inserting into California's Constitution was that which prohibiting anyone fighting a duel from holding political office. As noted earlier, the delegates voted it down. Nonetheless, they rewarded him for his hard work with one of the state's two U.S. Senate seats.

In Washington, Gwin exercised his uncanny knack for "give and take" with other senators, and over the next four years secured more appropriations for his state than its two other senators and four congressmen combined. One of his most important successes was passage of the "California Land Act of 1851." The bill established a board of three land commissioners to determine the legality of Mexican land grants, many of which lacked proper documentation, and granted California settlers the right to appeal the commission's decision. This single act, more than any other gesture, earned Gwin the undying gratitude of the state's rank and file voters.

His success, good looks, and polished manner however gained him the envy of many back home, particularly David Broderick who had notions of becoming a U.S. senator himself. In the cleavage within the Democratic Party that began to widen in 1851, it was only natural that Gwin became the leader of its Chivalry wing. While Broderick held a solid lock on state patronage positions, he had a similar hold on federal offices. His habit of dispersing political plums without consulting others made him many enemies beside Broderick—among them Congressman Joseph McCorkle.

McCorkle was raised in Piqua, Ohio, studied law at Kenyon College, and in 1849, with the Robichaux wagon train, crossed the great western expanses into what is now Butte County. He was a big, quarrelsome man whose most notable feature was a pair of thick-lensed spectacles. Gwin ran afoul of McCorkle in Washington in the spring of 1853, when he drew several patronage appointments from President Pierce without consulting him. Learning that he had once again been bypassed, McCorkle, who had his own patronage promises to keep, was furious.

Even before his term in Washington ended, McCorkle also learned that his own Democratic Party had chosen Milton Latham—one of Gwin's closest friends—to replace him in the House of Representatives. Worse yet, he discovered that Sophia Birdsall, with whom he had fallen deeply in love, had chosen to marry the same Milton Latham. This disappointment was compounded by the fact that Sophia's father, Lewis Birdsall, was another Gwin crony; he had been appointed superintendent of the California branch of the U.S. Mint. Though furious with Latham, McCorkle became convinced that Gwin was his real nemeses.

That April on board the same steamer for California, he refused to speak to Gwin. A week after arriving in San Francisco, he confronted the senator at the Pioneer Race Track, and before a large crowd he called him, among other things, "a deceitful coward." Gwin was so shaken by the outburst he left the racecourse without a word. That evening he wrote McCorkle a letter claiming that he did not understand the source of his anger, and demanded a retraction of his tirade. The congressman retorted with a letter of his own, claiming that Gwin "god damn well" understood the source of his anger. He also refused to retract his tongue lashing.

After consulting with friends, the thoroughly humiliated Gwin sent McCorkle a challenge. It was accepted. Thus did the most respected figure in all of California, the man who once insisted that all duelists be prohibited from holding public office, blunder onto its field of honor.

For a second he chose U.S. Attorney, Samuel Inge, one of those patronage appointments McCorkle most objected to; McCorkle named his close friend, Frank Stewart, as his. The date of the duel was set for June 1, 1853—the site near San Mateo, far beyond the trifling arm of San Francisco law. For weapons the congressman borrowed from gun shop owner, A.J. "Natchez" Taylor, the very same Mississippi Yagers that would be employed two weeks later in the duel between John Nugent and Thomas Hayes. There was some dispute about the distance, Gwin arguing for a very lengthy eighty paces. This was deemed unfair owing to McCorkle's shortsightedness, and in the end it was agreed that the two would stand with their backs to one another at forty paces. At the word "fire," both would whirl, aim, and squeeze their triggers.

Even though the two were already deadly shots, they spent the entire week before the duel honing their marksmanship before large crowds. Many friends of both wandered away from their respective shooting ranges shaking their heads, convinced that neither would return from the dueling ground alive. Gloom fell over San Francisco as even those who were not fond of Gwin or McCorkle wondered aloud about California's future as a state—a state whose governor had already shot it out with a newspaper editor, whose first congressman had been killed in a duel with a state senator, and yet another state senator who had shot it out with a municipal judge.

Could California sustain its reputation as a viable state, worthy of representation in Washington, if its most powerful senator and yet one more congressmen met violent death by gunfire? Some of the less informed doubted it could. But the fact remains that even though the Eastern states regarded California as a drain on the federal treasury, they were not about to cut lose America's golden outpost on the Pacific Coast.

Late on the morning of the May 30, astride a burro and leading another loaded with camping gear and grub, Gwin left San Francisco for San Mateo, followed by a party that was expressly limited to thirty partisans. Earlier in the morning the senator had been barely able to tear himself away from his wife Mary and his two daughters, whom he had left behind in hysterics.

Just ahead of him was McCorkle, astride his own burro, and with an equal number of followers in tow.

Even though the dueling site was less than twenty-five miles from town, largely because Gwin insisted on a leisurely pace, it took two full days to reach San Mateo. The parties finally arrived on the chosen ground, a grassy ridge overlooking the tiny town, before noon on June 1.

Within their respective camps Gwin and McCorkle unloaded their panniers, spread out tablecloths, and for the next hour munched on sausages, coleslaw and doughnuts; both quaffed several tumblers of wine. It was altogether a highly irregular proceeding, considering the deadly work awaiting them. Members of both groups discussed a settlement around their respective tablecloths, and Gwin appeared to be willing to make one. But the wine appears only to have inflamed McCorkle further.

Finally at noon Inge and Stewart roused themselves, strode to the center of the dueling ground and conferred. Minutes later Stewart turned and shouted, "Let the battle begin!"

The duelists rose and as one observer put it, "Full of wrath, wine, sausages and coleslaw," trudged to their respective positions where they turned to glower at one another. Moments later their attention was diverted by a noisy argument among the seconds and surgeons. In an error beyond anyone's comprehension no one in either party had packed ammunition for the Yagers. At the insistence of both enraged principles, Inge and Stewart sent a youth off on horseback to San Mateo for the ammunition. He returned an hour later with the required shot.

The rifles were loaded and at ten minutes to two, with Gwin facing east toward San Francisco Bay, and McCorkle west toward the Pacific Ocean, Inge called out, "Gentleman, are you ready?"

"Ready!" shouted both.

"Fire!"

Gwin and McCorkle whirled and fired. Both missed by wide margins. The chroniclers have it that Gwin, under the influence of several glasses of wine, brought down a passing raven. McCorkle's blast is said to have barely missed Samuel Inge, and to have landed on the back of a jackass, grazing a half mile away.

The Yagers were reloaded and the duelists resumed their positions. At the second call, both whirled and fired. This time their aim was frighteningly close to the mark, both bullets tearing shreds of cloth from the other's coat sleeves.

Again with their Yagers loaded Gwin and McCorkle turned to await the call. Again Inge called out "Fire!" Again the Yagers boomed, their echoes rippling down the slopes. And again each tore a wad out of the other's coat. It was then that Gwin, tormented by thoughts of never seeing his wife and daughters again, and over the prospect of never returning to the U.S. Senate, shouted across the thirty paces, "Why do you persecute me?"

"Because of your injustice!"

"But I did you no injustice!"

The duelists turned their backs to await the next call, initially heedless of the fact that Inge and Stewart had left their stations to mingle with others in hushed conversation. Puzzled by the delay, Gwin and McCorkle turned toward each other just as their seconds emerged onto the center of the dueling ground, Inge waving a crumpled piece of paper. A formal document, roughly stated it declared that Gwin had misunderstood McCorkle's grievances, which were genuine; and that the congressman had withdrawn the insulting language he had used at the Pioneer Race Track.

From their positions, in turn, Gwin and McCorkle read the statement and pronounced themselves satisfied. To the relief of all present the duel was over, the decanters reopened and their contents polished off. An hour later members of both parties, in various stages of intoxication, mounted their animals and left for San Francisco.

Word had already reached town that the duel had ended without bloodshed. Tradition has it that Mrs. Gwin, on learning that three shots had been exchanged without effect, rose from her chair and in a state of euphoria exclaimed, "I think there has been some mighty poor shooting out there!"

On their approach to San Francisco scores of residents mounted on horses and jackasses, or crammed into carriages rode out to meet Gwin and McCorkle. The revelers placed each into separate carriages and drove them into what many felt was the happiest night in San Francisco's short life.

In truth the two never got over their dislike for one another. At the Democratic Convention of 1857, in a move against both Gwin and Latham,, McCorkle offered himself as a candidate for U.S. senator, confidently assuming that Broderick would support him. He did not learn until after the convention that Broderick, after winning the nomination for one senate seat, had thrown his support to Gwin for the other. Thereafter he disappeared from the California political scene and in the early 1860s moved to Virginia City, Nevada Territory, to practice law. He later moved to Washington, where he made a tidy living preparing cases for presentation before the U.S. Commission on Land Disputes. He also entertained the establishment with many reminiscences about that far off, lawless land called California. He died on March 18, 1884, at the age of 65 and was buried in his home town of Piqua, Ohio.

Gwin, whose reputation was tarnished by his duel with McCorkle, resumed his senate seat, and in 1857, with his term expired he worked behind the scenes with Broderick in order to draw the short four-year senate term. Never as barefaced or relentless as Broderick in his pursuit of public plunder, he nonetheless was suspected of involvement in the U.S. Mint scandal. He was also accused of instigating both the Ferguson-Johnston, and Broderick-Terry duels. There is no truth to any three charges.

State Supreme Court Justice Alexander Wells was involved in numerous escapades before his early death in 1854.

Even though dueling was against the law in California, San Francisco Sheriff Jack Hays, formerly of the Texas Rangers, declined to intervene in any of that city's affairs of honor.

Governor John McDougal was so furious over an editorial penned by newspaper editor Andrew C. Russell he resigned his seat in order to challenge him.

JOHN NUGENT.

John Nugent, editor of the *San Francisco Daily Herald,* took the field of honor on three occasions, a record that stands to this day.

Colonel Thomas Hayes nearly killed John Nugent in their duel with
Mississippi Yagers. Afterward they became the best of friends. In the
words of Ned McGowan, "How I like a man after I have fought him once."

U.S. Congressman Edward Gilbert was also editor of the *Alta California*.
His disgrace at the hands of another newspaper editor led to his untimely
death on the dueling ground, against a foe who had no personal animosity
toward him.

Alta California editor Edward Kemble, left, served as a second for both
Henry F. Teschemacher in his duel with Lieutenant Bonneycastle and
Harry De Courcey in his duel with William H. Carter. After the violent
death of his partner, Edward Gilbert, right, Kemble renounced dueling and
returned to New York.

State Senator James W. Denver agreed to face Edward Gilbert on the dueling ground only with reluctance. Thee he was forced to apply his deadly marksmanship.

Perhaps the most grueling duel ever fought on the frontier was between
U.S. Senator William Gwin, above, and Congressman Joseph C. McCorkle.

One of early California's most colorful characters, Judge Edward
McGowan served as a second in four duels, was a witness to several
others, and became a prime target of the San Francisco Vigilance
Committee of 1856.

Governor John Bigler threatened to have District Attorney Phillip W. Thomas killed should any harm befall State Marine Hospital physician Joseph Dixon in their meeting on the dueling ground.

As a federal boundary commissioner, John B. Weller was wounded in a general shootout that resulted in his removal from that office. This had no effect on his political career as he went on to serve California both as governor and U.S. senator.

During the Gold Rush Era, Milton Latham served as both California governor and U.S. senator. His romance with Sophia Birdsall was a major factor in promoting the duel between Joseph C. McCorkle and William M. Gwin.

20

The Dentist and the Grocer

During the early 1850s the most respected dentist in San Francisco was Alfred B. Crane, a native of Louisiana. Like almost everyone who arrived in California, Dr. Crane had gone west to dig for gold. But he had been in the mines for a few months only when he discovered that he could make a lot more money driving gold into the teeth of his fellow emigrants than in extracting it from the ground.

He left mining country for the Bay City, fitted out an office on Dupont Street near California Avenue and aided by numerous letters of reference, built up a lucrative profession. Everybody liked Dr. Crane, the terms "genial," "kind," and "whole hearted" commonly being used to describe him. Though he had brought a pair of dueling pistols with him, perhaps not too much should be read into the fact, since almost everyone who arrived in the state brought some sort of firearm with him.

Among Crane's friends was a fellow Louisianan, Edward Tobey. Another San Francisco success story, by 1853 Tobey had become co-owner of a grocery store chain. One day he appeared in Crane's office and asked him to work on his teeth. Crane agreed, but in exploring Tobey's mouth found them to be in appalling shape. He nonetheless went to work and after three months perseverance placed his teeth in good order. He then handed him a bill for several hundred dollars.

Crane waited in vain for payment. Finally he sent a collector over to Tobey's store to inquire about the bill. The grocer told the collector he would make a payment on the day the next steamship arrived. But the next steamer day passed, as did several more and no payment was ever made. Finally Dr. Crane sent the same collector over with instructions to collect the bill at once. In response Tobey said, "Tell Dr. Crane that I'll pay the bill when I get good and ready. Do you hear? Tell him that!"

On learning of his response the dentist decided to call at the store himself. There, a heated argument erupted in front of several shoppers, during which

Tobey made some disparaging remarks about Crane's dentistry. In turn the dentist accused Tobey of "giving the lie."

The following day witnesses to the argument were not surprised to learn that the hot-tempered Tobey had sent Crane a challenge. His chosen second was San Francisco District Attorney, Calhoun Benham. His partner in the grocery business, William I. Hoyt, was named as auxiliary second. Benham, a Kentuckian and one of California's foremost authorities on the code, was a real stickler on formality, which is perhaps why the Crane-Tobey duel was among the first to employ auxiliary seconds.

Crane accepted and chose Brandt Seguin, a boyhood friend as his second; Ross A. Fishu, a clerk at the U.S. Customs House was his auxiliary. For weapons the Dentist chose his own set of dueling pistols—distance, ten paces. The site was a small ravine at the far end of Treat's Ranch, today at the corner of 23rd and Capp streets. The time of the duel was set for 6 a.m., June 11, 1853.

Crane and Tobey, and their followers arrived on the site early and were preparing for the duel when someone in the crowd shouted, "The Sheriff! The Sheriff is coming!" The duelists and most of the crowd quickly dispersed; though a jail term was most unlikely, the risk of being hustled off to post bond was an annoying prospect at best. But the cry proved a false alarm, set up by several in the crowd who raised objections to the duel. After some confusion the duelists returned and resumed their positions. A gold dollar was tossed to determine who would make the call. Benham won.

Benham's insistence on formally reading off the "*code duello*" gave the duel all the trappings of an embroidered European affair. His speech finally over, he rolled up his scroll and then lectured the crowd on other, lesser known aspects of the *duello*. Finished at last, he drew back and asked the customary, "Gentleman, are you ready?"

"Aye" sounded Crane and Tobey.

"Fire—one, two, three—stop!"

Hemmed in by the ravine, the pistols went off with a thunderous clap. Within moments it was apparent that both had missed. While Fishu and Hoyt reloaded the pistols, Benham and Seguin tried to arrange a settlement before the next shot. They failed, but persuaded Crane and Tobey to end the duel after one more fire.

Again the duelists took their positions and the word was given. This time while Crane's shot sailed high, Tobey's tore into the dentist's right side, passed through his stomach and out his left side. The ball's path in fact was just below the one that had killed Edward Gilbert ten months before. Nonetheless, the plucky Crane remained on his feet several moments before sinking to the earth.

"Is he dangerously hurt?" asked Tobey, turning to Benham.

"I think not. You only winged him."

"Thank God for that!"

Tobey strode over to where Crane lay prone and said, "I am very sorry you are hurt, Doctor. I earnestly hope that your wound may be but slight."

Crane extended his hand and said "The affair was honorably fought."

As the grocer left the dueling ground he was unaware of how badly the dentist was hurt.

Crane's doctor, knowing that he was seriously injured, quickly dressed his wound and ordered him driven to the Oriental Hotel. There, after a second examination the doctors declared the wound fatal. He died the following morning and was buried the day after at the Yerba Buena Cemetery. On learning of Dr. Crane's death, Tobey went into a deep depression, sold his portion of the grocery business and left California never to return.

21

The Surprise Acceptance

From America's beginning the pen and the press were brothers to the gun, the Bowie knife, the horse whip, and the fist. During the 1850s Marysville, California, certainly claimed its share of newspaper wars, horse whippings, knife fights, and shootouts. Perhaps the most exciting of the newspaper wars was the one that resulted in a duel in June of 1853 between Judge Oliver P. Stidger, editor of the *Marysville Herald*, and Colonel Richard Rust, editor of the *Marysville California Express*. June was a banner month for California chivalry, the Gwin-McCorkle, Crane-Tobey, and Hayes-Nugent duels also having been fought under the same moon.

Oliver Perry Stidger was a hardworking Ohio farmer with an unusual fondness for reading literature and studying law—until he learned about the California Gold Rush. After dropping his plow, he sold the farm, tossed his books into a trunk, swung aboard a horse-drawn wagon and headed west. Upon his arrival in the northern mines only a short time passed before he turned his energies from mining to law practice. Despite the fact that he had no formal training, he was appointed a Yuba County Justice of the Peace. Soon after, he became editor of the *Marysville Herald*. A member of that rare breed, Stidger was a Whig in a state awash with Democrats.

His opponent in that memorable duel was Richard Rust, a native of Vermont who in his youth had migrated to Virginia. When the Mexican War broke out Rust joined a Virginia regiment and went off to fight, rising to the rank of colonel. Like Stidger, upon arriving in California he found mining not at all to his liking and turned to journalism. The recently established *Marysville California Express*, with Richard Rust at its helm, became a solid Chivalry Democratic newspaper.

Through the early part of 1853, Rust and Stidger became engaged in a violent editorial war. Rust was a solid newspaper man, but when it came to applying the ironic twist of a pen to a piece of paper he was no match for Stidger. Many around Marysville claimed that Stidger could write more mean things in a single minute than Rust could think of all day. So exasperated did Rust become at one point he approached John C. Fall, to whom Stidger was deeply in debt, and asked him to foreclose on the *Herald*. Fall declined, and the editorial pounding continued.

Finally Rust sent a fellow Virginian, Assemblyman Charles Fairfax, into Stidger's office with a challenge. Sources have it that Rust was aware that Stidger was a crack rifle shot. But he also knew that he was from Ohio where dueling was regarded as a serious felony; he thus reasoned that Stidger would likely decline his challenge. Having declined, circulation of the *Herald* would plummet and he would be forced to leave Yuba County to earn a living elsewhere.

Fatuous thinking indeed: Had Rust not been tracking the numerous duels that were being fought elsewhere in the state? If he had, he would have known that migrants from above the Mason-Dixon Line were not at all reluctant to accept a challenge—and were more than holding their own in the gunfire that followed.

Much to his dismay, Stidger sent a fellow Ohioan, Judge Gordon Mott, back to his *Express* office with an acceptance; He had chosen Buckeye rifles at sixty paces. The two seconds sallied forth in search of Buckeye rifles, but in all of Yuba County no two of the same caliber could be found. Prodded by Fairfax, Mott persuaded Stidger to settle on .54-caliber Mississippi Yagers, a weapon he was not familiar with. Stidger's fortunes took a further tumble when Fairfax and Mott, in testing the Yagers, found that one was more accurate than the other. In determining the choice of rifles by lot, Mott lost that gambit as well.

The duel was to be have been held on a Sunday morning at sunrise, over the border in Sutter County. But the night before Stidger received a surprise note from Rust asking that the duel be postponed until the following Sunday. The colonel claimed to be ill. The editor had no choice but to accept the postponement. In fact Rust, aware that Stidger could blow a squirrel out of a tree at sixty paces, spent the entire next week honing his marksmanship.

The following Sunday morning, as the sun rose to the east, Stidger and his seconds, Gordon Mott and Judge T. B. Reardon, and his surgeon Dr. McDaniel, approached the chosen ground, a grove of oak trees two miles south of the Yuba County line. Waiting under the trees was Rust, his seconds Charles Fairfax and Lee Martin, and his surgeon brother, Dr. Rust.

Because the duel had been the talk of Marysville for the past two weeks, a crowd of several hundred, one of the largest ever to witness a duel, had already assembled. Years later Fairfax, in his reminiscences recalled that Rust, Stidger, and their seconds and surgeons—all men of great presence—presented one of the most imposing sights he had ever seen.

Fairfax and Mott walked off the sixty paces, then tossed a coin to determine position. Mott lost. Another toss was made for the call. Mott lost that one too. Thus, though Stidger was considered much the better shot, Rust had the advantage in weapons, call, and position. While he stood beneath the shade of a large oak, Stidger stood with the rising sun full in his face.

Turning away from the sun, he squinted at the huge Yager in his hand and said to Mott, "If I get hit there won't be a grease spot left of me." Mott made no audible reply. Having lost every point, on every coin toss, in preparing for the duel, he had every reason to believe Stidger was right. He later admitted to have muttered,

"My man *is* going to get killed."

Moments later Fairfax called out, "Gentleman, are you ready?"

"Aye," Stidger cried aloud

"Ready," shouted Rust

"Fire, one—two—three—stop!"

At the word "two" both rifles roared. Stidger, squinting into the sun, sent his shot into the tree tops while Rust's ball ripped through his coat tail pocket, tearing the pocket and a handkerchief within to shreds. Much laughter erupted from the crowd after one wit observed that Stidger's pocket had been "rifled."

Dr. McDaniel approached Stidger and asked if he was all right. He nodded. Then the doctor, knowing that Stidger had thrown his shot away, said, "Now there must be no more foolishness. You must kill him, or he will kill you."

"I do not want to kill him. I don't want his blood on my hands. He has a family to maintain and I don't want to rob them of their support."

"That may all be very fine in theory, but the fact is that he is trying to kill you, and you must kill him."

Seconds later Mott and Reardon who had been consulting with Fairfax, returned to report that Rust demanded another shot. Reardon, also aware that Stidger had thrown his shot away, warned, "I will abandon the field if you do that again."

"Very well, I am willing," said Stidger. As Reardon loaded his Yager, Stidger turned to Dr. McDaniel and whispered, "I said I would shoot at Colonel Rust, but I did not promise to kill him, and I won't."

"You must kill him, or he will kill you."

Stidger and Rust took their rifles and moved to their positions as the murmuring crowd fell silent. Once more Fairfax called out, "Gentlemen, are you ready?"

Both shouted ready and Fairfax began the count. Seconds later both Yagers roared at once, the boom rippling through the trees and across the plain. Still standing, amidst bright sunlight and gray smoke, Stidger abruptly shouldered his weapon and eyed Rust. His quick move jarred Fairfax, who because the guns had gone off simultaneously, thought Stidger had not taken his shot. "Stop! Stop!" he shouted.

As Reardon and Mott strode over to find what the shouting was all about, Stidger slammed his Yager to the ground and growled to McDaniel, "Doc, this gun ain't worth a damn. I had a splendid shot at his arm, and I got a pretty good sight along the barrel. If this gun had been worth a damn I would have struck his elbow."

"Why didn't you shoot at his body?"

"I would have killed him, and I didn't want to do that."

"If he demands another shot what will you do?"

"I will kill him! I have now given him two fair shots at me. I could have killed him if I had desired to. I spared his life because of his family and because I did not want his blood on my hands."

Moments later Mott and Reardon returned to announce that Rust demanded a third shot with the distance reduced by ten paces. After remarking that he could better fire at Rust if the distance was lengthened to 120 paces, Stidger handed his rifle to Mott who returned to confer with Fairfax.

Minutes passed and the crowd grew noisy as Stidger paced back and forth at his position waiting for his seconds to return. Suddenly a Yager boomed, signaling that Rust had withdrawn his demand for a third shot.

Relieved, Stidger strode to the center of the dueling ground, exchanged bows with Rust and turned toward his carriage. Both parties drove back to Marysville followed by a straggling, but largely satisfied throng of spectators. On the ride into town Mott told Stidger that his second shot had clipped a lock of hair just above Rust's ear. On learning of this Fairfax, fully aware that Stidger was willing to make a settlement, and also sensing that Rust would almost certainly be killed by his next shot, insisted on an immediate end to the duel.

Thus did end the last of the widely trumpeted tests between Northern and Southern pluck. Having already been a witness to several duels involving the men of the North, Fairfax, in the ornate language of his day and accent of his home state commented on Stidger's courage, and the courage of Northern men in general:

> There wasn't a wilt or a shadow of unease about him. He took to the field
> by God, sah, as if it belonged to him. People who tell me after this, that men

born in the North are cowards will run the risk, sah, of my telling them they are asses. I know better. It don't do to monkey with such men. No, sah, they are plucky and will die game, sah . . .

Fairfax, Stidger and Mott remained friends for many years after. Mott in fact named one of his sons, Faxton, in the Virginian's honor. Though Judge Stidger and Colonel Rust never really became friends, in the months that followed the editorial war between them wound down. In 1857 Rust sold the *Express* and became a partner at the *Amador Sentinal* in Jackson before purchasing the *Calaveras Chronicle*. He afterward moved to Washington, D.C. to take a position with the Buchanan Administration. After the Civil War he returned to California and settled outside of Mokelumne Hill where he resided until his death in 1872.

Stidger's life in the years immediately after the duel, were not so prosaic. In 1854 two attempts to bushwhack him were made. One of those implicated in the first ambush was a local desperado named Plummer Thurston. His assailant in the second failed ambuscade was Yuba County Judge William Barbour. That same year Stidger sold the *Marysville Herald* to his brother-in-law, James Allen, and moved to North San Juan, Nevada County where he founded the *North San Juan Times*. There, free from ambuscades and affairs of honor, he edited his paper in relative quiet until July 2, 1888, when he died at a ripe old age.

22

The Fatal Friendship

When the Mexican War broke out in 1846 great numbers of young Americans rushed to enlist in their state regiments. Aside from Texas, the state most fervent in its embrace of the cause was Mississippi. Among perhaps half a dozen regiments raised in that state was the First Mississippi, commanded by Jefferson Davis, within whose unit Alfred G. Scott and Peter Smith served.

Peter Smith was the son of Pinckney Smith, a noted jurist who for many years served on the Mississippi Supreme Court. Alfred Scott was also well connected, his father owning one of the largest plantations in the South. The two grew up together, sharing many boyhood adventures. When the war broke out they made no use of their social standing to gain officer commissions; rather, they enlisted as privates. During the conflict both rose to the rank of first lieutenant.

After the war Scott and Smith returned home. A year later when word arrived that gold had been discovered in California, Scott immediately left. Smith intended to do so, but instead found his attention diverted by a revolution that had broken out in Cuba. After landing in Cuba with a contingent of Americans, he made contact with the revolution's leader, General Narcisco Lopez, and showed him his war credentials. Lopez immediately commissioned him a major.

He served in the revolution with distinction, but Lopez's upheaval failed when he was captured by the Spaniards and executed. Smith was badly wounded in the same battle and lucky to escape the island with his life. Only after a long convalescence at his home in Mississippi did he start for California in search of his old friend, Alfred Scott.

He arrived in the Bay City in 1851, easily found Scott and the two resumed their friendship of old. Despite occasional outbursts, Smith was an amiable glad-hander who made connections easily; in 1852 he was chosen clerk of the State Assembly. After the 1853 session ended, he returned to San Francisco where he and Scott resumed their role in making the town an exciting and convivial, if not exactly respectable place to live.

One evening in late July, the two ended their evening rounds at Frederick Kohler's Blue Wing Saloon. There, while under the influence of too much alcohol they got into a heated argument over the merits of Smith's Cuban adventure. While Smith spoke of the glory inherent in his mission to free Cuba from its Spanish yoke, Scott insisted it was a fiasco from start to finish. One word led to another until Scott, raising his voice over the bar room din, shouted, "Smith, all I have to say is that you were a damn fool, risking your life for a band of half breeds and niggers!"

"You lie! you infernal scoundrel!" shouted Smith, rising from his stool and bulling head first into Scott, knocking him to the floor. Smith's rage was such that it took six fellow drinkers to pull him off. Even then he broke lose a second time, again knocking Scott to the floor. This time he was ejected from the saloon.

Even though he had been in an absolute fury when last seen, most Blue Wingers felt that Smith and Scott would return the following evening, their differences patched over. In fact neither would ever enter the Blue Wing again. The following morning Smith, through Monterey Assemblyman William J. Tighlman, sent Scott the following message: "I demand the satisfaction usual among gentlemen."

Scott was surprised by the challenge and turning to his familiar friend, George Davidson, asked him to help settle his quarrel without resort to arms. For several days after Davidson and Tighlman worked on an array of adjustments, each one of which Smith rejected. Thus was set in motion a duel that in its senselessness surpassed even that of the recent affair between Dr. Crane and Edward Tobey.

With no alternative, Scott accepted the challenge, borrowing a pair of dueling pistols from the celebrated gun dealer, "Natchez" Taylor. His distance was ten paces. Doctor Joseph P. Dixon of the state marine hospital agreed to serve as a surgeon for both men.

At two o'clock on August 3, Scott and Smith met with their supporters and seconds at the Pioneer Race Track. Both were considered good shots, but Scott thought to be the better. In signaling their continued opposition to the duel, Tighlman and Davidson walked off the distance arm in arm. Tighlman won the toss to give the word, while Davidson won the toss giving his man the choice of pistols.

Moments later as Scott and Smith, wearing broadcloth coats and dark, wide brimmed hats stood facing each other, Tighlman called out, "Gentleman, are you ready?"

"Ready," replied both.

"Fire—one, two, three—stop!"

Scott got off his shot first, but it went high; Smith, who had drawn a better bead, narrowly missed his fire. Tighlman and Davidson then made one last effort to end the duel, but Smith insisted on another fire.

In resignation Davidson, who suspected that Scott had thrown his first shot away, returned to his principle and whispered, "Scott, you must shoot to kill, or at least disable him. If you do not promise me this I must withdraw from the field. Smith intends to kill you if he can. You purposely missed him, but you now owe it to yourself and your friends to protect yourself."

"I did fire in the air, hoping one shot would satisfy him," said Scott. "But as he now demands another fire I promise that I will look out after myself."

Scott and Smith took their positions, pistols loaded and in hand.

"Gentlemen, are you ready?" called Tighlman.

"Ready," answered both.

"Fire—one, two, three—stop!"

As before Scott squeezed off the first shot, while Smith held back to steady his aim.

Within that microsecond Scott's ball smashed into Smith's neck just below the ear. Dropping his weapon, he threw both hands into the air and cried out "I am hit," before pitching head long onto the earth.

Scott rushed over, and kneeling lifted and placed Smith's head into his lap. With his head thus cradled, Dr. Dixon extracted the ball and dressed the wound. The badly injured duelist was afterward lifted into a carriage and driven to the home of a friend, where he remained unconscious until the morning of August 7, when he died. He was buried the next day at the Yerba Buena Cemetery. During Scott's four day vigil he never left Smith's bedside except to eat. Following the funeral, overwhelmed with remorse he left California by steamship. Like Edward Tobey and John Morrison before him he never returned.

Among the lesser known duels of 1853, on February 11 Charles Somers and Thomas D.P. Lewis, both of Sacramento, fought with derringers at ten paces. Somers received Lewis's ball in the left arm which had to be amputated.

On May 26, in a duel of which disappointingly little information has come to light, two French nationals, Jules de Tournier and J.R. Saulnier, fought with swords. A large crowd watched as Saulnier badly wounded de Tournier in the first sword duel fought in California.

On October 19, 1853 Assemblyman Charles E. Carr and Justice of the Peace John H. Hayes were preparing to duel near El Monte, Los Angeles County. But moments before the call to fire sounded, the sheriff hove into view and ordered them to lay down their weapons. Carr and Hayes complied, and on the sheriff's orders settled their dispute with a foot race.

On November 3 a duel was fought near San Andreas, Calaveras County, between two German nationals, C. Krug, editor of the *Freie Presse*, and Dr. Loehr, editor of the *California Democrat*. The two met with Colt .36s at just six paces and exchanged three shots. On the last fire Krug's ball struck the base of Loehr's left hand, forcing amputation of his thumb.

And on November 9, outside of Weaverville, Trinity County, State Senator William May fought a duel with express agent Edward Rowe. The two met at 7:30 a.m. with Colt .36s at twenty paces. On the fourth fire May brought Rowe down with a bullet to the neck, causing a painful, but not fatal wound.

23

The Fool Alternate

Of the some half dozen affairs of honor fought in Sacramento during the 1850s the Thomas-Dixon duel rattled the roof of the State Capitol more than any other. This was in part because the antagonists were so well known, and because the duel, as in the Smith-Scott and Crane-Tobey affairs, was so pointless.

In those days one of the most popular characters in Sacramento and nearby Auburn was Joseph Rutland, a Southern-born sport with a weakness for faro and monte. Another popular figure was Phillip W. Thomas, district attorney for Placer County, a native of Maryland, who had spent most of his life in New York before emigrating to California.

As a member of the Whig Party, Thomas was remote from the state's political power centers, the Broderick and Chivalry wings of the Democratic Party. He nonetheless had ambitions and was anxious to secure the position of state treasury clerk for a personal friend. When Rutland outmaneuvered him and secured the post for himself, he was furious and before a large crowd in Sacramento denounced him as a "low down gambler, unfit to associate with gentlemen."

On learning of Thomas's tirade, Rutland sought out Dr. Joseph P. Dixon, resident physician at the State Marine Hospital. Despite the fact that Dixon was a native of Tennessee, by 1854 he had aligned himself with the Broderick wing of the "Democracy," as the party was commonly referred to in those times, and become a close friend of Governor John Bigler. Dixon had earlier served as a surgeon in the fatal duel between Lieutenants Alfred Scott and Peter Smith.

The day after meeting with Rutland, Dixon appeared in Thomas's Auburn office with a note, demanding that Thomas either apologize for his words, or face Rutland in a duel. Thomas quickly read the note, then informed Dixon he would not bother to answer Rutland on the grounds that he was "not a gentleman." Citing the wording of his letter alone as evidence enough, he concluded, "I cannot give the lie to what every sensible citizen of Auburn and Sacramento knows!"

Interpreting Thomas's refusal to meet Rutland as cowardice, and incensed by his contempt for his friend, Dixon challenged him on the spot. Raising his arm, he shouted, "And if I am not gentleman enough, a gentleman will be found!" Thomas immediately accepted. Thus did two fairly worthy public figures stumble onto the state's field of honor.

Shortly after Dixon chose as his second the renowned Edward McGowan. "Ubiquitous Ned," as he later became known, had already served as a second in several duels, most recently for Captain Nugent in his affair with William H. Jones. A native of Pennsylvania, by 1854 he had emerged as one of the most scandalous, if personable, characters on the state scene. The following, penned by his friend Judge Alexander Wells, is an apt depiction:

> You rusty, broken down hack horse, spavined, wind galled politician, infernal old schemer—you dreadful and to be dreaded shoulder striker—you melt of wax. You who resides at a French boarding house of equivocal character—you luxurious dog who lives on the fat of the land, and never said grince once. You ex-member of the judiciary department . . ."

No longer a judge, McGowan was now director of the State Marine Hospital where Dixon was serving as a physician. The two in fact had set up a shooting gallery inside the building. There, after the doctor had made his afternoon rounds, between droughts of whiskey, and within thunderous earshot of the patients, the two would target practice through the long evening hours.

For his second Phillip Thomas chose San Francisco Treasurer Hamilton Bowie. A descendant of an old Calvert, Maryland, family, Bowie too had already employed his services as a second in several duels. Like McGowan, he was another one of those "precious rascals," having just been relieved as treasurer for embezzlement. Angered by his indictment just three months before, Bowie had threatened to shoot the entire grand jury who had brought charges. He was also a close friend of McGowan's. The two in fact worked long and hard to bring about a settlement between Dixon and Thomas, to no avail.

Also working for a settlement was Governor Bigler, who valued Dixon as a liaison with the Chivalry wing of his party. When Bigler learned the duel was imminent he warned that if Dixon was killed, he himself would see to Thomas's demise.

For weapons Thomas chose the very same set of dueling pistols used by Harry De Courcey and William H. Carter in their famous shootout two years before. Distance was thirteen paces—the site, a meadow half way between Sacramento and the Oak Grove House (today near El Camino Real, between Howe and Business 80). Three shots were to be exchanged, each commencing with the call.

With all the arrangements in place, early on the afternoon of March 9 Thomas and Dixon, in the company of their seconds and followers quietly left Sacramento in separate buggies. The sheriff of Sacramento had nonetheless been alerted of the duel and dispatched two deputies to stop it.

As the parties approached the dueling site, they found the officers quietly waiting, astride their horses. A hurried discussion followed, during which it was decided that while Dixon and Thomas, and a few followers took shelter inside a nearby building, a mock duel would be fought between Frederick Kohler, acting for Dixon, and Dr. H.O. Ryerland, for Thomas. The two, flanked by Bowie and McGowan, immediately took their positions, exchanged harmless shots, were arrested and escorted to the Sacramento calaboose where they posted bond.

Having foiled the law, Dixon, Thomas, and their followers emerged from the building and onto the dueling ground. Unknown to McGowan, Dixon, while closeted with his friends, had tossed down several glasses of whiskey. The two duelists gravely bowed to one another as they crossed paths and strode to their positions. Both wore dark trousers, wide-rimmed black hats, and broadcloth coats buttoned to the chin.

Moments later as Dixon and Thomas stood facing each other with pistols pointed toward the ground, Dixon suddenly announced that he wanted to write a letter to his sister back east. His followers converged on him, and while one held his hat to write on, the others milled about him. Thomas, thirty-nine feet away, had raised his pistol and was raising and lowering his sights on Dixon in search of the perfect shot.

Finally finished with his note, Dixon took his hat and weapon. Here McGowan, who had won the toss to call "Fire" advised him to wait for Thomas to answer the preliminary question, "Gentleman, are you ready?" before answering himself. But no sooner had McGowan asked the question, than Dixon blurted "Ready!" Thomas, never taking his eyes off Dixon, shouted, "Give the word again, if you please!"

It was about 4 p.m. when McGowan cleared his throat and again called out "Gentlemen, are you ready?" Thomas, lips drawn tightly over his teeth, face slightly flush, answered "Yes."

Dixon followed with "Ready."

"Fire!" shouted McGowan.

A single explosion appeared to split the air. A second later Dixon toppled to the ground as if poleaxed. Thomas's ball had ploughed under his right arm, smashed through his spine and come to a rest against the far side of his rib cage. At the moment he was struck Dixon's shot landed harmlessly in the dirt a few feet in front of Thomas. As McGowan and his surgeon reached Dixon, he called out, "I have been killed by a coward!"

Thomas also approached, but McGowan, realizing a reconciliation was impossible, waved him off. Later, after learning that Dixon had quaffed several glasses of whiskey beforehand, he swore that had he known, he would never have permitted the duel to be fought that day. Dixon was carried to his buggy and driven to the Jones Hotel in Sacramento where he remained conscious and in agonizing pain until quarter past midnight the following morning.

His death threw Sacramento into such tumult, that when his funeral was held two days later much of the state legislature turned out. Stricken with guilt, Thomas's original challenger, Joe Rutland, declared that he would shoot Thomas on sight. Warned by Governor Bigler and others there had been too much "effusion" of blood, already, he withdrew his threat.

Thomas meanwhile set out for neighboring Yolo County where he remained while murder charges were pending. His attorney easily dodged the prosecutor and the indictment was dropped. By then acknowledged even by enemies as a dead shot, he was praised by friends as "A star of the first magnitude, in the constellation of great California duelists."

He was twice re-elected district attorney of Placer County and in 1860 to the State Senate. With the passage of time however he began drinking heavily. His many binges at the state capital wore away his more gentlemanly attributes and in 1862 he was publicly horsewhipped by State Senator James W. Coffroth for making "ungentlemanly" advances toward Coffroth's wife. Thomas resigned from the Senate shortly afterward and returned to Auburn where some years later he died penniless.

24

Requiem by Moonlight

In January 1854 a furious political battle erupted at the California state capital in Benicia. It was a struggle that would culminate on March 1 after the state legislature moved itself and set up shop in Sacramento. Early in January, the backers of State Senator David Broderick introduced a bill that would move the 1855 election for U.S. senator up to 1854. In those days, prior to passage of the Seventeenth Amendment, the legislature, not the voters, made the choice of U.S. senator. Broderick feared that the fast growing Chivalry Wing of the Democratic Party, combined with the remaining members of the Whig Party, would be able to block his election the following year.

His bill was bitterly opposed by those groups: "If California can hold its 1855 elections in 1854, why not hold the *1856* elections in 1854?" became their mustering cry. Broderick's move reverberated all the way back to Washington, D.C., where seasoned senators shook their heads in disbelief. Over the next six weeks, ignoring all other issues, Broderick and Chivalry Democrats waged a vicious struggle over the senatorial bill. One of the key players in the battle was the Palmer, Cook and Company Bank, at the time the most powerful in California.

Joseph Palmer, director of the bank, was also paymaster for the Broderick wing of the Democratic Party. Through the enormous resources of his depository, as well their own forceful personalities, Palmer, and his partners George Wright and Abia A. Selover, were able to bribe eight assemblymen into voting for the bill, thus securing the Assembly for Broderick.

Not all their efforts among the state senators were as successful. One of those they attempted to bribe was a member of the Whig Party, Elisha Peck of Shasta County. Having failed in their attempted bribe, Palmer, Wright, and Selover instructed one of their employees, a man known only as Haines, to take the senator for a carriage ride. In the midst of what proved to be a very circuitous outing, Haines lashed his horses and drove his vehicle into a ditch. Baffled, mud-encumbered, and limping badly, Peck hobbled back to Sacramento in time to cast his vote against the Broderick Bill.

Another thought to be an easy mark for the election bill was State Senator Jacob Grewell of Santa Clara County, also a Whig. On March 5, after being toasted at the Union Hotel by Palmer and Selover among others, in a state of intoxication he pledged his vote for Broderick. Shortly after, he was whisked off to a room to be kept under guard by Assemblyman Martin Rowan of Calaveras County, and former San Francisco jailer Billy Mulligan. Unhappily for Broderick and Palmer, Rowan and Mulligan drank themselves into a stupor every bit as deep as Grewells's.

In the early hours of the following morning Grewell was stumbled upon and rescued/kidnapped by a Dan Aldrich, who escorted him to the office of State Senator Henry Alexander Crabb, the most influential Whig in the state. Crabb prevailed upon Grewell to turn his "yes" vote into a "no." Later that morning the senator was shoved into a hack and driven to chambers where, his hands still shaky, he cast what was indeed a shaky "nay" vote. Thus did Broderick's election bill go down to defeat by an 18 to 16 margin.

Strangely enough it was only after the political battles ended that the blood began to flow, in what developed into the bloodiest political month in California history. The first of the three duels to arise out of Broderick's attempt to fast forward the 1855 election occurred when John McBrayer, a Broderick Democrat, posted a notice in the *Sacramento State Journal* charging that J.W. Parks, a Chivalry Democrat, had passed a bribe to secure a vote against the bill.

Parks heatedly denied the charge and demanded an apology, or satisfaction on the dueling ground. McBrayer opted for satisfaction. But on March 18, on the ground near Sacramento the county sheriff hove into view and arrested both. Within the hour each posted bond, but that evening as they again prepared to duel, the Masonic Fraternity, of which both were members, worked out an "adjustment" that was satisfactory to both.

No such adjustment would be found for a second "card" that appeared in the *Sacramento State Journal*, claiming that two state senators from El Dorado County, Hollister and Livermore, were each offered $10,000 to vote against the election bill. The following day, Hollister and Livermore placed their own notice, claiming that the card was a malicious lie. Two days later a Broderick operative, David E. Hacker of Placerville, published a card in the *Coloma Argus*, claiming that the bribes had indeed been made, and they had been placed by Joseph S. Landon, an influential Chivalry Democrat.

Landon denied the charge and demanded a retraction. When Hacker refused Landon called him a "liar, slanderer, and a coward." A challenge was immediately sent. The newspapers carried very little personal background about either principle in this duel. As so many members of the Chivalry wing of the party were now from Northern states, and Broderick and been successful in prompting large numbers of Chivs to join his wing of the party, it is not known which section of the country or which states Hacker and Landon hailed from.

For his second Hacker chose Judge W.W. Wright of Yuba County, while Landon chose Captain A.C. Cory, a Mexican War veteran. Over the next several days Cory and Wright trudged patiently back and forth across Placerville, exchanging notes between the pair. The hostility between the two was so great it seemed as if the terms of the duel might never be settled upon; yet it was this very hostility that ensured the duel was inevitable.

After expending much of Wright and Cory's energy, Hacker and Landon agreed to meet under the following terms: the weapons would be Colt six shooters at a distance of five paces; each would fire a single shot commencing with the call "Fire—one, two, three—stop." The dueling ground was Volcano Bar, an abandoned mining camp on the Middle Fork of the American River. Hacker at first objected to the extraordinarily short five paces, calling it "barbaric." But Landon, the challenged party was insistent, in his words, "I do not propose to fight a farcical duel; the distance named means that one of us, perhaps both, may be killed, but I intend to adhere strictly to my original proposition."

In addition to the short span between the duelists were two other unusual provisos: aside from the surgeons and seconds, only three associates of each duelist were to accompany them to the site. Finally, the duel was to be fought at eleven o'clock at night, under a full moon.

The site of the duel was a well-kept secret, but news of the face-off swept through El Dorado County like a range fire. Even though the Sheriff knew empaneling a jury that would convict was remote, he arrested both. To no one's surprise friends of Hacker and Landon posted bond. On the day of March 20, 1854, the two, with their seconds and surgeons, left in separate wagons for Volcano Bar. Of the ten who arrived at the Bar that night the most noted was former San Francisco Mayor, Stephen Harris, serving as Landon's surgeon.

No sooner had the duelists left their wagons, than Cory and Wright began walking off the fifteen feet that would separate them. Hacker won both the coin toss for position, and the toss giving his second, Judge Wright, the privilege to call "Fire!" A witness later recalled the scene as the duelists stood grimly facing each other under a brilliant moon. Nearby, piles of tailings from the river bed gleamed white, and beyond, in the forest an owl hooted. At eleven fifteen, with the breath of everyone hanging in the cold air, Wright called out, "Gentlemen, are you ready?"

"Ready!" answered both.

"Fire—one, two, three—stop!"

Both Colts cracked simultaneously and the surgeons stumbled forward to their respective duelists, only to find them unscathed. Wright and Cory moved off to consult. Moments later they returned and proposed ending the duel without another shot being fired. Hacker was willing to discuss the proposal, but Landon insisted on one more shot. The seconds reloaded the revolvers, handed them back to the duelists and stepped back. Moments later Wright called out "Fire—one, two three—stop!"

Landon fired first, his bullet whining harmlessly into the shadows. A split second later Hacker's bullet struck Landon in the heart. The stricken duelist sank slowly, dead before he reached the ground. Years later the writer quoted earlier recalled the fright that had gripped him as he helped place Landon's body into the wagon for the long, shadowy drive back to Placerville.

After the duel Hacker fled El Dorado County for remote Los Angeles to avoid charges. Some months later he returned to Placerville, and then appeared in Sacramento where he was toasted by the political establishment. But like a number of triumphant duelist he slowly drifted into anonymity. Nothing is known of Captain Cory's life afterward. Judge Wright was later elected Sheriff of Nevada County, and in November 1856 was shot and killed while pursuing the notorious stickup man, Jim Webster.

25

Our Founding Father's Nephew

In December 1853, David Broderick, in preparing to pass his 1854 Senate bill, purchased the *Alta California* and the entire building in which it was housed; he then installed two fellow New Yorkers, George Wilkes and Charles A. Washburne as his editors. Prior to the Broderick purchase, the *Alta* had been a Democratic newspaper of independent leaning, and under the stewardship of Edward Gilbert and Edward Kemble had forged quite a reputation for itself. But with Washburne and Wilkes at its helm the *Alta* began strongly towing the Broderick line.

The Chief's plan to move the 1855 election forward to 1854 was opposed by not only the Whigs and Southern supporters of Senator Gwin, but by most rank and file Democrats in the mining counties—most of whom were from Northern states. In attempting to drive a wedge between the Southerners and their mining country allies, who preferred calling themselves "The Mountain Democracy," Washburne and Wilkes began referring to the Southerners as "That Customs House Crowd," in reference to the large number of Gwin appointees employed there. Broderick himself coined the even more imaginative term, "Virginia Poor House."

But the *Alta*'s tactic failed completely among the "Mountain Democracy" simply because Gwin's abuse of patronage was but a minor offense compared to Broderick's Senate scheme.

John Nugent, editor of the *San Francisco Daily Herald* fiercely opposed moving the 1855 election to 1854, but Broderick's harshest editorial critic was Benjamin Franklin Washington of the *San Francisco Times and Transcript*. In 1849, in the company of several other Virginians, the great-great-grandnephew of President George Washington trekked to California. A lawyer by profession, in 1853 he was hired by publisher George Kerr to edit the *Times and Transcript* and soon became one of the most influential writers in the state.

In early March 1854, Charles Washburne, the *Alta*'s senior editor, wrote an unsigned column in which he claimed that Washington once proposed that if Broderick would support the Chivalry candidate for state printer, George Kerr, the *Times and Transcript* would support his election to the U.S. Senate. Washburne then asserted that Washington had told Broderick that he deserved to be U.S. senator because of his tireless work on behalf of the Democratic Party. He then closed out the column by claiming that Washington owed Broderick $6,000, the amount the Chief had loaned the editor after his printing office was destroyed in a fire.

Washington quickly denied ever having proposed exchanging a pledge of support for U.S. senator for that of state printer. To equate the importance of the two offices was preposterous. He also insisted that Broderick had loaned him $1,000—not $6,000, and that the loan had been repaid. Further, he demanded to know who the real author of the editorial was. When Washburne declined to divulge the author's name, Washington asked the *Alta* editor for a retraction. He refused, whereupon Washington sent him a challenge. It was accepted.

The Washington-Washburne duel was another highly formalized affair, as evidenced by the fact that each duelist had two seconds. Washington's were Assemblyman Philemon T. Herbert, and another close political associate, Jo Beard. Washburne's seconds were his co-editor George Wilkes and Assemblyman Benjamin Lippencott. He chose Wesson rifles at fifty five paces; five shots were to be exchanged, each after the call was given.

Of the two, Washington was much the better shot, and despite Washburne's choice of weapons, favored to survive the duel. He was further aided by his seconds: Herbert was an Alabama hotspur, well-grounded on the code, as was Jo Beard whose personal set of dueling pistols had killed several duelists in his native Louisiana.

On Washburne's side, only Assemblyman Lippencott brought any knowledge of the code to the field. A native of New Jersey, he had come west with the Donner Party and served with the California Battalion in 1846–47. It appears that Washburne had initially approached Broderick and McGowan to serve as his seconds. For unknown personal reasons both declined. They nonetheless lent Washburne considerable counsel, and their presence on the field furnished him with some badly needed confidence.

With the recent death of Joseph Dixon on everyone's mind, (news of Landon's death in El Dorado County had not yet reached San Francisco) efforts to reach a settlement continued into the small hours of March 21. Failing to reach a satisfactory adjustment, well before daybreak Washington and his party rode off down the El Camino Real to San Bruno, site of the duel. They arrived at 5 a.m., three full hours before the firing was to begin.

Washburne arrived with his crowd at precisely eight o'clock and promptly took the field. Despite the gravity of the occasion, the duel took a comic twist when on Lippencott's first call Washington mistook a sudden move by Wilkes as a signal to hold fire and handed his rifle off to Herbert. Much to his surprise Washburne's shot hummed past his ear.

A long parley followed before the principles readied themselves for the next shot. On this call Washburne artlessly fired his rifle into the ground while Washington gallantly held fire. On the third call Washington blew Washburne's hat off, while the latter once more missed. On the fourth call both missed. Finally, on the fifth and last call Washington sent a bullet through the underside of Washburne's left arm into the fleshy portion of his back, knocking him to the ground. Several surgeons rushed over to the editor, discovered that his wound was not fatal and extracted the bullet.

Washington and his crowd waited for the operation to end before leaving. Upon leaving the *Times and Transcript* editor was overheard to say, "It was like shooting at a tied bird." Most observers felt that prior to his remark he had been the consummate gentleman on the field. And Washburne, though he had by no means proved himself a rifleman, had shown "true grit."

B.F. Washington later became Senator Gwin's third Southern-born collector of the port, succeeding Richard P. Hammond, and remained a key political figure on the state scene until 1861. Never the Federalist his great-great-uncle the president had been, with the outbreak of the Civil War he supported the South's bid to secede, and as the war progressed was eclipsed from the public scene. After war's end he helped to establish the *San Francisco Examiner* and soon recaptured much of his old popularity.

Charles Washburne remained a close associate of Broderick's even after the San Francisco Vigilantes smashed his political machine in 1856. In 1858 he followed his mentor into the newly formed Douglas Wing of the Democratic Party and launched a newspaper of his own, the *San Francisco Times*.

Six months after the duel, George Wilkes, who was the brain behind Broderick's Senate bill, had a violent row with him. The Chief had pledged him the State Supreme Court seat vacated by the death of Alexander Wells. To Wilkes's great bitterness he learned that Broderick had also promised the seat to State Senator Charles Bryon—in writing. He left for New York and did not return to California for some years.

Washburne's primary second, Ben Lippencott, returned east to remain, while Washington's auxiliary second, Jo Beard later became clerk of the California Assembly. The pair of French dueling pistols he had brought to California would one day play a pivotal role in the fatal duel between David Broderick and David Terry.

Just two months after the Washington-Washburne duel, Washington's primary second, Phil Herbert, served as a second in the fourth affair of honor to arise from the senatorial fight. The affair was between the clerk of the Assembly, Chris Dowdigan, a Broderick man, and James Hawkins a Chivalry assemblyman. Provoking the duel were some scathing remarks Hawkins made about Broderick. Though furious over the name calling, Broderick considered Hawkins much too low in status to personally deal with. He was therefore pleased when Dowdigan stepped forward to challenge the Assemblyman.

The duel was fought near Sacramento on May 19 with rifles at fifty paces. While Herbert stood in for Hawkins, Billy Mulligan (of Coyote Hill fame) seconded Dowdigan. In the exchange of shots Hawkins brought Dowdigan down with a bullet to the arm.

26

The Hubert-Hunt Duel

Every duel lays claim to several factors that are uniquely their own. The duel between George T. Hunt and Numa Hubert (pronounced Hubayer) is a curiosity for two reasons: it was fought between a Frenchman—admittedly a naturalized American—and an Englishman; and, it was the only duel in California ever fought over seating arrangements.

Numa Hubert was born in France but grew up in New Orleans, where he gained American citizenship and became one of that city's shrewdest lawyers. In 1849, accompanied by his beautiful octoroon wife, he took steamship for California. Even though he was an American citizen Hubert dressed like a Frenchman, and indeed represented France's interests at the state capital. He nonetheless spoke the American language with a Louisiana accent, cherished American customs, and strode about town in the same manner as those of his adopted country. In 1853 he was elected to the State Assembly, representing San Francisco.

Less is known of George Hunt, other than that he was an Englishman and a lawyer who had met with little financial and social success in the Bay City. According to Ned McGowan, Hunt's many financial embarrassments made him more sullen than he otherwise might have been.

One night in May 1854, on one of his few occasions out on the town, Hunt attended the same dinner party Hubert had been invited to. As chance would have it, he encountered and took a fancy to a young woman. Shortly after meeting her, Hunt overheard the easy-going Hubert, who had known the woman for sometime, make some offhand remarks he considered salacious. Already carrying several chips on his shoulder, he decided to call Hubert out at the first opportunity.

The scene was the Metropolitan Theater on Montgomery Street, just below Washington, then managed by Catherine Sinclair, divorced wife of the famous tragedian Edwin Forrest. The house was full and when State Supreme Court Justice Hugh Murray, who had reserved a number of seats, saw Hunt alone, looking for a place to sit, he invited him over to sit in his section. Hunt obliged, and Murray, a few minutes later, spotting Hubert in the hallway, similarly waved him over.

Hubert joined Murray in a lively conversation, then took one of the two seats left in the box; there he found that he could barely see the stage. Rising, he turned to Hunt, sitting one seat away, with his leg resting on the chair between them, and informed him he would like to have the seat. Hunt ignored him, and refused to move his leg.

By then the *prima donna* had begun to sing and Hubert felt compelled to resume his seat. When the song ended he again rose and turning to Hunt said, "Will you kindly let me occupy that chair, Mr. Hunt? I can see better there than I do from here."

"I shall not give up the chair."

Hubert then attempted to pull the chair out from under his foot. "You damned puppy!" shouted Hunt, rising. "Don't you dare move that chair!"

The attention of everyone in the theater immediately turned on the two men, and the acutely embarrassed Hubert resumed his old seat. But minutes later, still unable to see the stage, he once more attempted to drag the chair out from under Hunt's foot. In response Hunt leaped to his feet and with clenched fist struck him in the face.

Seconds later Hubert replied with a punch of his own that sent Hunt sprawling onto the floor among a clatter of folding chair legs. Several women screamed, the manager ran the curtain down and the theater was thrown into pandemonium. Minutes later the police arrived, arrested the pair and hauled them off to court where both pled guilty to disturbing the peace and paid $50 fines.

The next morning Hubert sent a challenge that Hunt accepted. He then picked Tom Tighleman as a second, with Charles Fairfax as his auxiliary. Tighleman had served as Peter Smith's second in his duel with Alfred Scott the year before; Fairfax had of course served Richard Rust in his duel with Oliver Stidger.

Because Hunt was such a loner he had difficulty finding a second, finally settling on a young Englishman named Hughes who was not well versed in the code. Feeling sorry for Hunt, the Washington lobbyist and chef Sam Ward asked Ned McGowan to serve as his second. McGowan agreed that Hunt badly needed help, but declined Ward's request because of a brawl he and Hubert had only recently engaged in. The fisticuffs had almost led to a duel; since then differences had been patched over, and Ned was not desirous of reopening old wounds. Nonetheless, he persuaded William Knox, a gambler with good knowledge of the code, to fill in as Hunt's auxiliary.

On the advice of Knox and McGowan, Hunt decided to borrow a pair of dueling pistols from Natchez Taylor's gun shop. The distance would be twelve paces—site, the celebrated Pioneer Race Track. A limit of three shots in all would be exchanged, the call commencing before each.

At 5:30 on the morning of May 21 Hubert and Hunt, and their followers, totaling about eighty, met at the track. The business of marking off the distance and other preliminaries was done very slowly and seemed to take a toll on Hunt's nerves; by the time he had taken his position he had lost much of his composure. That Fairfax won the toss to make the call only made him that much more nervous.

Moments later, following a few words of encouragement from Hughes, Hunt indicated he was ready. At the call of "Fire, one two three—stop!" he and Hubert raised their pistols, fired and missed. Troubled over the missed chance, Hunt flung his pistol onto the dewy grass. Knox strolled over, picked the weapon up, reloaded it, handed it back to him, and offered enough encouragement to allow Hunt to regain some composure. On the second call the duelists again missed. Left to face death by fire one more time, Hunt was again in despair.

But once more, coached by Hughes and Knox, he regained confidence. As he awaited Fairfax's last call, McGowan noted that he appeared almost cool.

At "two" Hunt's shot once more flew wide of the mark. Conversely, Hubert's ball stuck him in the stomach, knocking him onto the turf. Hughes raced over to Hunt's side and grasping his head solicitously cradled it in his arms. Hubert approached, reached down, took Hunt's extended hand, and shaken by the severity of the youth's wound, burst into tears.

After he departed, Hunt was driven downtown and carried to his room where he lay in great agony. McGowan, Hughes and Dr. Wake Briarly remained at his bedside until death, at sundown that evening. McGowan later wrote that Hunt, despite twice losing his nerve on the ground, showed more grit in the face of certain death than anyone else he had ever witnessed.

Hubert continued to reside in San Francisco after the duel. Though sobered by Hunt's passing, he resumed his glad-handing manner of old and continued to be fondly recognized as California's most Americanized Frenchman. He died in Chicago in 1872 while returning to California from a visit to France. His death came so suddenly that friends thought he had been poisoned; an autopsy revealed that he had died of smallpox. Hubert was then carried by train to his beloved Bay City where he was buried.

27

A Longshoreman's Affair

From the very beginning San Francisco was a maritime city, its harbor far and away the best and busiest on the Pacific Coast. Because the transcontinental railroad had not yet been laid out, the city's life blood was almost completely dependent upon the steamers and clipper ships that plied the seas. Its docks were perhaps the most bustling part of town.

From 1849 onward competition between the stevedore firms was fierce, but by 1853 two Scotsmen, Blyth and Menzies, had gained almost complete monopoly over the city's dock work. Early in 1854, however, a new firm, Foster and Benson, was placed on the stevedore list and within months the competition was again intense. So intense that Blyth & Menzies, and Foster & Benson began undercutting each other's prices, both firms on occasion undertaking work for nothing in hopes of denying the other an opportunity for profit.

Matters came to a head in May 1854 when a large English ship, the *North Fleet*, arrived in the harbor. During the negotiations that followed, the ship's captain led Foster and Benson to believe they had gained the stevedore's contract; the next day, to their dismay they found that Blyth and Menzies had secured it.

Benson, a 24-year-old Englishman, went in search of Blyth, found him on the deck of the *North Fleet* and before onlookers swore at him furiously. Only the interference of bystanders prevented him from assaulting Blyth. A few hours later he sent an American named Michael Coghlin into his office with a challenge.

As a Scotsman, Blyth refused to consider the challenge, infuriating Benson even further. Beside himself, he once again boarded the *North Fleet* and this time finding Stewart Menzies at work began piling on the abuse. In the midst of his tirade, Menzies rose and with one punch knocked him evenly onto the deck. Benson managed to pick himself up, leaving the ship in a state of humiliation. A few hours later Coghlin appeared in Menzies's doorway and handed him Benson's second demand for "satisfaction."

"Duel be blowed," shouted Menzies. "Let him come down on the dock and take his coat off, and I'll give him all the satisfaction he wants!"

Benson saw no gain in losing yet another round of fisticuffs, and sent Coghlin back a third time with the challenge. By now the trouble between the stevedore firms was the talk of San Francisco and Menzies found Benson's challenge impossible to ignore. He was so deeply troubled, he entered the office of city tax collector, William A. Matthews, and asked him his thoughts on the matter. Matthews quickly informed him that despite the fact that he was a Scotsman, he was obliged to shoot it out. Failure to face Benson would only bring himself disgrace, which in turn would lead to his firm's ruin.

Convinced he had no alternative Menzies sought out another American, Captain Cottrell, a veteran of the Mexican War and an authority on the code. Cottrell agreed to serve as his second and after asking a series of questions, decided that Menzies's best chance lay with Navy revolvers, borrowed from Natchez Taylor. The time would be 7 a.m., May 24, 1854—distance fifteen paces. The location was Chris Lilly's Lake House, three miles beyond Mission Delores. The Lake House, operated by former heavyweight boxer, Chris Lilly, did serve as a restaurant of sorts, but in fact was a house of prostitution.

On the evening before the duel Menzies, Cottrell and company drove over to Lilly's where they spent the night. All were out on the ground well before 7 a.m. waiting for the Benson party to appear. At nine o'clock, deciding they were not going to show, Menzies and company climbed into their wagons and started back to town. On the way in they met the Benson Party, which had apparently taken the wrong road and gotten lost. Menzies turned around and followed Benson back to Lilly's.

There, the fifteen paces were measured off and Captain Cottrell, on behalf of Menzies, won the coin tosses for both the word, and choice of position. After backing off the customary eight yards, he asked, "Gentleman, are you ready?"

"Ready," said Menzies.

"All ready," said Benson.

"Fire, one, two, three—stop!" The hammers of both revolvers dropped, but only Menzies cap exploded, his shot narrowly missing Benson.

At this point several in the crowd noticed the disparity in the size of their weapons. Menzies held a large, long barreled Navy revolver in his hand, while Benson had a small caliber Colt with a five-inch barrel in his. In accounting for the great disparity, Menzies explained that he had obtained his pair of revolvers from Natchez, as was his prerogative, but that Benson had turned down his choice, insisting on using his own much lighter weapon. Indicative of his ignorance of weaponry, and what an easy mark he was, Benson had earlier declared that his revolver could deliver a deadly shot at the fantastic distance of fifty paces.

On learning of his misconception, partisans on both sides tried to arrange a settlement. They had almost succeeded when Coghlin, hardly the ideal second, suddenly took Benson by the arm and led him away some distance away. There he turned and literally shamed him into taking another shot. Benson, who now doubted the wisdom of continuing the duel, only reluctantly succumbed to Coghlin's prodding.

The duelists took their places and the revolvers were again loaded. Again Cottrell gave the word. Both fired at the same time, but while Benson was wide of the mark, Menzies bullet tore into his right side just under the arm pit. "I am shot!" cried Benson falling heavily to the earth.

Seconds later Menzies was standing over him, tears streaming from his eyes. "I could not avoid it. And I hope you have no hard feelings toward me."

"I have not. This settles the difficulty."

Benson was placed in a carriage and driven to a house on Greenwich Street where the following morning he died at ten o'clock. The inquest that followed urged that Menzies be indicted; many felt an indictment of Coghlin would have been more suitable. Nothing of course ever came of either arraignment.

28

California's Don Quixote

Rasey Biven often boasted that he would "fight anything on earth." Indeed, growing up so tiny left him with a Napoleonic complex unlike that of any other Western migrant. Born in Albany, New York, into a family of Welsh origins, as a young man he often found himself in trouble. Following one altercation, which apparently involved gunfire, he was forced to flee the state capital to avoid arrest.

Somehow he wound up in a backwoods newspaper office in Arkansas setting type. In 1849 he joined the California Gold Rush and two years later, in partnership with his brother, William, set up a general store in Stockton. It wasn't long before both Bivens became acquainted with Stockton attorney Henry Alexander Crabb, the son of a Tennessee planter. In 1853 Crabb and Rasey Biven became shirt-tail relatives when they married sisters, Filomena and Catarina Ainsa, daughters of Captain Agustin Ainsa, who had earlier fled Mexico because he had sided with the Spanish government during that nation's war of independence.

Henry Crabb and William Biven—relatively speaking—seem to have exuded a steadiness of purpose in going about their lives; in 1854 they co-founded the *Stockton Daily Argus*. But the diminutive Rasey, at just five feet two, was too restless to settle into any particular avocation. Still, he was persuasive, and in part owing to his brother-in law's influence at the state capital, for a short time was placed in charge of arms at the state armory in Benicia. He later became superintendent of the Tejon Indian Reservation.

In a state filled with characters almost as eccentric as himself, the younger Biven had a bold, strutting manner. He was extraordinarily handsome, sporting a thick, drooping mustache which reminded many of Van Dyke's painting of England's Charles I. Like numerous recently arrived Americans, he took to wearing the attire of a Mexican hidalgo. Most noticeable was an enormous, vicuna haired sombrero that crowned his head, and which seemed almost to press him to the ground.

His bluster was near endless. On one occasion he challenged a state functionary to a duel with double-barreled shotguns, loaded with buckshot at ten paces. He and the object of his ire, however, could find no one willing to serve as their seconds in such a murderous exchange of fire. On another occasion he challenged State Senator Eliot J. Moore, who in a lighter moment had likened him to a cross between Don Quixote and Tom Thumb. Because the senator's assessment was regarded by most everyone as on the mark he easily pooh-poohed the challenge.

Biven's first real encounter on the field of honor occurred in August 1854 following an inspection tour of the Tejon Indian Reservation. His antagonist was Hillard P. Dorsey, a native of Georgia and a Mexican War veteran. Then owner of the Centinela Adobe, Dorsey was in fact the first to begin the practice of walnut cultivation in California. Recently he had been appointed registrar for the U.S. Land Commission in Los Angeles. For reasons that can easily be imagined, he and Biven had a violent altercation at the Bella Union Hotel of that town, after which Biven passed a challenge. Dorsey accepted.

But the site of the duel would not be Los Angeles; rather, they would shoot it out in San Francisco where both had business pending, and where their preferred seconds were present. A week later at the Pioneer Race Track, as they stood eying one another, San Francisco Sheriff David Scannel rode into their midst and ordered a halt to the proceedings. The two were escorted to jail where they posted bond.

On September 19 the two and their entourages steamed across San Francisco Bay to Clinton, a town since absorbed by Oakland. For seconds Biven had chosen his own brother-in-law, Henry Crabb, and the well-known attorney, Edmund Randolph. Only one of Dorsey's seconds is known—former governor John McDougal. In part because of Biven's natural inclination to bluster, one of the largest crowds to witness a duel was on hand.

At high noon Biven, who had surrendered his hidalgo chaps, *serape* and sombrero for a broadcloth coat and trousers stood ten paces from Dorsey, derringer in hand, waiting for Crabb to give the call. At "Fire," both leveled their derringers at each other and pulled the triggers. Dorsey's ball smashed into Biven's left forearm, forcing him to drop his weapon, wheel, and grasp it with his right hand. Biven's shot had meanwhile torn a furrow across Dorsey's stomach that left him grimacing with pain, but still on his feet. The ball did not penetrate his stomach lining, and he escaped, by fractions of an inch, the horrible death awaiting so many duelists suffering a stomach wound. As for Biven, despite talk of amputation, his badly mangled arm healed. Both were expelled from the Masonic fraternity for engaging a fellow Mason in a duel.

Dorsey, whose disposition was as quarrelsome as Biven's, was given to physically abusing his wife, Civility. In 1858, following one such incident he was confronted by Civility's father, William Rubbottom inside his own El Monte home. Enraged by Rubbottom's meddling in what he felt was a private affair, Dorsey pulled a knife, and lunged at him. His elderly, alert and very agile father-in-law quickly dodged him, pulled a revolver and shot him to death.

Even before Dorsey's demise Biven experienced another incredibly close shave with death. In November 1856, with his brother-in-law, Henry Crabb, Biven set about organizing a settlement plan for Americans in Sonora, Mexico. Whether it was an outright filibustering expedition in the tradition of William Walker or an arrangement agreed upon with Sonora Governor Ignacio Pesquiera has never been satisfactorily determined. Still, with Walker's filibustering expedition into Baja California three years prior, still fresh on the minds of many Sonorans, Crabb urged Biven to leave for Mazatlan three months before the expedition got underway. His mission there was to monitor the political situation in Sonora at large.

Some of Biven's dispatches made it back to Crabb, but others were intercepted by Mexican authorities. In March 1857, Henry Crabb, with some very poor intelligence, led ninety Californians across the Arizona border into Sonora. At Caborca they were surprised by an overwhelming Mexican force, captured, and massacred before a firing squad. Crabb himself was decapitated after being forced to witness the execution of his own men.

In Mazatlan meanwhile Biven was arrested, charged with filibustering, and also sentenced to death. But within minutes of his meeting with a firing squad, the pleas of his sister-in-law, Filomena Crabb, brought about his release. He returned to San Francisco in September, where his appearance was regarded as a miracle. He was one of just four Californians to survive the Crabb debacle.

He afterward worked as a reporter for the *Sacramento Union*. In 1859 he and his family left for the Dalles, Oregon, to open a general store. In 1866 he and Catarina and their five children returned and settled in Monterey where he began publishing the *Monterey Democrat*. An incurable romantic, he wrote a novel based on his own life. The following year he fell ill. Picaresque until the end, he wrote his own obituary, predicting the day of his death, May 18, 1867. Despite his boastful swagger, most writers dwelt sentimentally on the diminutive Rasey Biven, who had cut such a swath through a land filled with characters almost as large as himself.

29

An Affair of the Heart

At first glance the duel between William Knox and Thomas Allen seems hardly worth noting. One was a gambler—admittedly a successful, high toned gambler—but a dealer of monte and faro all the same. The other was just a miner. Yet the duel bears telling in large part because it was one of the few duels fought over a woman for which a good record exists. The other reason the Knox-Allen affair bears telling is because it was between a Massachusetts gambler—a rare commodity indeed—and an Irishman.

In early 1854 a young Mexican woman named Anita Frates moved to Columbia, Tuolumne County. Though women were scarce everywhere in California they were particularly rare in the southern mines, and Anita's beauty soon attracted the attention of several miners. Her studied indifference however soon discouraged most of them from calling, until only Thomas Allen remained. Often, on summer evenings he and Anita could be seen seated on her tiny front porch. She in fact proved so receptive to his attentions many in Columbia were sure a marriage was in the offing.

But that summer Allen's road to marital bliss was blocked by the appearance of William Knox, a well-dressed gambler, whose good looks matched Allen's, and whose "unfeigned suavity" far surpassed his own. Knox, you will recall, had served as a second for George Hunt in his duel with Numa Hubert the previous May.

Knox was soon spending almost as much time on Anita's front porch as at his faro table. That October he confided to a friend that the two were indeed planning to marry later that year. Learning of their plans, many in Columbia predicted there would be trouble. Most of them sympathized with Allen, not only because he had lay first claim to Anita, but because miners, even full blown Irish miners, always evoked more sympathy than a gambler.

A few nights after Allen learned of Knox's plans he sought him out in his favorite saloon. Quickly spotting him at the faro table, he strode over and shouted, "Knox, give me personal satisfaction!"

Looking up, Knox in a statement that startled many present, coolly replied, "Name your weapons, second, place, and I will be there."

"We'll fight here and now," said Allen who had intended to settle the matter in fist-to-skull fashion. Friends immediately pulled him away from Knox, whom he had almost dragged out of his chair. Several then persuaded him that the gambler was right; the issue ought be settled according to the code. This was particularly so in view of the fact that Knox had surrendered his right of weapons, distance, and site.

Underscoring this point was a miner from Louisiana named Warren Holmes, who in front of Knox offered to serve as Allen's second. When Allen accepted the offer, the gambler, who had resumed dealing, turned to his close friend Doc Ramage, and said, "Doc, fix this thing up for me, will you?"

"All right," said Ramage.

After conferring with Allen, who had chosen Colt revolvers at ten paces, Holmes retired with Ramage to discuss the duel's other terms. In the end they agreed that the pair would stand with their backs to one another at ten paces, and at the word turn and fire. Three shots were to be exchanged, each commencing with the word. The site chosen was a level piece of ground between Columbia and Sonora—the time, sunrise the following morning. As no surgeon resided in Columbia, the services of Dr. A.I. Hughes of Sonora were obtained.

By midnight both antagonists had declared themselves satisfied with the arrangements and gone to bed. But with excitement running high, Columbia's gambling halls and saloons remained crowded until daybreak. As the eastern horizon began to lighten, a good part of town followed both parties over to the site. The ten paces were marked off and Allen and Knox took their positions. A coin toss gave the choice of position to Allen; another gave the choice of Colts to Knox, a concession by Allen for his earlier favor. A third toss gave Holmes the right to call fire.

"Are you ready," called Holmes

"Ready," answered Allen and Knox.

"Fire—one two three—stop!"

Knox wheeled, fired, and missed. Allen, firing at the same time, sent his bullet through the crown of Knox's hat, whirling it to the ground.

The hat was retrieved and the pistols reloaded. In the meantime several of Knox's friends advised him to make a settlement; Allen they felt was the better marksman and he stood a good chance of being killed on the next fire. But the gambler was so incensed by their poor opinion of his marksmanship, he angrily insisted on another call.

Once more the men took their positions. Again the word was given, again they whirled, again the revolvers barked. This time, as Allen's shot plowed into the earth in front of Knox, Knox's slug slammed into his chest. Without a word the miner fell forward onto the earth dead.

A large, somber crowd gathered around Allen as Knox hurried off to Columbia where Anita awaited him. A few days later the couple left for San Francisco, where they boarded a steamer for New York and were never heard from again.

30

The Democracy
versus the Know-Nothings

With the demise of the Whig Party all across America in 1854, there came the rise of the American, or Know-Nothing Party. Though the American Party's big success in California did not come until the following year, by mid-1854 many former Democrats and not a few former Whigs were joining in droves. The party acquired its derogatory tag because of the secret meetings held inside its lodges. Upon being questioned by non-members about what they were discussing, the members invariably replied, "I know nothing"; hence the name.

The Know-Nothing Party's rise in California sundered quite a few friendships. One of those friendships it forever sundered was that between Achilles Kewen, a San Francisco attorney, and Devereux Woodleif, a San Joaquin County judge.

Colonel Woodleif was a Mississippian who as a youth left home to join the Texas Rangers. He fought with the Rangers through the entire Mexican War and during that epoch established a remarkable record as a duelist. Though quite probably an exaggeration, it was claimed that in eight shootouts he killed three of his antagonists, while on three other occasions he suffered serious wounds himself. Following his last duel Woodleif departed for the West Coast, arriving in 1850.

Even at chivalry's height, most Californians felt dueling should be resorted to only after the worst of insults. Not so Devereux Woodleif, who thought dueling was a good means of settling any number of personal scores. Even so, most people respected rather than feared him. Off the dueling ground he was friendly, if in a reserved, punctilious way, insisting that proper etiquette be followed not only by himself, but everyone around him. At a time when it was very common for one man to literally give another the shirt off his back, he was also extraordinarily generous.

Achilles Kewen too was from Mississippi, brother to Assemblyman Edward J.C Kewen who had recently published *Adeliana*, one of California's first volumes of poetry. Tall and handsome, "Kiel" as he was known, practiced law in San Francisco. Unlike Woodleif, the Kewen Brothers were reluctant adherents of the code, their father having been killed in a duel in their home state.

By late 1854 the American Party had established itself in San Francisco. Because California had already attracted many Irish, German, and Italian Catholics, and because, theoretically speaking, Mexicans were allowed to vote, in contrast to the other states California's Know-Nothing Party soft-pedaled the national party's discriminatory platform on immigrants and Catholics. Rather the party turned its fire on the rampant corruption within the state's Democratic Party—Broderick and Chivalry alike. Among the thousands joining its ranks were the Kewen Brothers.

Like the Scott-Smith affair, the Kewen-Woodleif duel originated in the Blue Wing Saloon where in November 1854, the denizens of that place were discussing the merits of the American Party. Present were Kewen and Woodleif, who had been friends for many years, but who had not seen each other since Woodleif had become a judge in Stockton. They were soon drawn into the general conversation, their talk becoming animated, then boisterous, then clamorous. Finally Woodleif, a life-long Democrat, still wondering how his old friend Kewen could have bolted the "Democracy," lost control of himself and called him a "damned know nothing."

Kewen reacted by striking Woodleif in the face with an open hand. The slugfest was on, and only after a violent brawl were the two separated. Though Woodleif departed the Blue Wing red-faced, silent, and grim, most of those present thought the two would soon heal their rift. Not so Kewen—who knew Woodleif better than anyone else. The next day he personally sought him out and apologized for slapping him. But as he had feared, Woodleif refused to accept his apology. Kewen then offered to place it in writing. He again declined. Only blood could wipe away the disgrace of that open-handed blow.

The next day Woodleif, through his two seconds, Mexican War veterans Captain Skerrett and Major McDonald, sent him the challenge. Kewen quietly accepted. But still hoping for a settlement, he asked his two seconds, Dr. Wake Briarly and Robert N. Wood of Tuolumne County to make every effort to reach an adjustment. Briarly had of course attended the Denver-Gilbert duel of 1852, the Crane-Tobey duel of 1853, and more recently the Hubert-Hunt, all three times serving as a surgeon.

But Woodleif rebuffed all overtures. Thus, in resignation Kewen selected Mississippi Yagers at forty paces. The chosen ground was to be in what is now East Oakland; the date, November 8, 1854.

The afternoon before the duel the two parties crossed the Bay on the steamer *Red Jacket* and early the next morning met on the ground. But while they were preparing, Deputy Sheriff Simmons of Alameda County drove his sorrel into their midst and called out, "Gentlemen, this cannot go on. If you attempt to fight here I will arrest everyone concerned."

Kewen and Woodleif withdrew to their carriages and the deputy, having done his duty, galloped off. After shuttling their seconds back and forth several times between carriages, Kewen and Woodleif agreed to fight across the Alameda line in Contra Costa County (possibly near the present day Huckleberry Regional Preserve).

Their carriages rattled off. The drive took them through a heavily populated rural area, dotted with small farms and ranches where scores of locals, having gotten wind of the duel, joined the procession in such numbers that by the time Kewen and Woodleif reached their ridge top over 150 were trailing. The ridge offered numerous bucolic and panoramic views to the east and west, scenes in marked contrast to the anxiety roiling inside of Kewen, and the cold fury in Woodleif. As the two left their carriages witnesses noted that Woodleif appeared determined, while Kewen looked deeply troubled. Like Alfred Scott sixteen months before, Kewen was fighting a duel he could not win.

With the Bay below on one side and the East Bay Ranges on the other, Briarly and Skerrett measured out the distance; Briarly won the toss for position, and to give the word. Kewen and Woodleif then took their places, forty paces apart, backs to one another. It was 1 p.m. when Briarly drew back and asked, "Gentlemen, are you ready?"

"Yes," shouted both.

"Fire—one, two, three—stop!"

At the call Kewen and Woodleif swung round, drew their beads and pulled the triggers, their rifles roaring at the same instant. While Kewen remained erect at his post, one hundred twenty feet away Woodleif tumbled to the earth, a bullet through his chest.

As Kewen approached Woodleif's form he began to uncontrollably recite the efforts he had made to reach a settlement. Try as Briarly, Wood and the others might, they could not console him. Finally they led Kewen back to his carriage, gently forced him inside, got inside themselves, and ordered the driver to move out.

Woodleif's body followed shortly after and was transported across the Bay to a hotel room in San Francisco where his wife was waiting. Mrs. Woodleif had prepared for this occasion many a time, but miraculously her husband had always appeared in the doorway—if not exactly hale and hearty, at least breathing. This time, as he was carried through on a litter, she was already weeping. He was buried two days later in the same clothing he wore to the dueling site.

With the Kewen-Woodleif duel ended, Dr. Briarly retired from the dueling ground for some years, declining on one occasion to even serve as a surgeon. Aside from practicing medicine, he occupied himself by baking and selling peach pies. Kewen's other second, Robert N. Wood, was one of just four Californians to survive the ill-fated Henry Crabb expedition into Sonora in 1857.

Achilles Kewen never recovered from his duel with Woodleif and shortly after joined William Walker in Nicaragua. During the battle of Rivas he was captured by guerrillas, dragged into the town plaza, and burned to death.

31

Galahad Shot Again

Since his 1851 duel with Will Hicks Graham, William Walker's political wanderings, like his military wanderings, had become one of California's great odysseys. Once an inseparable friend of John Nugent, politically aligned with William Gwin, by 1854 he had joined the Broderick wing of the Democrat Party.

It is quite possible he did so because Broderick had promised him some hard cash for his upcoming filibustering expedition to Nicaragua. In return for what is unclear: the pledge of a Central American *hacienda*? a role in shaping the government Walker intended to forge in Nicaragua? the hope that more influential Southerners would follow him into his wing of the Party? Possibly all three: but of the three points only the last is verifiable.

Among the Southerners to join the Broderick camp the most noted—aside from Walker—were some of the state's most able lawyers: Frank Tilford, A.P. Crittenden, and Edmund Randolph. Within the Broderick Democracy these newcomers linked up with such longtime Southern stalwarts as legislators Anthony J. Butler and James Estill. In addition was the Chief's confidential aide Visecimus Turner, and the notorious newspaper editor, politician, and murderer, Parker H. French.

At 3 p.m. on July 18, 1854, one of the most singular events in state history occurred when the Democratic Party convened inside the Sacramento Baptist Church to make its nominations for Congress. The Broderick faction, led by Broderick himself, Ned McGowan and William Walker entered the church first, and while such "shoulder strikers" as Billy Mulligan, Bill Lewis, and James Casey guarded the main entrance, Broderick called the convention to order.

Suddenly a large phalanx of Chivalry Democrats, led by Judge David Terry, former Governor John McDougal, Assemblyman Joseph C. McKibbin, and famed settlers John Bidwell and George Coulter, stormed through a side door. Forcing their way past the front pews onto the platform, they placed another chair and rostrum next to Broderick's. While their followers continued to stream through the door, they too called the convention to order.

Most confounding to anyone attempting to measure the pulse of Golden Era politics is the fact that of the five Chivalry Democrats who led the charge through the door, all but David Terry were from Northern states. Indeed, with so many migrants from Northern states enlisting in Chivalry's ranks, and with the Broderick Democrats dependent on so many Southerners, by the mid-1850s the old North-South axis, so often alluded to by historians, was a concept without real meaning.

For the next six hours Walker, McGowan, and Broderick alternately threatened and pleaded for the Chivs to yield, to no avail. Pandemonium reigned as some 350 heavily armed delegates from both wings of the Democracy, packed inside a church intended for half that number of parishioners, pushed, shoved, and bellowed, all the while tippling one dram of whiskey after another.

At one point a delegate was dragged out of the chamber into an anteroom to be treated for an epileptic fit. At yet another moment, so many delegates simultaneously reached for their revolvers and cocked the hammers that the church sounded very much like the inside of a New England clock factory.

Minutes later a shot indeed rang out when a Broderick Democrat, Reuben Maloney, his hand wound too tightly around his pocketed revolver, accidentally pulled the trigger and sent a bullet down his trousers past his ankle, through the floor and into the earth beneath. But the shot, rather than precipitating the feared bloodbath, prompted numerous delegates to plunge through the church windows onto the ground, fifteen feet below. A number of twisted ankles, hobbled knees, and scraped elbows resulted, but that was all. Even J. Reuben Maloney, who insisted that his boot was welling up with blood, was found to be unscathed by his own shot.

When night fell the angry and embarrassed church rectors refused to turn on the lights, leaving the delegates to roar on in full darkness. Two flickering candles were brought to the fore, and placed on each rostrum, enabling the cursing and cajoling to continue under the grim visages of McGowan, Walker, McDougal and Terry. Finally the delegates of both Democracies, in various stages of exhaustion and intoxication, filed out the front door, leaving the interior of the church in shambles. The Baptist rectors vowed never again to lease their building to the Democratic Party.

The following day the two factions met in separate buildings. At Carpenter's Hall, with Walker and McGowan presiding, Broderick announced his choices for Congress. But because his senate bill had brought such disrepute upon himself among rank-and-file Democrats, his own nominees refused to run. Instead the Chivs, meeting at Music Hall, saw their choices for Congress,

James W. Denver and Philemon T. Herbert, win the nomination. In an otherwise disastrous year for Democrats, both narrowly defeated the Know-Nothing candidates in the fall elections.

Amazingly, no challenges were issued in the wake of what since has become known as the "Baptist Church Riot." But in the Byzantine world of Golden Era politics, as William Walker moved into the Broderick camp, William H. Carter moved out. No one will ever know why this once staunch supporter of Broderick and John Bigler suddenly departed. Recall that the former editor of the *Democratic State Journal* had seriously wounded Harry De Courcey in a duel outside of Sacramento three years before.

At 7 a.m. on March 13, 1855, Carter fought his second duel, this one with Walker. It had nothing to do with politics. Rather, it was prompted when Walker overheard Carter make what he considered were abusive remarks to the wife of a personal friend. In that friend's absence, he chivalrously decided to challenge him. Carter accepted, picking James Quinn and John McDougal as his seconds, while Walker chose Edmund Randolph and A. C. Crittenden as his. Weapons were dueling pistols at twelve paces—location, the *Sans Souci* House, San Francisco.

The night before the duel, Broderick, aware of what a deadly shot Carter was, asked Ned McGowan and the visiting Sam Ward to aid Walker in any way they could. The two agreed, and the following morning arrived at the *Sans Souci* House to find Carter and Walker, and their followers standing in a driving rain. Leaving their carriage, McGowan and Ward made their way forward and tried to arrange a settlement. Despite their pleas and the inclement weather, both parties remained determined to shoot it out.

As Crittenden, who had won the toss, called out, "Gentlemen, are you ready?" Carter raised his pistol. Realizing his mistake—an error that could have prompted either Randolph or Crittenden to gun him down—he quickly lowered his weapon and answered "Ready," as did Walker. At the word "Fire," both raised their pistols and pulled the triggers. Walker missed. Not so Carter, whose ball struck Walker's right foot in the big toe.

Though in great pain, to hide his wound Walker grimly held his composure. McGowan strode over and while conversing with him, kicked mud over his punctured boot, thus concealing the flow of blood. A few minutes later Crittenden, who had been conferring with Quinn, returned to report that since one shot had been exchanged, negotiations for an adjustment could begin.

"As you please," said Walker, wincing.

The adjustment was made and shortly after the duelists and their partisans returned to San Francisco. McGowan later wrote that he and Ward, after changing into some dry clothing, repaired to Old Martin's restaurant for a fine French breakfast.

Posterity has not been as generous to William Carter as to his fellow Pennsylvanian, Will Hicks Graham. After the shootout with Walker his trail across the California firmament disappears.

Not so the state's most failed duelist, William Walker. Despite losing two affairs of honor, and his 1853 failure to carve out a "republic" in Baja California, his star continued to rise. The "gray eyed man of destiny's" magnetic personality continued to attract thousands of admirers. In late 1855 several hundred of his "immortals" accompanied him to Nicaragua to help set up another "republic." In January 1856 Walker's most successful recruiter, Parker H. French, departed San Francisco aboard a steamship listing with volunteers. In their bitterness over "this lost opportunity for glory," those left behind on the docks rioted.

Though Walker fancied himself as a sort of George Washington of Nicaragua, many in the ranks did not share his ideals. His ragtag army, which included a good many desperadoes and duelists, was no match for Nicaragua's disease-ridden jungles. His regime foundered, as did his second. Finally, in 1860, in the midst of yet a third attempt to set up a Central American "republic," he was captured by the British and turned over to the Hondurans, who shot him.

32

The Evils of Temperance

California's most sensational duel of 1855 was fought in Yuba County just beyond the Sierra County line. Eighteen fifty five was the year that Sarah Pellet arrived in California to launch her crusade against the evils of drink. A graduate of Oberlin College, Ohio, Miss Pellet was then one of a number of male and female reformers preaching against America's almost insatiable thirst for alcoholic beverages.

The state was still very much woman starved in 1855, but not quite so starved as for a woman like Sarah Pellet. Her unpopular arguments and priggish manner prompted many a discussion among miners as to whether she was more of "a pill than a pellet." In her canvass of the various mining towns she often encountered hecklers who made a point of bringing a bottle, or occasionally a keg of whiskey to her gatherings. A number of mining town newspaper editors treated her quite roughly.

One of the few journalists who did champion her was Calvin B. McDonald, editor of Downieville's *Sierra Citizen*. A former swiller of red-eye himself, McDonald had become a teetotaler, and was then recognized as one of mining country's most able newspaper editors. His vigorous defense of Pellet prompted the temperance leader to make a special trip to remote Downieville. Within weeks of her arrival she and McDonald had forged a thriving "Sons of Temperance League." Once a hard-drinking town, Downieville soon became a locale where a young man could toss down a cup of cold water without being thought of as a suspicious character. Temperance became the rage.

That summer, with Independence Day approaching Downieville's "Sons of Temperance" appointed a committee to schedule the afternoon festivities. It immediately decided to ask Sarah Pellet to give the Fourth of July oration. Their choice was resented by many who felt that it was not a woman's business to give a Fourth of July oration. Among those most opposed was Robert Tevis, a candidate for Congress who wanted to give the oration himself.

Tevis was a tall, agreeable-looking Kentuckian, fond of speechifying, horse racing, hunting and whiskey. Though personally likeable, many felt he lacked the steady temperament required for public office. Anxious to counter this impression, he urged the committee to appoint him orator of the day. After much discussion the committee confirmed Pellet as orator, but decided to let Tevis read off the Declaration of Independence beforehand, and then make a few additional remarks.

That Fourth of July afternoon nearly all of Downieville's 3,000 denizens gathered at the parade ground. The festivities commenced after a blacksmith applied a hammer and anvil to a packet of gunpowder. Seconds later every musket, rifle, shotgun, and revolver in the crowd went off in a thunderous salute to the flag. The town's brass band followed by crashing out several patriotic tunes.

Afterward Tevis mounted the rostrum and read off the Declaration of Independence. Finished, he took advantage of the few extra minutes granted by the committee to give a rambling lecture on several state and national issues. As he droned on the crowd grew restless. Finally several temperance leaders left the stand and proceeded to the blacksmith's bench, where they had little trouble persuading the smithy to, at the given signal, strike off another packet of gunpowder. The members then returned to the stand where Tevis continued at full cry.

Minutes later the congressional hopeful was cut short by the crack of a pistol and another thunderous explosion of gunpowder. Badly jarred, flustered and humiliated, he returned to his seat. Sarah Pellet then stepped forward and to an enthusiastic crowd delivered the Fourth of July oration.

In the days that followed Tevis's humiliation became the talk of Sierra County. The humor was not lost on Charles Lippencott, a state senator from neighboring Yuba County, and a political enemy of Tevis. A native of Illinois, Lippencott was a short, heavyset man with piercing black eyes and a deliberate manner. Since arriving in California he had established himself not only as a politician but as a grizzly-bear hunter. Testimony to the double lives led by many politicians, following the legislature's four month session of 1854, Lippencott spent the balance of the year in the wilderness hunting deer, bear, and elk. Highly amused by the Fourth of July incident, he took out a column in McDonald's *Sierra Citizen* and raked Tevis's performance over the coals.

Just hours after the column appeared Tevis entered McDonald's office in a fury. Face white, voice shaking with rage, he demanded McDonald publish a card calling Lippencott, among other things, "a liar and a slanderer." The editor read the card, then warned Tevis that his wording was so severe it would likely provoke a challenge. Tevis declared he would gladly duel and insisted the card be placed.

McDonald complied.

The day after the card appeared, as McDonald had warned, Lippencott, through his close friend, Edward "Ned" Smith, sent a challenge. As Lippencott explained in his letter, he had no wish to shed blood, but the nature of the public insult left him no choice. Tevis, through his second, former Congressman Edward Marshall, accepted and chose double-barreled shotguns with slugs, not knowing that the shotgun was also Lippencott's favorite weapon. Distance was set at forty paces.

Neither Tevis or Lippencott was a member of Sons of Temperance, but both belonged to the Odd Fellows Association. In the days before the duel this group tried to arrange an adjustment between the two. The Odd Fellows in fact spent the entire night beforehand patching together an arrangement that everyone felt would satisfy both. Their efforts were unhappily sabotaged by several "sports" who wished to see the duel come off.

On the morning of the duel Tevis and Lippencott both awed the crowd that had gathered, by unloading their smooth bores into several whiskey bottles, smashing them to bits at forty paces. Accompanied by Smith, Marshall and the crowd, they then left for the dueling ground, a flat near the mining camp of Brandy City.

No sooner had the duelists and their seconds assembled than the Sierra County sheriff galloped into their midst, reined in his horse, and threatened to arrest them. A lengthy *sotto voce* discussion followed between Tevis, Lippencott, and their seconds. At its conclusion they informed the sheriff and the crowd that they had reached a settlement. No duel would be fought.

In truth no such settlement had been reached, and shortly after the sheriff and crowd departed, Tevis and Lippencott, and their seconds and physicians quietly left for neighboring Yuba County.

It was late afternoon when they reached the chosen ground, a fairly level piece of land sloping slightly from one end to the other, surrounded by towering pines. Only the dropping of a few pine cones could be heard as Marshall and Smith walked off the forty paces. Moments later a coin was tossed for position. Tevis won and took his post, forty paces distant, a foot and a half higher than Lippencott's.

Moments later at the word "Fire!" their shotguns boomed, the roar crashing through the pines. A patch of hair flew from the top of Lippencott's head as forty paces away Tevis sank to the earth, blood spurting from his chest, a shotgun slug through his heart. He had drawn a good bead, but had somehow neglected to account for the higher ground he had chosen.

Tevis was buried among the pine trees, but the following day friends exhumed his body and carried it back to Downieville. A few days later much of the town turned out at the Hillside Cemetery for his formal services.

Of the other figures in the Lippencott-Tevis duel nothing is known of Ned Smith. Edward Marshall left shortly after to join William Walker's filibustering expedition in Nicaragua, and was killed in the fighting there. Lippencott returned to Downieville some weeks after the duel and asked for forgiveness. He was politely received by a few, but in a town that was not his own many treated him as an Ishmael. He finished out his term in the State Senate and returned to Illinois. When the Civil War broke out he enlisted in the Union Army and during the fighting rose to the rank of colonel.

Sarah Pellet left Downieville late that summer to spread the gospel of temperance to other mining towns. McDonald left to write for a newspaper in Sacramento, then departed for Weaverville where he edited the *Trinity Journal*, and again resumed drinking red-eye. With the departure of both, Sierra County's "cold water brigade" went into a decline and Downieville once again became an ordinary mining community.

33

Crawfishing in San Jose

One of the more curious duels that took place in 1855 was between two of California's most colorful pioneers, the infamous Parker H. French, and the far more reputable Lewis C. Belcher. Indeed, the life of French is so scandalous in its dimensions that, much like Ned McGowan, a biography of him would provide a first-rate textbook for anyone teaching a course on rascality.

French first appeared in California in 1852, one-armed and wiry, a Kentuckian with eyes as flinty gray as William Walker's. A lawyer by training, he was also handsome, reminding many of Napoleon III in the manner he trimmed his beard and mustache. Fast as he was with a gun, he was an even faster talker, possessing a gift of gab that rivaled P.T. Barnum.

It was probably this gift that enabled French to return to Missouri in 1854 to remarry his former wife, Lucretia, whom he had abandoned six years before. Doubtless it was also this fluency that convinced David Broderick and Edward McGowan that he was entitled to represent the city of Sacramento in the state assembly. They nominated him, he ran, and he won. But there is little doubt that he was stuffed into office with bogus ballots.

French took his seat in time to embroil himself in the tumultuous 1854 senatorial contest. He worked hard, prodding a number of reluctant Democrats to vote for Broderick's election bill. About that time it became known that he had been employed by the prominent Southern California rancher Richard Dana. After driving Dana's cattle to market in San Francisco, he sold the herd, but kept the receipts for himself. Although criminal charges were never filed, a civil suit found him liable for payment.

At about the time French took his seat in the state assembly, Supreme Court Justice Alexander Wells, another of French's cronies, suddenly died. In a tribute to the judge, French collected over $1,400 for his family, a gift that Wells's widow declined to accept. Rather than return the money to its rightful donors, French pocketed this sum too. Shortly after, more sinister rumors began to circulate, one connecting his missing arm to a long ago gun battle fought with a westering wagon train.

Other than his work for Broderick's election to the U.S. Senate, his stint at the state capital was unremarkable. Not so his conduct after the week's adjournment, particularly aboard the several steamboats plying the Sacramento River and Delta. On one occasion he engaged a passenger in a brawl that ended only after he pulled a gun and shot his adversary through the thigh. In yet another steamboat affray, he himself was shot in the thigh while trying to break up a melee between two other passengers.

After French's term in the Assembly ended in 1855, he was hired by William Roach to aid him in his legal bid to acquire the Jose Maria Sanchez Rancho in Monterey County, a dispute that had already led to four deaths. In July of that year Lewis Belcher, who was contesting Roach's claim to the Rancho, made some snide remarks about French—specifically he called him a "put up scare crow."

By then Belcher had made quite a name for himself in the state. Raised in Orange County, New York, as a young man he wandered to Missouri where he spent a number of years before moving on to California. Since settling in Monterey County he had established his own political organization and was known everywhere as the "Big Eagle of Monterey."

Upon learning that Belcher's was having a horse shod at a San Jose black-smith shop, French rode over and confronted him with the alleged quote.

Belcher readily admitted to calling him, "A put up scare crow."

To which French replied, "You must take it back in a public manner, and also privately to those to whom you uttered it."

"I never take back the truth after I have once given it utterance!"

French retorted that a duel was in order. The Big Eagle readily agreed, and then suggested that since both were armed with six shooters, and the two blacksmiths would be more than willing to serve as seconds, they could "have it out right now." French too agreed.

But on his way up the hill to the chosen site, he turned to Belcher and said, "You had better apologize and retract the offensive language, and settle the matter without a resort to arms."

Belcher said no and the ascent continued. The ground was finally reached and the blacksmiths were in the midst of measuring off the distance when French and Belcher took their approximate positions. Just as preparations ended, French announced that he wanted to talk over an adjustment. In the exchange that followed he once more asked Belcher to retract his insulting language.

"I did not come out to this place to retract the truth!"

"We both have families," continued French. "And I have already caused my wife a great deal of trouble and unhappiness, and I do not wish to further add to her sorrows. I am willing to let the matter drop and remain as it is."

"As you please," said Belcher, turning and striding off the hill. French trailed him down to the shop, mounted his horse and rode off. One witness later said that "French showed the 'white feather." Another, referring to that crustacean's familiar mode of backward retreat in the face of danger, claimed that he "Crawfished."

Despite his facing down of French, the Big Eagle's reign in Monterey County lasted less than one more year. In June, 1856 he was gunned down inside a saloon by an unknown assailant from without. He died the following day fully conscious, swearing vengeance on his killers. All evidence points to French's former employer, William Roach, with whom Belcher had been feuding over the Jose Maria Sanchez Rancho, as responsible for the killing. Even with the Big Eagle's death, over the coming years, the Roach-Belcher feud became the bloodiest in state history, ending only after the death of Roach himself.

French never underwent the disgrace suffered by Edward Gilbert and others who had groveled on the field of honor. This was partly because his crawfishing affair was witnessed by so few, partly because Belcher—with good reason—was so obsessed in his feud with Roach that he seldom spoke of it, and because French's mendacity was almost without parallel.

In the fall of 1855, in the company of another glib Kentuckian, James Estill, French began publishing the *Sacramento Tribune*, a Know-Nothing newspaper. Two months later he abandoned the paper to join William Walker's forces in Nicaragua. There, he suggested that the "grey eyed man of destiny" appoint him ambassador to the United States. Walker, an atrocious judge of character, who had already appointed him a colonel, obliged.

Ambassador French arrived in New York City in January 1856 to a friendly reception. A number of newspapers saluted him as Nicaragua's "One armed Paladin." As he raced from one reception to the next, raving about the glory of his "Nicaraguan Immortals," he enlisted hundreds of volunteers. But in the midst of his mission, he made the mistake of trashing the Franklin Pierce Administration for its "pusillanimous" stance toward the Walker regime. The attack, and rumors that were circulating about his past, prompted Secretary of State William L. Marcy to launch an investigation. The report, issued a few days later, vindicated the Secretary's suspicions, and profoundly embarrassed many of French's admirers. Much, but not all of what took place, appeared in the *California Chronicle* of February 21, 1856 in a feature titled "Adventures on the Plains; Parker H. French's California Express Train."

In late 1849 French organized a wagon train of 170 prospective settlers, pledging to guide them from east Texas to California. He financed the venture with forged drafts, courtesy of the banking house of Howland and

Aspinwall. Then in August 1850, in remote west Texas, members of the wagon train, angered by French's brusque manner and routine drunkenness, seized the wagons and ran him and his gang of fifteen off.

A week later as a portion of the wagon train paused at a spring in the wilds of northern Chihuahua, French and his well-mounted gang thundered down on them in a surprise attack. In the dramatic gun battle that followed, they ran off most of the stock, killed seven wagon train members and wounded nine others. In the midst of the bloody clash, one of the defenders fired off a round that struck French's wrist and tore up his forearm, exiting above the elbow and shattering it.

The pain-maddened French broke off the attack and with his gang fled to Coralitos. There, an unknowing and sympathetic doctor amputated his arm, cauterized the wound with charcoal, and restored his health. After his recovery he and his gang rode off for Durango where they remained two full years, during which time they had several brushes with the gendarmes, in one instance robbing a mail coach. Now a hunted man in both Chihuahua and Durango, French fled to Altar, Sonora, where he and the remnants of his gang ran the local *jefe* up a rope in an attempt to gain access to the city treasury. From there he made his way to California, where he made contact with the unfortunate Dana.

Marcy's disclosure rattled the continent from Washington, to California, to Nicaragua. On learning of the secretary's disclosure and that criminal charges were pending, French hurriedly left New York, leaving behind the following note for Marcy:

> Regretting that you should have misunderstood my last communication and that you authorized the arrest of my person in New York and thereby the indignity shown against the government I have the honor to represent, I therefore respectfully request that you will not consider my credentials as before your government at the present. I am sir, your most obedient servant. Parker H. French.

He returned to Nicaragua where he managed to persuade Walker to appoint him Minister of Haciendas. French's bullying of the natives with regards their homestead rights played a major role in Walker's plummeting popularity, and ultimate defeat in Nicaragua.

His sojourn on the field of honor was less than consequential. But Parker French practicing law, lobbying the state legislature, and voting in the state assembly, much like Ned McGowan practicing law, David Broderick organizing the state legislature, Billy Mulligan monitoring San Francisco's polling stations, and John McDougal ensconced in the governor's chair, offer a few suggestions as to what went wrong with California during its Golden Age.

34

The Salted Claim

Once again the question begs asking: why should a duel between two miners lay claim to an entire chapter? The Jacobs-Joiner Duel warrants telling, in part because it involved a salted claim, and in part because it was the only duel in California known to have been fought between members of the Hebrew faith.

William Jacobs was a native of Liverpool, England, who arrived in California in 1851 with dreams of making a fortune. After trying his luck at mining without success, he opened a general store in Nevada County. Like most mining town stores in the early '50s, Jacobs's was a canvas affair. And like many merchants, upon learning of a fresh bonanza, he would fold up his canvas store and drive off in the direction of the strike, his merchandise aboard several wagons. Often the first shopkeeper to reach the diggings, he always had a good assortment of dry goods and wares on hand. Within three years he was a fairly wealthy man.

The last part of 1855 found Jacobs back in Nevada County at a mining camp in Humbug Canyon. At the far end of the canyon lay a claim owned by Israel Joiner, a loner who seldom mixed with his fellow miners. No one knew anything of his past, and in accordance with the customs of the time, no one pressed him about his past. The only time anyone ever saw Joiner was on a Sunday when he arrived at Jacobs's store to lay in supplies. On several occasions, Jacobs, curious about his taciturn fellow wanderer, asked him what kind of luck he was having. Each time Joiner would reply "Poor."

But strangely there was always more than enough gold dust in his pouch to keep him going. Jacobs soon passed word that he thought Joiner owned one of the richest claims in Humbug Canyon.

Sometime in October Joiner appeared in town in the middle of the week, entered Jacobs's store, drew him aside, and informed him that he indeed owned the richest claim in Humbug Canyon. He then suggested that Jacobs become his partner. Jacobs hesitated, but when Joiner insisted that he look the claim over himself, agreed. What he saw on his inspection, so convinced him of its worth, that when he returned to camp he announced that he had bought half interest for $5,000 in cash.

For a few weeks after all went well. But by mid-November Jacobs was complaining to customers that Joiner had swindled him. For reasons unknown the mine was no longer paying.

One Sunday morning Joiner, learning that Jacobs had spread the word that he had salted his mine, strode into the store and in front of customers began a bitter if subtle quarrel. After some minutes of arguing in *sotto voce*, Jacobs suddenly shouted, "You're a liar and a swindler!" Pulling a revolver from his belt, he dealt Joiner a terrific blow to the head, knocking him out.

When the victim regained consciousness, several shoppers helped him to his feet. Still groggy and stroking his scalp, he turned to Jacobs and said, "You took me unawares, you cowardly assassin. I give you fair warning now that I will kill you on sight."

Jacobs's associates warned him that he meant business, warnings that proved very nearly prophetic. On three separate occasions Joiner attempted to take his life. In his most determined effort, he attempted to break into his cabin, but was disarmed at the window by Jacobs and a fellow occupant, who pulled him inside and thoroughly worked him over, before tossing him outside.

A few days later an American miner named Slocum approached Joiner and told him that if he wanted Jacobs dead, "You should kill him in a fair and just manner." Joiner listened, nodded, and asked Slocum to be his second. The following morning Slocum delivered a challenge. Jacobs accepted, and named as his second a Jewish miner named Wienman.

As the challenged party Jacobs insisted that he and Joiner meet two miles from camp, attended only by their seconds and one friend each. Weapons were Colt six shooters at ten paces. They were to hold their firearms with one hand, while with the other each was to wield a Bowie knife. At the word they would begin shooting, and shoot until all loads were expended. In the event that both were still on their feet, they were to end the contest with a flourish of Bowie knives.

When Slocum learned of the terms he rejected them as, in his words, "contrary to every consideration of humanity." Jacobs eventually agreed to dispense with the Bowie knives, but then insisted that the distance be reduced to just five paces. Slocum consented and the following morning the two duelists, with their seconds and one friend each, met on the ground. Fifteen feet apart, they waited for Slocum to make the call.

Moments later at the word "Fire!" both cocked their triggers and let fly. Joiner instantly fell to the ground, one of Jacobs's bullets lodged in his chest. His single shot narrowly missed Jacobs' shoulder. Later that day he was buried in a shallow grave to the rear of his cabin. A short time afterward Jacobs sold their claim, and with his canvass store in tow left Nevada County in search of better diggings.

35

The Grand Burlesque

Some duels are intense, filled with melodrama and dread, while others, no matter how murderous the intentions of the antagonists, lend themselves to farce. Setting the standard for mockery on the field of honor is the duel between Austin E. Smith and Henry B. Truett.

Austin E. Smith was a U.S. Navy officer and lawyer, brother to Judge Caleb Smith who had fought the duel with Broderick four years before, while Henry B. Truett, formerly the mayor of Galena, Illinois, was one of San Francisco's most successful wholesale merchants. Both were Chivalry Democrats of different stripes. One of the many reasons the Democrats went down to defeat in 1855 was because Chivalry itself had crumbled into two factions.

While Smith and most Chivs remained loyal to William Gwin, many others, such as former Collector of the Port Richard P. Hammond, Congressman George McDougall (not to be confused with John McDougal) and State Supreme Court Justice Hugh Murray were left seething with anger over the senator's patronage appointments. This faction included an unusually high number of migrants from Illinois, Indiana, and Maryland, of which Truett was one.

Despite their subtle political leanings Smith and Truett remained the best of friends. Early in October, however, Truett lost a considerable sum of money in a game of whist. Because he had also recently suffered a business reverse he was unable to pay his debts. His creditors hired Smith to retrieve their assets. Smith in turn delivered a writ of attachment for Truett's house at his doorstep, where the owner, who initially thought the call was social, became furious.

The next day Truett sought out Smith in his office and accused him of having acted in an "ungentlemanly fashion." A brawl followed during which Smith liberally applied his cane about Truett's head and shoulders. The following day Hamilton Bowie appeared in Smith's office with a challenge. With him was Richard P. Hammond, who Truett had chosen as his auxiliary. Like Bowie, Hammond was from Maryland and in the recent political struggle among Chivs, had sided with Truett's faction.

Smith accepted, chose Colt six shooters at ten paces, and named Volney E. Howard and Edward J.C. Kewen as his seconds. Kewen, an assemblyman from Southern California, was brother to Achilles Kewen who had killed Devereux Woodleif in a duel the year before. Howard was then a lawyer of some repute, and still committed to Gwin.

Because of foot dragging on the part of the seconds, who were loathe to see the duel "come off," Smith and Truett could not reach agreement on the manner in which it would be fought. Only after some days of intentionally protracted haggling between their seconds did they agree to fight just south of San Francisco. They would stand with their backs to one another at ten paces and at the word, whirl and fire away. Should both escape the expected riddling they were to finish each other off with Bowie knives.

The day before the duel, a close friend of Smith and Truett, Judge Harry Thornton, learned of the expected meeting. One of San Francisco's most respected jurists, he was quoted as shouting, "There is not cause enough for a duel between two such worthy gentlemen!"

Vowing to prevent bloodshed, on the morning of the fight he awoke early and with two others, through early dawn's light followed the duelists in his own carriage to a fenced pasture about a mile beyond city limits. He pulled up in time to see Smith and Truett take their positions. Descending from his carriage, the portly Judge hurried to the fence where his two companions helped him over. Lumbering across the pasture toward the duelists, Thornton shouted, "Hold up there men, don't shoot!"

Suddenly at the far end of the pasture an enormous black bull cantered through an open gate. The bovine's presence accomplished what Judge Thornton was unable to—draw the attention of Smith and Truett. The animal's own attention however immediately focused on Thornton. Snorting and bellowing, he thundered after the judge, who, unable to scurry more than a few paces, threw himself onto the ground. The bull pulled up short, but not short enough to avoid administering several punishing whacks with his hooves.

In an effort to draw the bull away from Thornton, Smith, Truett, and the throng set up an immense howl. Seconds later, as the animal lumbered off in their direction, puffs of gray smoke erupted in the air as the crowd emptied firearms of various calibers into him. Several were forced to vault the rails as the lead-ridden beast collapsed in their midst. The bull had stayed the duel, but paid for it with his life.

Members of the crowd meanwhile raced over to Thornton, lifted him from the ground, whisked off his dirt-encumbered coat, hoisted him onto a rail, and carried him to his wagon. An hour later, amidst great hue and cry, the judge's wife and daughters put him to bed, where it is claimed he remained an entire week.

Despite the efforts of Thornton and the now defunct bull, Smith and Truett were determined to fight it out. Much to their dismay, however, as they resumed their positions a mounted policeman loped into the pasture. Reining in his horse, he announced that Smith and Truett were under arrest. The two vented their fury at the officer, reminding him that he was out of his jurisdiction. For several minutes the lawman jawed back until U.S. Marshal Hampton North and his posse galloped into the corral.

The sight of North prompted Smith and Truett to leap the fence and disappear in opposite directions. Later that day Truett was arrested and forced to post bond; Smith, it appears was never captured. A calm settled over San Francisco as the next day several newspapers announced that the two had reached a settlement.

But the reports proved false. Early the next evening, accompanied by their seconds and some eighty followers, Smith and Truett drove off for San Mateo. Unlike William Gwin and Joseph McCorkle who had taken two leisurely days to wind their way down the Peninsula, Truett and Smith drove their carriages full tilt through moonlight and shadow, arriving at San Mateo the following morning. Since their aborted meeting in the pasture, Bowie, Hammond, Kewen and Howard had managed to persuade them to drop the two most savage aspects of their duel—advancing on each other while firing and finishing each other off with Bowie knives.

Well beyond the reach of even Marshal North, the two parties assembled on the banks of San Mateo Creek, an eighth of a mile to the rear of Dr. De Peyster's hotel. The crowd now had grown to 120, augmented by many *Californios* anxious to see an American-style duel for the first time. At one point the crowd grew so enthused Bowie and Kewen ordered its members to stand sixty feet back.

At their positions Smith and Truett both sported broadcloth coats buttoned to the chin; while Truett wore a black slouched hat, Smith sported his Navy cap. Both waited as Hammond ceremoniously read off the articles to the "code of honor."

Moments after finishing, he stepped back and began the call. At the word "Fire" both spun around and a rattle of exploding caps rent the air as they blasted away at each other. On Truett's third fire the cap caught in his cylinder, forcing him to fire his weapon with both hands. Having discharged all shots, he threw his pistol aside, and, in a move reminiscent of John Nugent, turned to face Smith directly, waiting for his last shot. Instead he watched in astonishment as Smith dropped his pistol and spun into the arms of the onrushing Kewen.

All four surgeons rushed to Smith's aid. An examination revealed that he had been struck in the right leg above the knee. He had fired five shots, but all had missed—other than the one that had, unknown to Truett, torn a ragged hole across the seat of his pants, leaving his posterior without a scrape.

Truett strode over to Smith, lying between the surgeons, reached down and shook his hand. Both pronounced themselves satisfied and the duel was over. After insisting that Smith use his more comfortable "rockaway" carriage for the trip back to San Francisco, Truett departed for town.

Among the major figures present, the duel proved to be Hamilton Bowie's last appearance on the field of honor. Within the year his untimely death would be mourned by many. Richard P. Hammond, in spite of recently being indicted for embezzlement while collector of the port, would go one to play a major role in establishing the University of California. Edward Kewen remained a popular assemblyman from Southern California for many years. Volney Howard, on the other hand went on to play a less than memorable role as a leader of the Law and Order Party during the vigilante uprising of 1856.

Henry Truett recovered from his squandered whist stakes and went on to financial success. He joined the Vigilance Committee of 1856 only because his brother, Miers Truett, was one of their leaders. In July, after the vigilantes decided to hang two desperadoes from the façade of his own building, he changed sides, joining Smith, Howard, Bowie and Hammond as "Law and Order Men." He later moved to Montana Territory.

Austin E. Smith opposed the Vigilance Committee from the start. In fact he and his old foe David Broderick, having placed their differences aside, were both captured by the vigilantes. The two were peering into their headquarters from a vacant room across the street with a pair of field glasses. They were apprehended by several committee members, and escorted to the edge of town with a warning: "Behave yourselves!"

With the outbreak of the Civil War, Smith returned east to fight for the Confederacy. He was killed near Richmond during the Peninsula Campaign.

36

A Fighting Editor Takes a Stand

The year 1855 was perhaps the most violent in California history, with a total of 497 homicides committed over the first ten months, an extraordinary tally for a state with less than 300,000 people. Just the year before the Golden State had registered 464 murders, while New York and Texas—the former with ten times the population—were distant runners up, recording 74 and 50 homicides respectively.

Yet the fact remains that in 1855 the number of duels fought declined. One reason for the decline was the ghastly toll of the dead. The cumulative deaths of such noted figures as Dr. Crane, Joseph Dixon, Edward Gilbert, Joseph Langdon, Peter Smith, and Devereux Woodleif, among others, had a chilling effect on the state. But there was also the widely circulated letter written by James King who later in the same year would found the *San Francisco Evening Bulletin*.

A native of Georgetown, Maryland, King arrived in California in 1848, and even before it became a state, with explorer Jacob Snyder established one of its first banks. Shortly afterward King sent for his wife and children. In 1854 he merged his bank with the Adams and Company Bank and Express firm and became one of its managing partners. Suddenly on February 22, 1855, a run began on the Adams and Company Bank's deposits. The following day the bank closed its doors and a receiver was appointed to manage its remaining assets.

Within a week King learned that Adams and Company director, Isaiah C. Woods, and his new receiver, Alfred A. Cohen, had covertly funneled $400,000 into the Palmer, Cook and Company vault. This was the same Palmer, Cook and Company Bank that in 1854 had withheld payment of California's bonds on Wall Street, prompting their value to crash. Using a front company, Palmer and Cook had hoped to purchase the bonds at a basement price. But before its kingmakers, Joseph Palmer, George Wright, and Edward Jones were able to do so, another financial institution came to the state's rescue.

Alfred Cohen was arrested and Woods, learning of his own impending indictment, sailed for Peru. An agonizing four months followed as King and the state of California strove to learn the particulars behind the Adams and Company failure. That summer King reported that prior to its collapse, Woods and Cohen had gone into the "barley" business. The two would purchase gold dust in the mining counties for $7.50 an ounce, debase its contents, and then sell it to the Page, Bacon and Company Bank for $14 an ounce. King's disclosure resulted in a suit by Page, Bacon and Company against Adams and Company's receiver Cohen, and brought him considerable renown.

The exposé in turn led to even greater acclaim for the failed banker, when Cohen accosted him on the street. In the fight that followed King soundly thrashed him. The next day Cohen, through his chosen second, John K. Hackett, sent a challenge.

King pondered the challenge. To flinch from the "Code of the West" was courting disgrace. But he had always opposed dueling in the belief that it almost never resulted in real justice being served; rather, it had too often resulted in the loss of a fairly valuable life. Just as important: whatever anyone else thought, he knew that he himself was no coward. It was this strong sense of himself that enabled him to write Hackett a letter, posted in several newspapers, key portions of which follow:

> Recent events have stripped me entirely of what I once possessed. Were I to fall I should leave a large family without the means of support. My duties and obligations to my family have much more weight with me than any desire to please Mr. Cohen or his friends in the manner proposed. I have ever been opposed to dueling on moral grounds. . . . Whilst nothing could induce me to change my principles on the subject of dueling, my conscience is perfectly easy as to my right [to] defend myself should I be assaulted . . .

King's refusal to duel made such good sense he received a tremendous outpouring of praise. Married men who had previously felt duty bound to honor the code now declined challenges, citing the same reason. Dueling would continue to take its toll, but in large part owing to James King, the number of deaths began to decline.

37

Year of Bedlam: 1856

In January 1856 the American Party, led by Governor Neeley Johnson, having swept to victory in the fall elections, took over the reins of government in California. Within weeks the party split into two factions, those who had formerly been Democrats and those who were former members of the Whig Party. In a raucous session punctuated by several brawls, the Know-Nothings failed to pass any legislation of importance. Most noteworthy was its failure to elect a U.S. senator to replace William Gwin, whose term had expired the year before. The state was thus forced to limp through its second consecutive year with but a single senator, John B. Weller, in Washington.

On May 14, 1856, San Francisco City Supervisor James Casey shot and killed *San Francisco Evening* Bulletin editor James King. In the wake of King's death an 8,000-man vigilance committee formed, dwarfing the 1851 vigilance committee in size. In the wake of its takeover of the city four men were hanged and some thirty desperadoes, including many of Broderick's henchmen, were either jailed or run out of town: among them were Bill Lewis, Alexander Purple, Charles P. Duane, and Billy Mulligan. Another, heavyweight boxer Yankee Sullivan, committed suicide in his jail cell. Other members of the Broderick clique such as Mayor James Van Ness, District Attorney Henry Byrne, and Sheriff David Scannel, while able to officially retain their positions, were stripped of all material power.

Meanwhile the state's political establishment—Broderick and Chivalry Democrats, Know-Nothings and old line Whigs—lined up against the vigilantes. Appointed by Governor Johnson to lead the "Law and Order Party" was none other than former governor, John McDougal. Also hastening to join "law and order" was State Supreme Court Justice David Terry. That June, in the company of Hamilton Bowie and J. Reuben Maloney, he left his bench in Sacramento for the streets of San Francisco in order to personally deliver a writ of *habeas corpus* for the jailed Billy Mulligan. In a wild brawl that was almost a foregone conclusion, Terry rammed his Bowie knife into the neck of a vigilante. He was shortly after captured and thrown into jail where he languished for most of the summer.

That same month in Sacramento, another law and order leader, Chief Justice of the State Supreme Court Hugh Murray, was arrested for severely thrashing a shopkeeper who had condemned his conduct on the bench. Murray entered a guilty plea before departing for Nevada in search of a silver mine. With Solomon Heydenfeldt, the state's third Supreme Court justice, off on a junket to Europe, the high court had effectively closed down.

In June 1856 an even greater disgrace befell the Law and Order Party when news arrived that another of its members, Congressman Philemon T. Herbert, had shot a waiter in Washington, D.C., during a fight over a breakfast order. Recall that Herbert had served as B.F. Washington's second in his duel with Charles Washburne, and as James Hawkins's second in his duel with Chris Dowdigan. Later in the summer, after a stacked jury found him not guilty of murder, Herbert returned to California. On his return he challenged *San Francisco Evening Bulletin* editor, Thomas King, who had succeeded his murdered brother James, to a duel. King, who had condemned Herbert's murderous conduct in Washington, declined the challenge.

Even worse than the Herbert debacle, in July the state learned that its most powerful banking house, Palmer, Cook and Company, had absconded with $250,000 in state funds. Though the bank had been barred from handling state finances since 1854, Joseph Palmer, kingmaker of the concern, had long been a friend of Know-Nothing State Treasurer Henry Bates. The prior January, within weeks of taking office, Bates had handed the keys to the Treasury over to Palmer. Over the coming months, he and his partners removed the bullion, and packing it into innocuously labeled crates, shipped it off to New York where it was transferred into the coffers of the newly formed Republican Party. Palmer, by then one of the most hated men in California, knew that his career in the state was at a dead end. He had hoped that should his long-time associate, John C. Fremont, win that year's presidential election, he would be appointed secretary of the U.S. Treasury.

Mid-1856 would be the last San Francisco would see of Ubiquitous Ned McGowan for some time. Accused by the vigilantes of passing James Casey the pistol he used to shoot James King, McGowan went into hiding inside the city. In early June he slipped through the vigilante dragnet and headed south along the coast, disguised as a priest intent on writing a book about California missions. Patrick Hull, a well-known city columnist, touches on McGowan's career with San Francisco's Court of Sessions, and the legal carnage he left behind:

> Within the old county building in front of Portsmouth Square, McGowan held court. The ubiquitous Ned here dispensed justice, equity and maritime law before Hall McAllister, Eugene Casserley, Calhoun Benham, James McDougall, Edmund Randoph and others. Harry Brown and Alexander Wells,

tenants of the same building, were his especial friends. It was understood that the Judge had an easy time of deciding all issues so long as these two attorneys were not arguing opposite sides of the same case. . . .

Judge McGowan's court was hampered by no questions of jurisdiction. Suits of law and equity were eagerly taken—ejectments from land, or bills for divorce. Suits in admiralty were disposed of when ship and cargo hung in equal scale. No amount was too small for him to adjust, no sum too great for him to determine. He thus continued to dispense justice and equity until forced to flee the persecutions of a populace who had never learned to appreciate the merits of Judge McGowan's statesmanship, or his administration of justice . . .

In the months that followed, McGowan's flight before the Vigilance Committee became the stuff of which western novels are written. He eventually returned to Sacramento under his own steam. There, greeted by throngs of law and order admirers, he persuaded the state legislature to change the location of his trial from unfriendly San Francisco to friendly Napa County. At his trial, held in June, 1857, he was found not guilty of passing James Casey the weapon used to kill King.

Eighteen fifty six was also the last anyone would ever see of Hamilton Bowie. A staunch member of the Law and Order party, Bowie had accompanied David Terry on his excursion into San Francisco. Following their wild brawl with the vigilantes, Bowie was arrested. But because, unlike Terry, he had refrained using a weapon, he was released the following day. Shortly after, he left the state to join William Walker in Nicaragua, where just two months later he died of an unknown tropical illness.

Event continued to pile upon event. In June of the year the "Big Eagle of Monterey," Lewis C. Belcher, was shot and killed in an ambush, and in November Sheriff W.W. Wright of Nevada County was shot to death while in pursuit of outlaw Jim Webster. Yet there were moments in 1856 when violence did pay dividends for genuine law and order men. In April members of the George Walker gang, which had earlier robbed the Trinity Mountain Express of $16,000, were trapped by a posse just outside of Folsom. In the violent shootout that followed Walker was killed. And in October another posse led by George Belt captured the famous stagecoach robber, Tom Bell, on the banks of the San Joaquin River and hanged him.

Thus through much of 1856 California—its treasury plundered by renegade bankers and Know-Nothings, its largest city rising in defiance of the law, lesser vigilance committees seizing Mokelumne Hill and Yreka, its Law and Order Party led by a former governor with a long history of breaking the law, one of its Supreme Court justices guilty of assault and battery, another languishing in a vigilante jail, one of its two members of Congress on the dock in Washington on charges of murder, and long stretches of its lonely highways stalked by highwaymen—staggered toward ruin.

Fertile ground for the dueling fraternity, one would have thought. Yet during the entire year of 1856 just two duels took place, both in remote sections of the state. Part of the decline can be attributed to the reasons already cited for the 1855 decline. But the near paucity of duels, to some extent can be blamed on the San Francisco Vigilance Committee. Most of those who joined the committee were reform types: solid, law-biding citizens who, like their fallen leader, James King, considered dueling an uncivilized practice.

On the other hand the Law and Order Party counted within its ranks almost every advocate of the "code of honor" in the state. Ferociously hostile to the vigilantes, those law and order men not being detained or pursued by the vigilance committee and those not residing in San Francisco were hardly disposed to quarrel among themselves. It might be said with some exaggeration that cleansed of its grifters, grafters, and peculators, the Bay City had no "gentlemen" left to issue challenges.

The first major confrontation was less a duel, than an impromptu gunfight between two newspaper editors. The shootout took place in February, in Weaverville, Trinity County, between J.O. Crowningshield, publisher of the *Trinity Times*, and J. Crawford formerly publisher of the *Trinity Democrat*; Crawford's *Democrat* had recently been absorbed by the *Trinity Journal*. When Crowningshield ridiculed Crawford's obsolescent newspaper, the latter vehemently called him out into the street.

There, without the benefit of seconds and surgeons, before scores of pass-ersby, they fired eleven rounds at each other. One of the shots entered a nearby bakery, nearly striking a patron. Crowningshield emerged from the fight unscathed, while Crawford was carried off with a bullet in his heel. Both were roundly condemned by the town for their poor marksmanship and endangerment of others.

The other duel was fought on October 11 at even more remote Troux's Flat in Siskiyou County. There, John Strong and John Grady, with six shooters in hand and backs to one another, just four paces apart, waited for the call. But before the word, Strong turned, fired, and sent a bullet into Grady's arm. Grady survived the wound, while Strong barely managed to survive the wrath of the crowd that had assembled.

38

The Doctors' Duel

Among the various professions, the medical calling played a particularly important role on California's field of honor, many duels counting at least one doctor in attendance. But as events eventually proved, not all doctors were content to remain on the sidelines. In February 1857 two fire-eating physicians, Doctors Samuel Langdon and Washington Ryer, squared off against each other outside of Stockton.

Samuel Langdon was a native of Wilmington, North Carolina, who after taking a medical degree at Bellevue College, New York, left to seek his fortune in California. Following an initial try at mining, he moved to Stockton where he came across two fellow Southerners, Porter Ash and David Terry. The three soon became the best of friends.

That fall Langdon was elected constable of Stockton, Ash won his race for sheriff, while Terry lost his campaign for mayor. Some writers have attributed Terry's defeat to a supposed North-South animosity in Stockton, claiming that because New Yorkers outnumbered Southerners, his loss was a foregone conclusion. Forgotten are the victories of Langdon and Ash. Their success indicates beyond doubt that the voters were simply looking for the best qualified, or at the very least, most personable candidates. After Langdon assumed the job of constable, he continued to practice medicine. Because he insisted on treating the poor without charge, he became a very popular figure indeed.

His opponent in the duel, Washington Ryer, was a native of New York State who, after the Mexican War broke out, joined the U.S. Army and went off to serve as a surgeon. After the war he returned home. But like Langdon, upon learning of the Gold Rush, he left to "see the elephant" for himself. And like Langdon, no sooner did he arrive in Stockton than he announced that he would give medical attention to any indigent in need, without charge. One of his most noted patients was an Indian chief named José Jesus, who had been shot by a drunken miner. Dr. Ryer saved his life and in appreciation of his effort, Charles Weber, Stockton's founder, presented him with $400.

Shortly after settling in Stockton Ryer formed a close friendship with Dr. Reid, president of the state's newly formed Society of Natural History. When the Stockton Insane Asylum was established in 1853 Reid was appointed its director and for several years all went well. Then in 1856 newly elected governor, Neeley Johnson, decided to replace Reid with Samuel Langdon. Like David Terry and thousands of others, Langdon had been lured into the Know-Nothing Party by its pledge to clean up corruption in politics.

The removal of Dr. Reid was denounced by many, including the influential *San Joaquin Republican* newspaper. Emboldened by his groundswell of support, he refused to vacate his office, claiming that Governor Johnson could not remove him without legislative authority. On May 18, 1856, District Judge Charles Creanor decided in his favor. The governor then took his case to the State Supreme Court, upon which sat two recently converted Know-Nothings, David Terry and Hugh Murray. They reversed the lower court decision by ruling in favor of Langdon.

After Langdon assumed the asylum directorship he produced a report charging Reid with numerous abuses of office. In response the legislature sent a committee to Stockton to investigate. At the hearing, when Dr. Ryer sharply questioned Langdon's motives for publishing his report, Langdon jumped to his feet, pointed his finger at Ryer, and accused him of unfairly slanting his testimony.

The next day the two encountered each other outside the courthouse, and severely battered one another with their canes. The day after Ryer, still smarting from the blows he had suffered, sent attorney Samuel Booker into Langdon's office with a challenge. Langdon accepted, declared dueling pistols at ten paces and named Thomas O'Neil as his second.

Learning that another Stockton physician, William Aylette, owned a pair of dueling pistols, Langdon asked O'Neil to see about borrowing them. Upon query Aylette assented. His pistols were sinister looking instruments with eight-inch barrels and hair triggers. Manufactured by the La Foucheux Firearms Company of Paris, France, they had been brought by the Jo Beard family to New Orleans, where they had figured in a number of duels. When Jo Beard, himself a Creole, left for California in 1850, he took the pistols with him. Several years afterward, while serving as clerk of the State Assembly, he sold them to Dr. Aylette.

In examining the pistols, Langdon and O'Neil discovered that the trigger of one of them was much more sensitive than the other—so sensitive a touch of the finger was not necessary to prompt a discharge. A sudden jerk of the hand sufficed. The two immediately chose the only pistol with an operational trigger.

The next day, upon receiving his weapon, Ryer was astonished to learn that he could not control its fire. Booker immediately sought out O'Neil and demanded a full day's practice for his principal. O'Neil agreed, but in spite of their practice, Ryer and Booker found they still could not control the weapon's trigger.

In the face of these murderous odds, on the morning of February 12, Ryer, Booker, and their followers settled into a boat and rowed across a slough to the dueling site, Mormon Island. Langdon and his party, trailed by a crowd of spectators, followed in their vessel. Shortly after, on the ground as Langdon and Ryer prepared to duel a canoe carrying three stragglers pulled ashore. One of the stragglers, who had been rowing with a shovel, hoisted his implement aloft and shouted, "Make haste now and shoot, we came to bury you."

The assembled crowd burst into such laughter that all trace of dignity was swept from the dueling ground. Ryer and Langdon had no choice but to return to Stockton. The next morning William Biven, editor of the *Stockton Daily Argus*, ran the following header: "Agricultural Instrument used to Break Up Duel."

A second attempt to fight took place near the San Joaquin-Contra Costa County Line. But Langdon's physician, Dr. Aylette, failed to show. While the parties were waiting for Aylette, San Joaquin County Sheriff George Webster galloped out of the fog, reigned in his plug, and shouted, "Hold your fire! Stockton is short of doctors as it is!"

For a second time the parties returned to town.

On February 22 Langdon, Ryer, Booker, O'Neil, their physicians (Aylette was replaced), and just six others sallied forth into the San Joaquin River Delta by steam boat. Disembarking at Rough and Ready Ranch, again shrouded in a thick fog, they once more prepared to shoot it out. In many respects, the strange pistols aside, the Ryer-Langdon duel was most peculiar. Among its provisos: prior to each shot Ryer and Langdon were to walk off ten paces in opposite directions, and turn with their pistols pointed toward the ground. A white handkerchief would then be dropped to signal the exchange of fire.

Samuel Booker won the coin toss to make the call, and drop the hanky. As his voice rang out, "One, two, three, four, five . . ." Ryer and Langdon marched off in opposite directions. At "Ten" they turned and Booker dropped his hanky. Both raised their pistols, but Langdon alone pulled his trigger. His ball whizzed past Ryer's ear as Ryer's pistol discharged into the ground without his having touched the trigger.

On the second hanky drop Ryer's pistol again fired prematurely, while Langdon's ball again blew by his ear. On the third drop the results were the same.

On the fourth hanky drop Ryer raised his weapon very slowly, but it again went off without his touching the trigger. He had nonetheless drawn an excellent line shot. His ball struck Langdon in the knee, knocking him to the ground and forcing him to discharge his pistol into the air. Still an adherent to the Hippocratic Oath, Ryer was the first physician to reach his side. The damage however was done, and Langdon would walk with a limp the rest of his life.

After recovering from the immediate effects of his injury, Langdon resumed his duties at the insane asylum. Despite the fact that all charges against Dr. Reid were dropped, and despite his unchivalrous conduct in foisting the malfunctioning pistol on Ryer, Langdon's generosity continued to win him many friends. His death in 1880 brought out the largest funeral procession in Stockton to that date.

Dr. Ryer continued practicing medicine in Stockton until 1863, when he moved to San Francisco and began speculating in land. When he died in 1882 he was a millionaire. But much sooner than the deaths of either Ryer or Langdon, Dr. Aylette's brace of pistols would become the center piece for the most famous duel in California history, and the third most famous in U.S. history.

39

When Chivalry Was in Bloom

The Ryer-Langdon duel, despite its outrageous weapons, did have its lighter points: the shovel-wielding straggler announcing his eagerness to bury the duelists, Sheriff Webster protesting the shortage of doctors in Stockton, and the effeminate hanky-dropping exercise. The same cannot be said for the Blair-Casey affair of September, 1857, also fought near Stockton, which ranks as one of the most desperate on record.

Very little is known about either Charles Blair or Colonel Edward Casey, or the women they fought over. Blair was a Virginian who owned a ranch in recently formed Merced County, while Casey was a Tennessean and a Mexican War veteran who owned a ranch in Stanislaus County. The cause of the duel was a young woman known only as Miss L., a flaxen-haired beauty "of prepossessing personal appearance and accomplishments," who resided on her father's ranch on the Stanislaus River. In those times the newspapers were reluctant to print the names of women unless they were married to a noted figure, or had established themselves independently as an actress, singer, or madam.

One can imagine Blair and Casey passing away alternate Sunday afternoons under the valley oaks bordering the Stanislaus River with Miss. L. With bamboo fishing poles in hand, behind them on a checkered table cloth, an empty peach pie pan may have been glinting in the dappled sunlight. Adjacent might have stood a jar of pickles, a wicker basket of hard-boiled eggs, a pitcher of punch, some cups, and a short stack of plates. Nearby perhaps a William Ainsworth novel lay open, face down in the tawny grass.

Sometime in early September, Miss L. decided that she loved Colonel Casey more than Mr. Blair. Though both Blair and Casey had knowingly been competing for her hand, until then their conduct toward one another had been gentlemanly. On learning of Miss L's preference for himself, Casey could not help but pay Blair a visit at his ranch. As the two leaned against a rail fence in the late summer light, Blair seems to have accepted the sorry news with calm skepticism. Late that day he called upon Miss L. to confirm Casey's account.

The following Monday Blair sought Casey out in the barroom of the Weber Hotel in Stockton. A courteous conversation followed. But as the minutes passed Blair, increasingly angered over Casey's cold indifference to his hurt feelings, harshly criticized his mode of courtship. In turn, the colonel rose from his stool and dealt Blair a blow across the face that sent him reeling backward. He then drew his revolver. Though disarmed by bystanders, he stormed after the still back peddling Blair, and dealt him a second blow to the face.

Strangely enough Casey's thrashing of Blair did not produce the satisfaction it should have. The next day he sent a challenge. Blair accepted and chose six shooters at ten paces. On the morning of September 15, 1857, the duelists, accompanied by their seconds and surgeons (names unknown), left for the San Joaquin County Race Track, three miles outside of town on the Waterloo Road.

There, as the sun appeared over the horizon, on the first call to fire the duelists leveled their revolvers at each other and fired. Both missed. A few minutes later, on the second call Blair inflicted a flesh wound on Casey's thigh, while the latter's bullet flew high. On the third call, as Blair fired and missed, a cap exploded inside of Casey's revolver, preventing his cylinder from further rotation.

Shooting was discontinued for ten minutes while the seconds cleaned the chambers of both Casey and Blair's weapons, then reloaded them. Passions during the interval, rather than cooling as might have been expected, had only grown more heated. At Casey's insistence, with the next "Fire!," both would discharge all six rounds at each other as rapidly as they chose.

Moments later the race track was ripped by a barrage of shots as Blair and Casey furiously unloaded their revolvers. Thirty seconds later, under two ashen clouds of smoke, before their confounded seconds and surgeons, Blair and Casey were still on their feet, at their positions. Blair then turned and informed his doctor that he had not been hit.

But thirty feet away Casey suddenly turned pale. His surgeon hurried over, unbuttoned his coat and pants, and found that he had been struck three more times, two bullets striking the same thigh that had been nicked in the earlier exchange. To the doctor's horror he then found the third bullet had entered Casey's right side, passed through his stomach, and then exited his left margin. Yet incredibly he remained on his feet, trousers loose, six shooter in hand, his attention still riveted on Blair. Puzzled by the surgeon's furor and Casey's gaze, Blair's second approached and asked, "Is Mr. Casey satisfied?"

"No! Load the pistols again!" cried Casey.

His second hurriedly countermanded the order. Only then did Casey tumble into his arms, and those of his surgeon. He was driven back to Stockton and carried to the Magnolia House where the doctors, knowing his wound was fatal, labored through the afternoon and evening to make him comfortable as possible.

As Miss L. had already made her preference for Casey known, it is quite likely she visited him. There, in the stylized fashion of the times, an emotional, fractured conversation, mingled with tears, likely followed, dwelling on the many pleasant days gone by and the colonel's unbounded courage. He died at five o'clock the next evening.

Of Miss. L. and Mr. Blair afterward, nothing is known.

Three more duels were fought in 1857. In one of the better known affairs, occurring in the same month as the Blair-Casey duel, Captain Frank Shafer took the field against James T. Wethered, who had fought the duel with Clinton Winters five years before.

The two men, Shafer, a Southerner, and Wethered, a New Yorker, were drinking at the Union Hotel at the corner of Merchant and Kearny Streets in San Francisco when they got into quite a row. In the midst of the argument, Shafer knocked Wethered to the floor. A challenge was quickly tendered and accepted, Shafer choosing shotguns with slugs at just fifteen paces with the duelists' backs to one another. For a second he chose John Spence, while Wethered chose George Stoneman—the same George Stoneman who later became governor of California.

Word of the impending duel rapidly spread across the town of 40,000 people. Late that afternoon, Ned McGowan, who had returned to San Francisco only recently, was representing a client in court. On learning that a duel was imminent, he asked the presiding judge for an early recess. The judge obliged and McGowan promptly left for the dueling site.

He arrived in time to hear the first count and see Wethered and Shafer wheel and fire their shotguns. Both missed. Shafer, who could hit a bird on the wing nine times out of ten, was so disgusted he threw his weapon to the ground and accused his second, Spence, of not properly loading it.

By then dark had almost fallen, and as the two prepared for a second round the crowd began urging the chivalrous Ned to end the duel. He agreed, moved forward, and in conferring with Stoneman enlisted his aid. Shouting at the top of his lungs, McGowan then demanded that Shafer and Wethered end their affair with a bow and a handshake.

Both obliged.

Earlier that year on May 30, Gallagher and Clark squared off in Benicia with double-barreled shotguns at thirty paces. Clark fired into the air while Gallagher missed. The following day at Iowa Hill an Irishman named Sheridan fought a duel with an Englishman named Ogilby with Colt revolvers. Neither was hit.

Stewart Menzies thought that because he was a Scotsman and a foreigner, he was exempt from accepting challenges. San Francisco Tax Collector William A. Matthews quickly informed him that he was mistaken.

A state senator, Nicaragua's ambassador to the United Sates, filibusterer, and consummate swindler, Parker H. French "crawfished" during his face-off with the "Big Eagle of Monterey County, "Louis Belcher."

A leader of the California Democratic Party who led three filibustering expeditions into Central America, William Walker also fought two duels.

Despite a bad temper, State Supreme Justice Hugh Murray
never engaged in a duel. Murray however approved of dueling,
and was a witness to several.

In 1850 Assemblyman George "Penn" Johnston pushed a bill through the state legislature providing strong penalties for anyone convicted of dueling. Eight years later Johnston took the field of honor, thereby breaking the very law he had authored.

All his life State Supreme Court Justice David Terry was unpracticed with
firearms. Yet through a phenomenal bit of luck and skullduggery, in 1859
he was able to gun down U.S. Senator David C. Broderick.

U.S. Senator David C. Broderick was steeped in the code of honor and was one of the state's best marksmen. Yet he was mysteriously killed in an 1859 duel he should have easily survived.

40

Duel at Angel Island

A number of writers have willfully subjected several California duels to misunderstanding. One of the worst cases of this manipulation of history is the Ferguson-Johnston duel of 1858, tossed off by one eminent historian as a fight between North and South over the issue of slavery. Though 158 years have passed, misunderstanding continues to obscure the duel between State Senator William H. Ferguson and Assemblyman George Pendleton Johnston.

Sectionalism and the feud over slavery indeed played a role in sparking the affair of honor, but in a peculiar back-door way only. The major cause lay in a personal misunderstanding between two very popular politicians.

Ferguson was a native of Pennsylvania whose family moved to Springfield, Illinois, while he was still a boy. There at the age of twelve he decided to become a lawyer. Young Ferguson read Greek and Latin fluently, and in the tradition of the orators of his day, often took to the woods to practice his "speechifying" on the trees. So booming a voice did he develop that in 1842, when Ferguson was 16, Springfield's town council chose him to give the Fourth of July oration. One source claims that he was picked over none other than Abraham Lincoln.

Two years later Ferguson graduated law school and after serving as Springfield's youngest city attorney ever, departed for Dallas, Texas, where he opened a law practice. By then he had mastered where then known as the "Four Ws"—wine, women, whiskey, and war. By war, Ferguson meant a good round of skull cracking fisticuffs. Strangely he never became practiced with firearms. Yet when one remembers that another famous duelist, David Terry, had little practice with guns, this characteristic is less surprising.

In 1853, prodded by cronies who had already been "to see the elephant," Ferguson left Dallas for California where he found his friends had not been exaggerating—the state's demand for lawyers far outstripped its demand for miners. Within a short time his back slapping manner and devastating wit made him one of its most popular attorneys, earning him such sobriquets as "Dipseedoodle" and "Uncle Ferggie."

In 1855 he won a seat in the State Senate, representing Sacramento County. There, in the company of the renowned lawyer, Edward Baker, and fellow state senator James W. Coffroth, he emerged as one of the three best orators in the state. In politics Ferguson generally sided with Broderick, not out of any special fondness for him, but simply because he so disliked Gwin.

A good bit is also known about George "Penn" Johnston. He was born in Breckenridge County, Kentucky, the son of a circuit-riding clergyman. While still in his teens he took a law degree and left for Mississippi, where he set up his own practice. Tall, lithe, with a remarkable gift for sizing others up, at the startling age of 21 he was elected sheriff of Issaquena County. It was about then he became a fast friend of William Gwin who was still serving as a U.S. marshal.

In 1850 Johnston received a letter from Gwin, just elected to the U.S. Senate from California, offering him the position of deputy U.S. marshal for Northern California. Therein lies the reason why Gwin, despite his legislative accomplishments in Washington, made such a host of enemies in his adopted state: there were thousands of fellow migrants already residing in California who were lusting for such a position. Johnston quickly accepted. A few weeks after arriving in San Francisco, he was also appointed to fill a vacant seat in the State Assembly.

Johnston served both as deputy U.S. marshal and as an assemblyman until 1853, when he landed a job in the U.S. Customs House. In 1857, once again with Gwin's aid, he was appointed U.S. judicial commissioner for California. It was while serving as commissioner that he became embroiled in the celebrated Archy Lee case.

In the spring of 1858 a slave named Archy deserted his Mississippi master, James Stovall, who was vacationing in California for health reasons. Taking asylum with several sympathetic attorneys, Lee claimed that because California was a free state he could no longer be held in bondage. His case went all the way to the State Supreme Court, where, in defiance of federal law, Peter Burnett ordered Lee returned to Stovall; David Terry wrote a concurring opinion.

Lee's attorneys next sought relief from U.S. Judicial Commissioner Johnston. Despite being a supporter of slavery in the South, he found Stovall's arguments legally unsound and in April 1858 ordered Lee's release. Johnston's decision so infuriated the anti-Abolition crowd that he was roundly insulted in public. Twice in the following two months he was challenged to a duel. But Johnston, who had fathered the state's anti-dueling statute in 1850, brushed the challenges aside. Between San Francisco and

Sacramento the word soon passed that he was yellow. Thus, in its own peculiar back-door way, the fight over slavery did play a role in promoting the duel between Ferguson and Johnston.

Ferguson was well aware of Johnston's decision in the Archy Lee case, and strongly backed it. He was also aware of the immense heat he had taken since his decision. One August evening the two were drinking with several other legislators at the Mercantile Exchange Saloon in San Francisco (corner of Montgomery and Washington). The Atlantic cable, connecting the United States with England, had just been laid and was then a common topic of conversation. In a lighter moment Senator Westmoreland remarked that the first message over the wire would likely be President Buchanan, announcing to Queen Victoria that "Mrs. Gwin, Lucy and the rest of the Gwin baggage had set sail for Albion's chalky cliffs."

Johnston, who owed more to Gwin than any other figure in the state, took offense and told Westmoreland that ridiculing a woman as remarkable as Mrs. Gwin inside a barroom was disgusting. Ferguson roared with laughter, repeated Westmoreland's joke in another variation, then told Johnston that he should be the last to complain about a woman's name being brought up in barroom banter.

Johnston nodded in agreement and proposed a drink to let the matter pass. But as the three reached for the next round, still smarting from what he regarded as one more, in a long chain of personal insults, Johnston turned to Ferguson and said:

> Before I drink with you, I have something else to say. You agreed with me that I was to use my influence in our convention [Chivalry Democrat] to prevent the nomination of a Congressman, and I did do this. You then pledged me that if the subject were proposed at your convention [Broderick Democrat] you would get up and do the same. *This* you did not do, notwithstanding your promise.

Ferguson replied that he had never made such a promise. Johnston called him a liar and Ferguson retaliated by punching him in the face. Enraged, Johnston drew his pistol but was disarmed by Westmoreland and others.

The following day, still seething from a public humiliation certain to dye him a deeper shade of yellow, Johnston sent a challenge. As unfamiliar with firearms as Ferguson may have been, his pride and stubbornness would not let him decline. He chose former superintendent of the state prison James Estill as his second; his auxiliary was Eugene L. Sullivan. Weapons were dueling pistols loaded and primed by Natchez Taylor—distance, ten paces.

Ferguson's primary second, Estill is an amusing story all by himself. Renowned for his mismanagement of the state prison at San Quenton, he was capable, on occasion, of being three-faced. Earlier in the decade, following his election to the State Senate from Napa County, he placed a copy of a speech he had prepared in a Whig newspaper, placed a second variation of the same speech in a Democratic newspaper, and the following day gave a markedly different variation of the same before the State Senate. Regarding the anger his triplicity had aroused in both parties and the legislature, the glib Kentuckian declared, "Oh thunder, I can lick 'em all!"

Normally jovial and easy-going, Estill also at one time, in an inordinate fit of anger, went after John Bigler with a shotgun. None other than State Senator James W. Denver encountered him just outside the state house, where he convinced him that it was not in his interest to empty the contents of his weapon into the governor.

If one needed a crash course in firearm use, Estill was as good a coach as any. He spent the next several days familiarizing Ferguson with dueling pistols.

Johnston meanwhile chose as his second newspaper editor Benjamin Franklin Washington. Recall that four years before, Washington had wounded *Alta California* editor Charles Washburne in a duel at San Bruno. His auxiliary was William B. Dameron, the date of the duel 5 p.m., August 21—the site, a flat on the northeast side of Angel Island, San Francisco Bay, behind a building owned by steamship captain, Frederick Waterman. Five shots were to be exchanged, each following the call.

That afternoon Johnston and his followers departed for Angel Island by sailboat; shortly after Ferguson and his party left by steamer. The parties met adjacent Waterman's house where a coin was tossed to determine position and whose second would call fire. Washington won the toss. Moments later as they presented their sides, pistols pointed toward the ground, Washington called out "Gentleman, are you ready?"

"Ready!" shouted both.

"Fire—one, two three, stop!"

At the word both raised their pistols and fired. Neither shot took effect. The distance between the duelists was then reduced to twenty feet, as previously agreed to. On the second fire both Johnston and Ferguson again missed; Estill and Washington reloaded the pistols while the duelists girded themselves for yet another shot. At the word Ferguson again missed. Two seconds later, Johnston, taking deliberate aim, also fired—and much to his dismay missed.

With but one more shot to fire, Estill and Washington proposed to immediately end the duel. But Johnston continued to insist that Ferguson apologize for striking him. Ferguson would not hear of it and the two prepared for the last shot.

At the word Ferguson fired first, his ball striking Johnston's left hand at the base of the thumb, spattering his clothing with blood. Johnston jerked his injured hand back, recovered his composure and took careful aim. As he did, Ferguson braced himself and announced, "I'm a gone community!" Seconds later Johnston's shot tore into his thigh, spinning him around into Estill's arms.

As Ferguson was lowered to the ground, Johnston approached and asked permission to shake his hand. Looking up, the senator replied, "I am in the hands of my seconds."

Estill nodded affirmatively, Johnston bent over and clasping Ferguson's hand said, "Uncle Ferggie, I'm sorry for you."

"That's' all right," the downed man whispered.

"That's enough said between gentlemen," replied Johnston, turning to leave.

At first Ferguson's doctors thought his wound was not serious, but they soon discovered that he had a compound fracture of the thigh bone. They recommended amputation, to which Ferguson replied, "I will not part with my leg for the whole of California."

He was carried back to San Francisco, protesting all the way that he had made no political promise to Johnston, but that Johnston had honestly believed he had. Meanwhile gangrene set in and over the next four weeks his health went into slow decline. On September 14, while doctors were frantically trying to amputate his leg, he died at the age of 33. Among his last wishes was that his shooter not be persecuted for his death.

The day he died a committee of notables was chosen to escort his body to Sacramento for burial. At his funeral, held on September 16, Colonel Edward Baker, within whose law office Ferguson once studied in Illinois, read the eulogy. He was buried on the grounds of the Sacramento City Cemetery.

Johnston meanwhile departed San Francisco on the revenue cutter *William L. Marcy*. Aboard he learned, with a great deal of irony, that the state was going to prosecute him under the very anti-dueling statute he had authored in 1850. He immediately returned to town and employed A.A. Crittenden as counsel. Crittenden and Johnston were able to fend off the only rigorous prosecution of a duelist to that date, managing to persuade the jury that Ferguson would not have died if he had earlier consented to have his leg amputated.

For a long time afterward Johnston was cold-shouldered by all but a few close friends. His ostracization was in part caused by an editorial in the *Sacramento Bee* charging that he was the trigger man in a plan hatched by Chivalry Democrats to seize a "scarlet letter," implicating Gwin in the deal he had made the previous year with Broderick to secure the election of both to the U.S. Senate. The editorial claimed that while Ferguson and Johnston were dueling at Angel Island, Ferguson's office had been ransacked.

There is no truth to the story. A scarlet letter implicating Gwin and Broderick in the senatorial bargain indeed existed, but it was in Broderick's file, not Ferguson's.

A decade later Johnston recalled that he passed the remainder of 1858 and most of '59 alone inside one of San Francisco's first Italian restaurants, reading magazines to pass the time because no one would speak to him. He spent the Civil War years in Central America. After the war he returned to San Francisco and took a position with the *San Francisco Examiner*, just established by his old friend, Benjamin Franklin Washington. He quickly regained his former popularity and went on to become one of the city's most successful journalists, editing the *Examiner* until a year before his death, March, 4, 1884.

41

Honorable Mention: 1858

Another duel of note fought in 1858 was that between Duncan H. Houser, justice of the Yuba County Court of Sessions, and Albert D. Turner, a businessman residing in Butte County. In June of that year the two went to court in a dispute over a business transaction and a verdict was rendered in Houser's favor.

Following the trial, on the street outside the Yuba County Courthouse, Turner approached Houser and pitched into him with some rough language. Despite the dressing down, Houser quietly turned and strode away. Thus everyone was surprised to later learn that he had passed Turner a challenge. He accepted, opted for shotguns, a slug in each barrel at fifty paces. Five shots were to be exchanged, each commencing with the call.

The duel was to have taken place across the border in Sutter County on June 5. But the sheriff of Sutter, learning the duel was imminent, was on the ground when Houser and Turner arrived, and put an end to the proceedings. On June 11 the two met at six in the morning, a quarter mile from downtown Marysville adjacent the hospital. Only twenty-five spectators were on hand, but so determined were all to see the fight "come off" they chased off two Marysville policemen.

On the first four shots Houser and Turner both missed. The poor shooting so rankled both of them that for the fifth fire they agreed to shorten the distance to forty paces. Both meticulously prepared for the last fire, and at the word Turner pulled his trigger first. His blast sent a slug into Houser's left arm above the elbow, shattering it. Houser glanced at his shattered limb, tossed his shotgun away and left the ground, while Turner rushed after him shouting, "Mr. Houser, I'm glad it is no worse. You are a brave man, and that I am willing to say for you."

California's third sword duel and first seaside affair of honor also took place in 1858. For some time the editors of two French newspapers, R.M. Thiele of the *San Francisco Spectator*, and A.H. Rapp of the *San Francisco Pharo* had been waging a violent editorial war. Rapp had brought several suits for libel, but all had been dismissed. That September, following yet another abusive editorial in the *Spectator*, he challenged Thiele to a duel with pistols at ten paces.

Thiele declined those conditions because of his shortsightedness, and suggested pistols at arm's length. Rapp's seconds refused to allow him to participate in "this bit of butchery." Eventually the two agreed to meet with swords. Accordingly, on January 25, Thiele and Rapp, their seconds and surgeons, and a sizable band of spectators left for the chosen site, a bluff in San Mateo County overlooking the Pacific Ocean.

On the ground Rapp discovered to his dismay that Thiele was left-handed. Nonetheless, realizing that he could not walk away without losing face, he threw aside his earlier notions of attack and sailed into Thiele with no particular line of attack. In the spectacular clash that followed he severely gashed Thiele just above the knee, while himself suffering a flesh wound to the stomach. Following the exchange of injuries the two editors pronounced themselves satisfied and the duel ended.

A month later a duel almost came off in far Northern California. The affair was sparked by former Siskiyou County Sheriff David Colton, who published a column in the *Yreka Union* highly critical of Dr. T.T. Cabiness's management of the Siskiyou County Hospital. Cabiness in turn published a card in the *Yreka Chronicle* ridiculing the charges. Colton sent a challenge that was accepted.

The doctor chose Mississippi Yagers at forty paces—the site, just across the Oregon border. On February 7, 1858, inside Oregon Territory (it became a state in 1859) Colton and Cabiness, in the company of their seconds and a large crowd of Siskiyou Golden Staters, dismounted. Just as the preliminaries got underway, Captain Goodall, acting for Colton, and William D. Fair for Cabiness, made one last attempt at conciliation. It was a success. Thus by minutes only did Oregon escape carnage on California's field of honor.

Eighteen fifty eight also saw the passing of A.J. "Natchez" Taylor, a San Francisco luminary, and the most popular gun shop owner in town. A native of Natchez, Mississippi, he had come west with the first gold seekers. Early on, however, he found that selling weapons and ammunition was much more profitable than mining. Upon returning to San Francisco, he set up a gun shop and shooting gallery on Clay Street, opposite the Plaza, and was soon not only selling guns, but loading them for the city's many gentlemen of honor. No gun primed by Natchez ever hung fire. Among those dependent on his services were Hamilton Bowie, David Broderick, William Ferguson, George Penn Johnston, Ned McGowan, John Nugent, William Walker, and many more.

Despite his fixation with death-dealing instruments, Natchez was a mild-mannered gentleman who never dueled in California. In fact, he was so affected by William Ferguson's death he swore afterward that he would never load another weapon for another duelist. He was also scrupulously honest. In 1855, on the heels of the Adams and Company bank robbery, transient miners began stashing their gold dust and coin in his safe. Natchez's shooting gallery was the *one* place in San Francisco they knew their valuables were secure.

On the afternoon of September 25, barely a week after Ferguson had died, John Traverse entered Natchez's gun shop and asked to examine one of the derringers in the display case. Gun safety not then being the issue it is today, the derringer, like all the other weapons in his shop, was loaded. Natchez bent over, reached for the weapon and handed it to Traverse.

While he turned his attention to a second patron, Traverse, in fondling the derringer, accidentally grazed its trigger. The gun went off with a deafening pop that sent a ball through Natchez's mouth into the back of his head, killing him instantly. His funeral, held two days later, was attended by hundreds.

42

Another Exciting Year: 1859

Eighteen fifty-nine is most properly remembered for the Broderick-Terry duel. Yet prior to, and after that affair, several clashes involving some of the most prominent figures in the state took place. One of the most infamous was that between Assemblyman Charles Fairfax and Supreme Court Recorder Harvey Lee. Fairfax, you will recall, had served as a second in the Rust-Stidger and Hubert-Hunt duels. Four years before, the genial Virginian, known to intimates as Lord Fairfax, had married Ada Benham, the sister of Calhoun Benham. The couple acquired a large piece of property in the North Bay they named Bird Nest Glen, later renamed Fairfax. At the time of the incident it would not be an exaggeration to claim that Charles Fairfax was the best-liked figure in California.

But the pace of life then was so intense that even such mild-mannered public servants as the Assembly speaker sometimes lost their tempers. By contrast, the target of his wrath, Harvey Lee, was a churlish individual whose work for the Supreme Court was so sloppy that he was the despair of all three justices, as well as much of the state legislature.

On the afternoon of March 25, Fairfax encountered Lee in front of the old St. George Hotel in Sacramento and upbraided him for his failure to again deliver a copy of the court's proceedings to the Assembly. The court reporter cut loose with a string of oaths and Fairfax slapped him. Whereupon Lee drew a sword cane from its sheath, and ran it through the assemblyman's chest.

Still on his feet, Fairfax drew his derringer and pointed it at Lee who cried, "Don't kill me, I'm unarmed!"

Fairfax held fire and shouted, "You miserable coward, you have murdered me—you have assassinated me! I have your worthless life in my hands, but for the sake of your wife and children I will spare you!" Several bystanders urged Fairfax to shoot Lee, but he put his derringer away, and allowed the court reporter to scurry off. Fairfax survived his badly punctured lung, but the resulting respiratory problems made him a semi-invalid for the rest of his life.

Another brawl, this one nearly resulting in a duel, was that between Congressman Joseph C. McKibbin and State Senator James W. Coffroth. McKibbin was a native of Pennsylvania who had served as an assemblyman from Sierra County before being elected to Congress. He had been William Speare's second in his affair with John Kelly. Until recently McKibbin had been a Chivalry Democrat. With David Terry and John McDougal among others, he had been in the phalanx of those who had burst through the side door of the Sacramento Baptist Church, stormed past the front pews, and placed a lectern adjacent the one erected by Broderick and McGowan. The events that followed that memorable event have already been told.

More recently, as a congressman, McKibbin had returned to his home state after learning that his deaf and dumb sister had been seduced by one Isaac Cray. There, at Pittsburgh's Allegheny Railroad Station, in one of the most spectacular gun battles in Pennsylvania history, McKibbin and his brother gunned Cray down. His offence, while not nearly as reprehensible as that of his predecessor Philemon T. Herbert—he who shot the waiter—did little to enhance California's reputation in the East.

Coffroth's political career was almost as checkered as McKibbin's. Yet another Pennsylvanian, for most of the decade he had served as a state senator from Tuolumne County, and with Edward Baker and William Ferguson had emerged as one of the top three orators in the state. Thousands turned out every year at Fourth of July festivities in Sonora to hear him speechify.

In 1854 a Sonora mob seized Jack Barclay, who had shot a personal friend of Coffroth's. The state senator turned himself into a vigilante prosecutor and played a leading role in Barclay's lynching. On yet another occasion Coffroth's eloquence fended off a mob, this time preserving the life of one Peter Nicholas, who had the good fortune to have shot someone Coffroth held no special affection for.

But unlike McKibbin who had aligned himself with Broderick in 1858, only after a bitter falling out with Gwin, Coffroth had been a Broderick Democrat ever since 1852. He was able to buck the anti-Broderick tide in Tuolumne County, only because of his eloquence and glad-handing manner.

In June 1859 as the Democrats gathered in Sacramento for their convention, they quite naturally coalesced into two wings, the Chivalry Democrats, and the Broderick Democrats—now more properly known as the Anti-Lecompton Democrats. Yet even within factions there were factions. While McKibbin's star was on the rise, Coffroth's was on the wane. Angered at McKibbin's growing stature within the Lecompton faction, angry because Broderick no longer consulted him on matters of significance, inside the

Barnum Restaurant, he shouted into McKibbin's face, "No one has a show in here unless he wears a collar marked B!"

When McKibbin warned that he would not permit such insulting language in his presence, Coffroth repeated the charge. McKibbin punched him in the face and in the brawl that followed gave Coffroth quite a pounding. Early the next morning, through his second Richard Irwin, Coffroth sent a challenge. McKibbin accepted and chose William Addison as his second. The duel was to be fought on June 23 at the Nye Ranch, twenty-one miles north of Sacramento. But on the night of the June 22 McKibbin was arrested and thrown in jail.

Broderick meanwhile sought out Coffroth. As he explained, their differences had all been a misunderstanding. Worse yet, a duel between Coffroth and McKibbin would badly divide his wing of the party, hurting his chances in the upcoming campaign against William Gwin. Coffroth listened, decided the Chief had a point, and asked Irwin to work out an adjustment. The next morning, after posting bond, McKibbin learned that Addison and Irwin had cobbled together an agreement that he too deemed satisfactory.

On November 21, 1859, a duel most bizarre in its origins was fought just below the mining town of Shasta. The affair was between two Trinity County officials, Judge R T. Miller, and District Attorney James Gallagher. The duel was sparked when Miller, in the midst of a disagreement with a Mr. Watson, made some disparaging remarks about him. In response Watson sent him a challenge through his chosen second, Gallagher. But the judge declined to accept on the grounds that Watson was "not a gentleman." Gallagher then asked the judge if he considered himself a gentleman. Miller readily agreed that he was, and the district attorney challenged him on the spot.

Unlike the Thomas-Dixon duel, in which there is some evidence of prior hostility, there had been no ill feelings between Miller and Gallagher. It was thus perhaps the only duel fought in the state solely over the matter of punctilio.

To avoid interference from the Trinity County sheriff, who had been alerted, the two crossed over into Shasta County astride their horses, trailed by a large throng of followers. On the ground near Shasta the judge and D.A. went so far as to shake hands before taking their positions. There, holding Colt revolvers at fifteen paces, on the first exchange the district attorney sent a bullet through Miller's legs, scraping both shin bones and toppling him to the ground. He then strode over, extended his hand and declared himself "perfectly satisfied." Judge Miller gladly accepted the proffered hand, and insisted he held no grudge against the D.A.

On December 21, in Shasta's second affair of honor within two months, George Godfrey, a powerfully built schoolmaster, and a man known only as

Levy squared off at sunrise with derringers. Both fired two shots without effect.

Suddenly Godfrey, sensing he had been "had," examined his derringer and found that it had been loaded with cork-tipped cartridges. Flinging it to the ground, he rushed at Levy, who took flight. Godfrey overtook him and dealt Levy such a blow that he was knocked unconscious. Still furious, he turned on a nearby public functionary and beat him up too. A half-dozen bystanders then seized the schoolmaster, but striking left and right, he broke free and thrashed them all. Godfrey was later arrested, charged with beating up eight men and fined one dollar. Thus did end California's third hoax on the field of honor.

The state's second hoax on the field of honor took place on September 20 of that year when Colonel J.E. Esterbrook and Major Sylvester Knight took the field in Sonora. The trouble between the two began several days before when Knight's partner at the United States Hotel, a man named Phelps, accused Esterbrook of stealing his boots. Esterbrook was so furious that he challenged him to a duel. But since Phelps was a "man of family," Knight offered to stand in for him. Esterbrook placed no objection.

Knight nonetheless wanted nothing to do with a duel, and working through his second "bought out" Esterbrook's second. The next day near Cannan Hill, just before the preliminary call, Esterbrook's pistol accidentally discharged. As he was insistent on continuing the duel, and no one had brought any more blanks to the field, the two seconds retired to discuss the matter. Finally they decided to risk handing Esterbrook Knight's still "loaded" weapon, and Knight the empty revolver.

Esterbrook took no notice of the change in weapons and at the word fired. Knight immediately fell to the ground, where he lay squeezing a sponge soaked in red ink, earlier inserted into his vest. Esterbrook was so pleased with his work that he cut loose with a thunderous "hurrah!" He left the field in a hurry, however, when the crowd began chanting, "Hang him, hang him, hang him!" Last seen he was racing down the road well ahead of the "mob," bellowing that given a fair chance he would shoot it out with any one of them.

43

Duel of Infamy: Part One

The most written about duel in California history is the Broderick-Terry affair of September 13, 1859. There were other duels that stirred excitement on the East Coast, but the Broderick-Terry face-off stirred up a positive uproar. Despite all that has been written, until recently many facts surrounding the shootout remained shrouded in mystery.

The fight between the two indeed reflected the North-South tensions then building in the state over slavery. By 1858 Broderick, who previously had never given the issue of slavery any real concern, had become a free-soil, Anti-Lecompton Democrat. As a Free-Soiler, he did not oppose slavery where it already existed, he simply opposed its extension into the territories, and the new state of Kansas.

His political machine had been smashed by the 1856 vigilante uprising, but since that time he had regained considerable public support in both the interior of California and the Bay Area. His support in the mining counties came from Democrats who had opposed the Vigilance Committee; his support in the Bay Area derived from the growing number of Free-Soilers who had recently settled there. These two factions, and his extraordinary backroom political skills were the reasons why in January 1857 Broderick was chosen by the state legislature as one of California's two U.S. senators.

In contrast to Broderick, and unlike most Southerners and Northerners who had emigrated west, Terry openly advocated slavery in the territories, *and in California itself.* His position placed him at odds not only with Broderick, but Gwin, who had voted against slavery's extension into the state and felt that in the territories it was a matter for local voters to decide. Here it is important to explain the issue of the Lecompton Constitution, admitting slavery into Kansas. The entire California State Legislature voted to order both Broderick and Gwin to support Lecompton in Washington, D.C. Gwin cast a yes vote, while Broderick cast a no. The latter's vote infuriated the legislators, who in those years expected their U.S. senators to abide by what they felt were their "commands."

In assessing Broderick's past, it should surprise no one that he fought a second duel; but that he wound up facing Terry is somewhat surprising. They had been brothers-in-arms during the days of the Vigilance Committee, and while Broderick had often spoken of Terry's integrity—a quality he himself sorely lacked—Terry in turn had often spoken of Broderick's courage, of which he indeed possessed a surfeit.

The first act in the drama that would culminate on that September morning occurred on June 24, 1859, at the same Democratic Convention that had brought on the near duel between McKibbin and Coffroth. Terry carried away from that convention a deep personal frustration over being turned down as the party's nominee for another term on the State Supreme Court—punishment for his having joined the now-extinct Know-Nothing Party. Filled with anger and with the slavery issue building toward the fall elections, the target of Terry's partly misdirected wrath was Broderick, upon whom he launched a blistering personal attack.

Two mornings later while eating breakfast at the International Hotel in San Francisco, Broderick came across Terry's speech in the *Sacramento Union*. Turning to Terry's law partner from Stockton days, Duncan Perley, seated at the next table, he tossed the newspaper toward him and said "Your friend Terry has been abusing me at Sacramento."

"What is it Mr. Broderick?" said Perley, looking over.

"The miserable wretch, after being kicked out of the convention, went down there and made a speech abusing me. I have defended him at all times when all others deserted him. I paid and supported three newspapers to defend him during the Vigilance Committee days, and this is all the gratitude I get from the damned miserable wretch for the favors I have conferred on him. I have hitherto spoken of him as an honest man—as the only honest man of a miserable, corrupt supreme court—but now I find I was mistaken. I take it all back."

"Who is it you speak of as a wretch?"

"Terry."

"I will inform the Judge of the language you have used concerning him."

"Do so. I wish you to do so. I am responsible for it."

"You would not dare use such language to him."

"Would not dare?" retorted Broderick in mockery.

"No sir, you would not dare to do it, and you shall not use it to me concerning him. I shall hold you personally responsible!"

When Perley demanded an apology, Broderick refused; Perley abruptly left the restaurant and shortly after sent a challenge to the senator's hotel room. Broderick responded by reminding Perley that he was a British subject, and that he was not about to waste his time dueling with, in his words, an *alien*. He then added that with his summer primary against Senator Gwin about to commence, he could not respond to any "call of a personal matter" until September 7, the day after the campaign ended.

Perley may not have had U.S. citizenship, but he was a North American and had resided in California as long as Broderick. Furious at being called an alien, he sought out Terry and told him of Broderick's remarks. History has since overlooked the bond that existed between the two, and the effect the senator's contemptuous treatment of Perley must have had on both. Angered by the comments about himself, and his best friend, Terry decided to challenge him. But mindful of Broderick's statement regarding the summer primary, he decided to mark time.

A few days later both Senators Gwin and Broderick hit the campaign trail through the mining counties, seeking votes for their respective slate of candidates. Despite Broderick's lengthy political career, this was the first time he had ever taken to the public stump. During the canvass for the first time he brandished the long rumored "scarlet letter"—the letter in which Gwin had not only pledged to support his effort to win a U.S. Senate seat, but had promised to turn his patronage rights over to him. In exchange Broderick assured Gwin that he would support him for the other Senate seat. So it was in January 1857, after a series of legislative caucuses, largely directed by Broderick, both were elected to the U.S. Senate.

In brandishing the letter before the public Broderick declared it irreversible proof of Gwin's corruptibility. Strangely, he never considered the immense damage the letter did to himself. So heated did the campaign grow that on one occasion Broderick forgot his statement to Perley and issued a thinly veiled challenge. But Gwin, playing the role of elder statesman, was too wily to be trapped into a duel by either the scarlet letter, or the cloaked challenge.

Apart from personalities, the campaign of 1859 also brought the issue of Free-Soil to the fore. Broderick declared his support for legislation barring slavery from the Western Territories, and the state of Kansas, but denied that he was an Abolitionist. Again Gwin argued that slavery was a question to be decided by the voters within the territories they resided. He also spoke of his vote in support of the Kansas Lecompton Constitution, as requested by the California Legislature.

On September 7 Broderick's slate of delegates went down to a crushing defeat. The defeat was not just a referendum on Free-Soil, it represented a perception among the voters regarding the capabilities of each senator. Gwin's talent for pulling pork out of the Washington pork barrel and carrying it home to California was proven, and would have presented an obstacle to any opponent, let alone Broderick. At the same time he had little trouble alluding to his opponent's misrule of San Francisco prior to 1856. In truth, the vigilantes had run him out of town. That he was able to convene a brokered convention just six months afterward and became a U.S. senator is but a tribute to his back room negotiating skills, so much greater than his skills on the stump.

Just two days after his defeat, the Senator received a menacing letter—not from Gwin as he might have hoped—but from Terry, rehashing his long forgotten remarks of the previous June. In the letter Terry asked Broderick to retract, not any specific words, but the intent of his words; to quote "The precise term however, in which the implication was made is not important to the question. . . . What I require is the retraction of any words which were calculated to reflect upon my character as an officer, or a gentleman."

Broderick answered the letter by stating that Terry himself was the best judge of which words carried the offensive meaning.

The judge replied with the following: "To this last letter you reply acknowledging the use of the offensive language imputed to you, and not making the retraction required. This course on your part leaves me no alternative but to demand the satisfaction usual among gentleman, which I accordingly do. Mr. Benham will make the necessary arrangements."

The above letters make a powerful statement about the now personal nature of Terry's animosity for Broderick. He was challenging a man who, politically speaking was dead, and who despite occupying a U.S. Senate seat, had no policies to pursue, and now no patronage leverage whatever. The challenge was tendered by Calhoun Benham on the evening of September 10 in San Francisco to several Broderick associates. They in turn took it to the Chief who was then staying with Leonidas Haskell at Black Point. On being awakened at 1 a.m. he accepted.

How Terry occupied himself during that long summer between Broderick's exchange with Perley and primary day has long been a mystery. All accepted accounts ignore the fact that he was not remotely the crack shot the senator was. Thus they ignore this very important time frame, suggesting only that Terry obtained the Aylette pistols at about the time he sent the challenge. He is then said to have fired off a few test rounds. In fact, between his face-off with George Belt in 1852, and the summer of 1859, he had not practiced one jot with a firearm of any kind. As at the Democratic Convention of 1854, and his brawl with the vigilantes in 1856, until then he had continued to rely upon his enormous presence, great physical strength and Bowie knife to make his point.

Quite probably the following took place after the June confrontation at the International Hotel. On learning of Broderick's contemptuous treatment of his friend, and denunciation of himself, in a state of fury, the judge decided to challenge him. He then sought out Calhoun Benham, California's leading authority on the code, and asked him what his chances of obtaining the choice of weapons were—despite being the challenging party.

Benham doubtless told him that they were very poor, but that there was always a possibility. Terry then left for Lodi to seek the advice of another friend, State Senator Benjamin Langford. Langford in turn took him to Stockton to see Dr. Aylette, still in possession of the Jo Beard pistols used in the Ryer-Langdon duel of two years before. The trio went outside to practice with the pistols. As Langford later confided, Terry's first attempts to fire the pistol with the *correct* trigger were so bad he could not hit the side of Aylette's barn.

This statement puts to rest the long held belief that the judge was a hit man for Gwin, or a hit man for the pro-slavery party of California. Aside from Gwin, there were twenty thousand duffers in the state better with a gun than Terry.

But that was June. Terry practiced with Aylette's pistols through July and August not only in Stockton, but at the state capital. Assemblyman Charles Knox, who knew both Terry and Broderick, was astonished to see him that summer in Sacramento wearing a brace of pistols. Never before had he known the judge to go about with firearms in his possession. Back in Stockton, Dr. Washington Ryer was surprised to see him target practicing. So were others. By September Senator Langford was able to pronounce Terry's use of the single operational Aylette pistol as *improved.*

As his pistol accuracy progressed Terry continued to consult with Benham and another authority on the code, Samuel Brooks. Just as important was his third second, Thomas Hayes. A personal friend of Broderick's for many years, like many pre-1856 Broderick Democrats, he had gone over to the Chivs after his Chief joined the Free-Soil Democrats. In Hayes, Terry found a second who knew every quirk in his antagonist's nature.

Still he faced the problem of weapons. In the shooting galleries about the state, the Senator could "ring the bell" on 29 out of 30 shots. In order to stand any chance against him, the judge needed to carry the Aylette pistols to the field. Once there, even if his seconds were able to negotiate away his opponent's weapons prerogative with a coin toss, he still stood a 50-50 chance of losing. That he was willing to stake his life on a coin toss all the more underscores his unmitigated hatred for Broderick.

Terry has often been framed as a man of unbridled passion, filled with hatred, and committed to spreading the doctrine of slavery across the world. Yet through most of the 1850s he was regarded as one of the few judges in the state who could not be bought. Moreover, there was a tender side to his life regarding his marriage to Cornelia Runnels, formerly of Galveston, Texas. While he was fond of calling his wife—who incidentally was also his cousin—Neil, she had a passion for calling him Cousin, or "Cuz" for short.

To spare Neil any distress, from June to September Terry did not inform her of his intention to duel until the evening he sent the challenge from his Stockton home. He then went outside to water the garden, during which time Cornelia pleaded with the visiting Samuel Brooks to arrange a settlement. Brooks readily agreed to try, but as the record shows his efforts came to nothing.

Upon receiving the challenge Broderick chose his seconds, chief among them, Joseph C. McKibbin. Since his own election to Congress in 1857, McKibbin had quarreled with Gwin and thrown his lot with Broderick. He was certainly a good man with guns and "up on the code," but he was not steeped in it like Benham.

Nor was Broderick's auxiliary second, David Colton, former sheriff of Siskiyou County, who the year before had come close to exchanging gunfire with Dr. Cabiness across the Oregon Border. Like McKibbin, he knew his guns, but he did not know the code as did Benham. Broderick's other auxiliary, Leonidas Haskell, would prove to be an outright liability on the ground.

In determining why the senator and his seconds conceded the choice of weapons to a toss of a coin, the following is known: after his defeat at the polls, the most crushing defeat he had ever suffered, he went into a deep depression. Friends remarked that overnight he suddenly looked much older than his age, and that he walked about in a stoop. Beyond losing the popular vote, he was hated by the legislature, and so far as patronage was concerned, his leverage was gone. The impending duel therefore must have seemed almost like an incidental matter.

Added to Broderick's depression was his complacency. He knew Terry was a not a good shot, or worse. He had no further to turn than McKibbin, a former associate of the judge to confirm that fact. This very peculiar blend of despair, indifference and overconfidence led the senator and his seconds either to agree, or to suggest the following to Benham: they would concede a coin toss for the choice of weapons—provided of course they remained dueling pistols—in exchange for a short call. Instead of the traditional "Fire—one, two, three—stop!" the count would be "Fire—one, two—stop!"

Broderick would thus be placed in a win-win situation. Should he win the coin toss and his own set of pistols, he would be shooting at a "tied bird"; should he lose, he would still be able to cut down an inexperienced foe, forced to hurry his shot by the short count. He, McKibbin and Colton of course had never heard of the Aylette pistols—or the long summer Terry had spent with them.

James O'Meara in his otherwise fine book, *Broderick and Gwin*, in remarking on the terms of the duel, implies the short count, in clause five of the dueling agreement, and the coin toss for weapons, in clause eight, was normal procedure for the code of honor. Both clauses in fact were highly irregular, and could only have been inserted into the agreement with the expressed consent of both parties.

Five of the six seconds, Benham, Hayes, McKibbin, Colton, and Haskell (Brooks excepted) failed in one respect—hotspurs all, they failed to bring to the negotiating table, and dueling ground that sense of justice and respect for the other party. Many outside the two immediate circles felt the duel could have been avoided. When Edmund Randolph, for one, approached Colonel Anthony J. Butler, a Broderick confident with a proposed adjustment, Butler told him, "We intend to fight the giant, and pay no attention to the call to the herd by the pygmies."

44

Duel of Infamy: Part Two

The duel was to have been fought at one p.m., September 12 at the William Higgin's Ranch, adjacent Laguna Merced south of San Francisco. But on their way to the site both Broderick and Terry were arrested. For reasons unknown Terry was immediately released without posting bond, while Broderick was escorted to town where he was forced to post bond. Upon his discharge, the seconds for both conferred and agreed to meet at the same place at seven the next morning.

While Terry slept comfortably at Hayes's place, Broderick spent a restless night at Haskell's. Badly harassed by fleas, he was also suffering from diarrhea. Colonel Edward Baker sat up much of the night, trying to lift his spirits, without success; the senator's recent defeat had simply overwhelmed him. To make matters worse, before daybreak he learned that Haskell had run out of coffee. Deprived of his morning stimulant, listless as ever, with Baker, Colton, McKibbin, and Haskell, he left by carriage for Laguna Merced.

It was cold and damp when they arrived at 6:15 to find Terry and his entourage waiting. Their arrival brought the total number on site to eighty-five. The dueling ground was a level piece of ground near Lake Merced, then approachable only through a gap between two hills. William Higgins, owner of the ranch, later recalled the first carriage to rattle up: one of the riders asked if there was any whiskey available. When Higgins said no the rider replied, "Its a good occasion to have some."

"No it is not!" Higgins retorted.

Bernard Legardo, a San Francisco gun dealer, appeared shortly after with Broderick's set of pistols. Observers noted that while McKibbin and Benham marked off the agreed upon ten paces, Terry was visibly nervous. Only after the coin toss for the choice for pistol braces, which Benham won, did he regain his composure, assuming an almost arrogant manner.

Benham of course presented the Aylette pistols, drawing for Terry the only weapon in working order. Thus, through a phenomenal bit of skullduggery and good luck, Terry now faced Broderick with an enormous advantage. Even better, Bernard Legardo—no Natchez Taylor when it came to sizing up weapons—after testing Terry's pistol, was handed the one with the "tricky trigger." He carelessly snapped it, said it seemed lighter than the other, but declared it in good working order. While Brooks began loading Terry's pistol, he loaded Broderick's.

As was his fashion, Terry's physician, "Dr. No Show Aylette" never showed. In his stead Dr. William Hammond arrived. A witness recalled that Hammond, after shaking hands with Terry, casually spread his overcoat on the ground nearby and sat down to await events. By way of curiosity Hammond brought very little in the way of surgical instruments and exhibited a blasé manner about the entire business. Broderick's surgeon, Dr. Loher, on the other hand paced nervously back and forth on the sidelines, his open surgeon's bag bristling with saws, knives, tongs, and other troubling instruments.

Another coin toss followed to determine the choice of position, and to make the call. Colton won this one. As McKibbin was giving him some last minute advice, Leonidas Haskell untied Broderick's kerchief. In doing so, he turned away flicking his hand, as if he had completed a very unpleasant task. Ever after Haskell was referred to by Broderick men as "That bird of ill omen."

As was customary in searching the opposing duelists' clothing for foreign objects, McKibbin approached the judge, touched his chest as a formality and withdrew. No such courtesy was extended to Broderick. Benham worked his chest, stomach and sides over with scrupulous care. The gold watch that had saved the senator's life seven years before was very much on his mind.

Benham returned to the center of the ground, and taking a scroll of paper from Hayes, raised it high and read off the *code duello*. Broderick meanwhile tried to get a feel for the pistol in his hand. After Benham finished reading, Colton announced that he would make the call, "Fire, one two—stop!" Many were surprised that the customary "three" had been omitted.

As the duelists, similarly clothed in dark coats and wide-brimmed Palo Alto hats stood eying each other, they also assumed different postures. Terry, his hat resting comfortably back on his head, took a classic duelist's stance, showing Broderick only his right side, his left arm, and shoulder well behind him. Much preoccupied, Broderick adopted a careless stance, presenting a larger target. While trying to familiarize himself with his trick pistol, he unintentionally stepped over the line demarking the ten paces. McKibbin leaned over and returned his foot to its proper place. With everyone now drawn back to the sidelines, pistols pointed toward the ground, at a 6:45 a.m. Colton called out, "Gentleman, are you ready?"

"Ready," replied Terry.

"Ready," replied Broderick a split second later.

"Fire—one, two—stop!"

Broderick had scarcely brought his pistol to a 45-degree angle when it discharged into the ground, four paces in front of him.

A second later Terry, taking careful aim, fired. A puff of dust erupted from Broderick's coat as the ball plunged into the left side of his chest, through the upper lobe of his lung and out his arm pit. Clasping his chest with his right hand, he reeled to the left and before his seconds could reach him, sank to the ground, right leg doubled beneath him.

As Terry stood with arms folded, the still-smoking pistol in hand, he said to Brooks, "The shot is not mortal. I have struck two inches too high."

Broderick's surgeon, Dr. Loher, after opening his coat and shirt, hurriedly began stuffing cotton balls into his wound. Here again Broderick was not well served, and McKibbin called for Dr. Hammond. Hurrying over with a flask of brandy, Hammond knelt and gave the senator several swallows.

Despite his obvious condition, Benham strolled over and asked if Broderick wished for another shot. Told he was in no condition for a second shot, Benham returned and informed Terry. His manner was so arrogant that it provoked a Broderick partisan named Davis to shout "That is murder, by God!" As Davis strode toward Benham and Terry in a fury, he was blocked by his own partisans, who argued that more bloodshed was pointless.

But Davis had a point. The duel was no more a duel than Jim Lundy's murder of George Dibble at Industry Bar eight years before.

Only after Benham returned to inform Terry of Broderick's condition did he leave his post. Followed by most of the spectators, he left the site. A few minutes later the senator was placed in a litter, hoisted into his carriage and driven back to Haskell's house. There, he said very little. Among his few quotes was the following to Edward Baker: "Baker, I tried to stand firm when I was struck, but I could not. The blow blinded me."

Three days later, at 9:30 on the morning of September 16, he died.

Years later Colonel William Gift, a Chivalry Democrat and once a Terry partisan, said of the affair, "It was not a fair and honorable duel." Of the weapons, Jo Beard himself later told a friend, "There was something peculiar about those pistols—one of them was tricky—but the other always killed." Dr. William Ryer of course had his own thoughts on the matter.

Terry may have been! the most popular duelist on the ground, but in departing San Francisco for Oakland, and then Martinez by steamer, he began encountering unmistakable signs of hostility. By the time he reached Stockton, suspicion over Broderick's trick weapon and the deliberate, calculating manner in which he had been shot after his pistol misfired, was spreading. As days passed the anger toward him mounted.

Ten days later he was arrested and escorted to San Francisco where he placed a $10,000 bond. His lawyers pleaded for a change of venue, and the trial was moved to Marin County, where as chance would have it, a close friend of his, James H. Hardy, was presiding. On the morning of the trial, Hardy waited some minutes for both parties to appear in his courtroom. Claiming to be out of time and patience, he slammed down his gavel and dismissed the case. Some claim the judge set the clock ahead. Whatever, David Terry, once revered for his incorruptibility in a state filled with corrupt politicians, had forever exchanged his white hat for a black one.

Still, the inquest following Broderick's death failed to provide the public with any details of the negotiations leading to the duel. Under oath, McKibbin and Colton, simply stated that the question of whose set of pistols to use had been decided by the coin toss. Even though the public already regarded them both with suspicion, they evidently felt that to admit negotiating away the choice of pistols for the short call, would only have made them look worse.

Thus, thanks to their failed gambit, David Terry's long summer with the Jo Beard pistols, a stunning funeral oration by the silver tongued Edward Baker, and much hard work by revisionist historians, one of most unscrupulous figures of the Golden Era was transformed into a champion of virtue—an Abolitionist committed to ridding his state of its slave-loving Chivalry Democrats. Broderick accomplished in death what he had never attempted in life.

In the broad political sense there was no conspiracy to kill Broderick. But in a narrow sense there certainly was in that David Terry, Benjamin Langford, Calhoun Benham, Duncan Perley, Thomas Hayes, and others plotted an "affair of honor" that was nothing of the sort.

Among the major figures affected by the duel's fallout, Gwin suffered damage second only to Terry. He had never been close to the judge, nor was he a part of the narrow conspiracy, but as a Southerner his enemies found it easy to cast him in the same mold. He spent the war years in Mexico, where he invested in the silver mines of Sonora. Unlike the tragic Henry Crabb five years before, he induced so many Americans to settle in the area with complete safety, he became widely known as "The Duke of Sonora." After the war he returned to California, where he was welcomed by many old friends. Far more popular than he was in the days leading up to the Civil War, he prospered socially and financially. On September 3, 1885 while on a trip to New York City he died of pneumonia. His body was returned to California, where he was given a funeral at Grace Cathedral in San Francisco. The overflow crowd included the state's governor and two U.S. senators. He was buried at the Lone Mountain Cemetery, not far from Broderick.

With the outbreak of the Civil War McKibbin returned east to join the Union Army. During the conflict he rose to the rank of colonel, and with his brothers became known as one of the "Four Fighting McKibbins." Edward Baker also joined the war for the Union, dying a hero's death at the battle of Balls Bluff. Leonidas Haskell took the Union side too. In November 1861, when John C. Fremont was relieved of command under multiple charges of corruption, he too was removed. At the time he was still being referred to as that "bird of ill omen."

Thomas Hayes served as Dan Showalter's second in his fatal duel with Charles Piercy in 1861, and remained in California during the war years. Calhoun Benham returned east to take his stand with the Confederacy. He rose to the rank of colonel, and by dint of a miracle, survived the horrendous bloodletting at the Battle of Franklin. After the war he returned to California, where he practiced law until he died in 1884.

During the same war Terry served under Braxton Bragg, and was wounded at the Battle of Chickamauga. With the fall of the Confederacy, he left for Mexico where for several years he engaged in ranching. In 1868 he returned to Stockton, where he resumed law practice. In 1879 he became a prominent member of the California Constitutional Convention, which rewrote the 1849 state Constitution. Fractious as ever, in 1889, upon encountering a long standing legal adversary, Justice Stephen J. Field at an eating house in Lathrop, he slapped him in the face. In turn he was shot dead by Field's bodyguard, David Nagle.

45

The Duel at Moonlight Flat

Not many readers of Western history are familiar with the Gatewood-Goodwyn duel, largely because it was fought within four days of the sensational Broderick-Terry affair, which in fact triggered several copycat face-offs, none of which amounted to anything. But there was nothing copycat about the Gatewood-Goodwyn duel, its origins having sprung from a violent quarrel the month before. Like Broderick and Terry, the duel had its sectional components, North and South, but when all is said and done it was more a matter of alcohol and egos.

Jefferson Gatewood was born in Gallatin County, Illinois, in 1830. At the age of 16 he joined one of that state's regiments and went off to fight in the Mexican War. Although his friends often referred to Gatewood as "the Colonel," there is no evidence he ever obtained that rank. Regardless, at five feet nine, of average build and light complexion, his even temperament made him a well-liked figure. By the time he arrived in Mokulumne Hill in 1853, he was a successful lawyer. Three years later, when he ran for the office of district attorney, he won.

In 1857 Gatewood married Mary Crosthwaite, described as a tall, very good-looking woman. The couple moved into the Odd Fellows Hall in San Andreas to share an apartment with an old friend from Gatewood's Mexican War days, Robert Pope. A native of Georgia, Pope was a natural-born storyteller and a good fiddler. Because Gatewood was talented with a flute and Mary with a guitar, the trio was soon in popular demand at Calaveras County's many dances and socials.

Gatewood's antagonist in the duel was 34-year-old Peterson Goodwyn. Six feet tall, slim and dark-eyed, Goodwyn was a native of Petersburg, Virginia, who had taken a degree in medicine. He arrived in Calaveras in the early 1850s, established a medical practice, and like too many frontier doctors became a hard drinker. In reminiscing about Calaveras's pioneer days, one of its settlers recalled how Goodwyn had "gotten into his cups" while attending to his pregnant mother. His father arrived home before she gave birth, angrily thrust the tangle footed doctor out the door, and drove to San Andreas in search of a sober physician.

In fairness to Goodwyn, when on the wagon, he was a good practitioner.

In August of 1859, while Gatewood was in Salt Lake City on business, another of his friends from Mexican War days, Colonel Edward Baker, made a political swing through Calaveras County. Baker, a close friend of Broderick's, had recently joined the Free-Soil Republican Party.

Outside the Bay Area, Republicans in California were about as popular as polecats, and Calaveras was no exception. Baker could not find a single volunteer in the entire county to set up a speaking schedule. When Gatewood returned to San Andreas in late August, he was unaware of how shabbily Baker had been received. That day on Main Street, in front of Favelle's Saloon, the first person he encountered was Peterson Goodwyn; following a hale greeting, with much laughter he informed Gatewood of Baker's humbling visit to San Andreas.

Gatewood listened, looked coldly at Goodwyn and said, "I was personally acquainted with Colonel Baker in Mexico. If I had been here, I would have acted as chairman through courtesy."

"Then you must be a damned old Abolitionist!" shouted Goodwyn.

"No, I am not!" retorted Gatewood.

"You're a liar!"

Gatewood let fly with his fist, knocking Goodwyn onto the street. Enraged, the doctor picked himself up and went for his gun. Gatewood seized his arm and as they struggled, two passersby disarmed Goodwyn and told him to go home and cool off. Humiliated, he climbed into his buggy and seating himself said, "You will hear from me again, Mr. Gatewood."

Though the warning was veiled, Gatewood understood its meaning and the next day, through Robert Pope and another friend, former assemblyman Martin Rowan, informed Goodwyn their dispute could be settled without resort to arms. Goodwyn's second, Calaveras State Senator Buck Lewis, agreed and worked hard to sooth his ruffled feelings. But his principle insisted a duel could not be avoided, unless Gatewood publicly admitted to being "a liar and a coward."

Gatewood was fully supported by his wife and Captain Pope, who felt there was no way he could avoid an encounter. Thus he chose Mississippi Yagers. But because of numerous public engagements on his schedule, he insisted the date of the duel be postponed until September 16.

As a rule the women of California looked upon dueling with dread. But feeling that her husband had been driven to the wall, on the evening before the shootout Mary Gatewood personally handed Gatewood the slug she hoped and prayed would end Goodwyn's life. Unknown to either, at that moment Goodwyn was intoxicated. Those who knew the doctor well were not surprised to learn that he had been drinking ever since he challenged Gatewood. That very afternoon, in a moment of drunken pity, he had told a friend he didn't care if he lived or died.

Early the next morning five carriages carrying Gatewood, Goodwyn, and their seconds and physicians rolled out of San Andreas toward the dueling ground, Moonlight Flat, near Foreman's Flat in southern Calaveras County. On the drive Gatewood was told that his opponent was drunk, and had been for days. Turning to Pope he said, "I don't think Goodwyn can hold his rifle up. I'll fire over his head."

"Don't be a fool!" said Pope. "Goodwyn has already said he will not be satisfied with less than three or four shots."

The two parties arrived at the Flat where the duelists exchanged courtesies as they left their carriages. The forty paces were measured off and the pair took their positions. Two coin tosses followed, Goodwyn winning the first, giving Buck Lewis the right to call fire, Gatewood wining the second for position. At 7 a.m. the pair, each standing beneath a large oak tree, rifle butts on hips, awaited the call.

"Are you ready?" called out Lewis.

"I am," answered both.

"Fire—one two three—stop!"

Between "two and three" both rifles thundered. Goodwyn's shot, to no one's surprise ploughed harmlessly into the earth in front of Gatewood. At that instant the bullet Mrs. Gatewood had chosen for her husband, tore into Goodwyn's right side, passed through his intestines and out his left hip, staggering him to the ground. As he lay in the grass Gatewood strode over, extended his hand and said, "Doctor, I am very sorry that this affair has terminated so—very sorry indeed."

"I am glad to know that you acted like a gentleman," the doctor replied.

Gatewood left his larger buggy behind to carry Goodwyn to San Andreas, mounted a horse and rode back to town alone. The doctor arrived an hour later and was carried to his room where he died in agony the same morning. His death followed Broderick's by just hours. Two days later, before a large crowd, he was buried in the Odd Fellows section of the San Andreas Cemetery.

An inquest was conducted on the death of Goodwyn. Despite the best efforts of Judge J.A. Smith and Justice of the Peace James Barclay to pressure witnesses into testifying against Gatewood they were unsuccessful. Some admitted to seeing Gatewood and Goodwyn driving toward the dueling ground; others saw Goodwyn with a gun; others saw him lying in the grass. But no one saw Gatewood shoot him. Barclay was forced to sum his inquest up in a manner quite typical of the times:

> We the undersigned jurors, summoned to examine the cause of death of Dr. P. Goodwyn, upon and examination of the body, find that his death was occasioned by a wound in his abdomen caused by a gunshot fired by some person unknown to the jury . . .

Though it was still too early for even the most seasoned observers to foresee, California's age of chivalry was drawing to a close. Of the duel, Samuel Seabough, the editor of the *San Andreas Independent* wrote, "So long as the public continues to lavish its praise on the duelist, while scorning those who shun the code, the state will be forever cursed by the obnoxious 'code of honor.'"

In the tradition of many late-nineteenth-century writers who abhorred dueling, several claimed that Gatewood afterward led a life of dissolution. One reported he died in a poor house. In fact, only a few years afterward he founded the *San Andreas Register* newspaper. In 1868 he and Mary moved to San Diego where together they founded the *San Diego Union*. A few years later Gatewood was elected city attorney. An ideal couple in every other respect, they never had any children. Mary died August 27, 1881 and Jeff March 26, 1888. Both are buried at the Mount Hope Cemetery in San Diego.

46

Shootout in Visalia

Many of the challenges issued by California's gentlemen of honor never resulted in a duel. The state's newspapers report a number of incidents where the challenger and challenged reached an agreement before ever reaching the dueling ground. On the other hand, there were run-ins that resulted in many gunfights before ever reaching the formal duel stage. One of these occurred in the San Joaquin Valley town of Visalia in November 1860. The combatants were two well-known state figures, William Gouverneur Morris and John Shannon.

Among the legion of bad-tempered journalists who made their way west with the Gold Rush, was John Shannon, publisher of the *Visalia Delta*. A native of Ohio, upon arriving in Auburn in 1850 he established the *Placer Democrat*. Shortly after, he returned to Ohio to court Mary Eulalie Fee, the daughter of a wealthy Kentucky family. Prompted by Shannon's better than average looks and rough charm, Eulalie succumbed to his accounts of California's salubrious climate and amazing scenery, married him, and left for the new El Dorado.

For the most part Shannon's *Placer Democrat* was a very unremarkable mining-town newspaper. Through 1854 however it became quite popular because of several poems that appeared in its columns written by Eulalie. Among them was her acclaimed *Home, or the Pastoral Present*. Unhappily, this first of California woman poets died the day after Christmas, 1854, while giving birth. Shannon, already a hard drinker, surrendered the baby boy to adoptive parents, sold the *Placer Democrat* and left for Mokulumne Hill where he purchased the *Calaveras Chronicle*.

Over time Shannon's numerous quarrels made him so unpopular in Calaveras County that he was forced to sell his paper. The purchaser proved to be Colonel Richard Rust, former editor of the *Marysville Express*. In search of a more tranquil locale where he would not be subject to so many misunderstandings, Shannon departed for the ranching down of Visalia, two hundred miles south. There, in October 1859, in partnership with C.

Killmer, he launched the *Visalia Delta*. It wasn't long before Shannon had a falling out with his partner/editor and fired him.

A few months after the *Delta* was established, Hugh M'Lean began publishing the *Visalia Sun*. Though hairs split the two newspapers politically—both were Breckenridge Democrats opposed to Lincoln—Shannon reacted angrily to the *Sun*'s inroads on his readership. His feelings toward Visalia at large soured when he failed to obtain the board of supervisor's printing contract. With circulation falling and the 1860 presidential campaign in full swing, he tried to bolster his sagging readership by publishing a series of bitter editorials, attacking anyone even suspected of failing to support Breckenridge.

In response M'Lean hired a local attorney named William Gouverneur Morris to ghost write several editorials for the *Sun*. Morris was the great-grandson of Lewis Morris, one of the signers of the Declaration of Independence, and great grand-nephew of Gouverneur Morris, New York's first governor. Morrisiana was in fact the title of the family's Westchester County homestead, granted them by King Charles II of England in 1670. Since his arrival in California in 1855, Morris had cut quite a path for himself, having immediately landed a clerk's position with State Supreme Court Justice Joseph Baldwin. After spending two years with Baldwin, he resigned and moved to Visalia where he set up his own law practice. Shortly after, he became a prosecutor.

In manner and appearance Morris was as polished as Shannon was crude, and considered a gentleman. But like most California gentlemen he possessed a rough side to his character. In 1858, while trying to extract a confession from a swindler, he ran the accused up a rope. When word of the mock hanging became public, he was severely condemned. Nonetheless, because most of Visalia's business establishment backed him, and because the swindler later confessed to his crime, Morris was able to salvage his reputation.

One of his columns in the *Visalia Sun* dealt with Shannon's inability to write a coherent newspaper column. Morris had a point. Without an editor Shannon could not produce a readable newspaper. He followed this attack with another in which he reported that a prominent local Democrat complained that Shannon's violent electioneering style had cost Breckenridge thirty known votes in Tulare County. In typically crude fashion Shannon retorted, "That is a fib. The prominent Democrat (not a very prominent one at that) is telling a lie. The odor emitted would lead one to believe he was sleeping with the editor of the *Sun* or some other black republican dignitary."

About a week before election day 1860, Shannon learned that Morris was indeed ghost writing the *Sun*'s editorials. He retaliated by accusing Morris of prosecuting the same criminals that his law partner was defending. Morris reacted by sending R. Atwell into his office with a challenge to duel. With Shannon absent, Atwell thoughtlessly left the challenge on his desk. Some minutes later, Shannon returned and found the note. Furious over Atwell's lack of etiquette, he charged out the front door, down the street, overtook him, and in the knock-down, drag-out brawl that followed, soundly thrashed him.

Later that day he accepted Morris's challenge, but because his hand had been badly sprained in the fight with Atwell, he was forced to postpone the duel until the hand recovered. A few days later, November 4, for reasons unknown, Shannon abruptly decided to pay Morris a visit. Shoving a revolver into his coat pocket, he strode down to the courthouse square, burst through Morris's front door, pulled his gun and shouted "Are you armed?!"

Morris, unarmed, but on his feet, bulled into Shannon head first before he could pull the trigger. In the struggle that ensued Shannon struck Morris on the head several times with his gun, and knocked him to the floor unconscious. As he leveled his revolver at him, Morris's partner seized the weapon and in yet another brawl disarmed him. Some minutes later, upon regaining consciousness, Morris was helped to his feet. Suddenly he shouted, "Where's that damned rascal?" pulled a revolver from his desk drawer, and raced out the doorway into the street.

Across the square, Shannon heard Morris's shouts and turned in time to see him take cover inside a shed next to his law office. Morris fired at him without effect; Shannon returned the fire and missed too. Morris then bolted from the shed and leaped over a picket fence before flicking off a second shot. Just as Shannon loosed another round, Morris's bullet struck him in the stomach.

The publisher dropped his pistol and clutching his wound staggered up the street into his office, where he collapsed on the floor. Before his death two hours later, he asked that he be carried back to Auburn and buried next to his beloved Eulalie. But the people of Tulare were not about to underwrite the cost of hauling Shannon's body all way to Placer County. Rather, they buried him in Visalia. Later they exonerated Morris of any wrongdoing.

The Morris-Shannon gun battle drew state wide attention only because it was fought between two well-recognized figures. Hundreds of such shoot-outs took place between 1849 and 1861, most of them receiving but a few lines of notice in local newspapers.

Despite Gouverneur Morris's early support for presidential candidate John Breckenridge, he went on to become a strong supporter of the Union during the Civil War. As a major in the state militia he played a role in suppressing a secessionist revolt in Santa Clara County without the effusion of blood. He afterward operated a pony express, running war dispatches from Southern California to New Mexico Territory. After the war he became a U.S. marshal. He spent his last years on a ranch in Napa County, where he was regarded by his neighbors as a fine example of California pioneerhood.

47

Sunrise on Mount Tam

The Broderick-Terry duel did much to hasten the end of chivalry in California. Yet aside from the Gatewood-Goodwyn duel and the Morris-Shannon shootout, several little known, bloodless affairs followed. On April 12, 1860, two Stockton store owners, Oppenheimer and Frankenthal, squared off over some insulting language and exchanged three shots at fifteen paces, without effect.

The following month two Nevada City residents, Morris and Van Hazen, blasted away at each other with six shooters, missed all shots, shook hands and rode back to town in the same wagon. In July, on the road between Mokulumne Hill and Stockton, two Frenchmen, Dauphin and Pach exchanged single shots with rifles at forty paces. Both missed, shook hands, and retired to the North American House for breakfast.

The following year, in Tuolumne County another mock duel took place, when Moore and Davis exchanged blank shots near Sonora. Moore fell to the ground unharmed and sprayed himself with red ink. Unaware it was all a prank, and sighting the sheriff, Davis—who had slipped on a suit of mail beneath his clothing—attempted to mount his horse. Unable to climb astride the animal because of his encumbrance, he was seized, and amid much laughter, escorted back to shake hands with Moore.

Bringing a formal end to the age of chivalry was a much less amusing affair— the Piercy-Showalter duel of May 1861. Daniel Showalter was a native of Greene County, Pennsylvania, who as a youth attended Madison College in the same state. Well over six feet tall and powerfully built, his most startling feature was a flaming red beard set against a pair of coal black eyes. In 1852 this rugged young man set out for California. Arriving in Mariposa County, he began mining, and meeting with some success became a familiar figure around the mining camps of Horseshoe Bend, Red Banks, and Coulterville.

Showalter was literate, hardworking, and a natural-born leader with a taste for politics. He also had a temper, a taste for red-eye, and verbally and physically was a match for most men. In 1855 he was elected to the State Assembly as a Democrat, representing the Mariposa-Merced region. He served a second term before stepping down in 1858. Two years later he was reelected to the Assembly as a Union, or Douglas Democrat, opposed to abolition on the one hand and Southern secession on the other. While serving in the Assembly his hard work and diligence temporarily won him the post of Assembly speaker pro tempore.

One of his acquaintances at the capital was San Bernardino Assemblyman Charles Piercy, a native of Illinois. Tall, slender, and exquisitely polite, he quite naturally expected his Assembly associates to conduct themselves in the same manner. The record shows that like Showalter, Piercy was a political middle of the roader who sought to conciliate the Assembly's Union and Secession factions. Despite this common ground, the two did not get on well.

By May 1861 America was at war with itself, and California was still straddling the fence. But an increasing number of Douglas Democrats, including Charles Piercy, had swung to the side of the Union. Among the few Douglas Democrats moving into the Secession camp was Dan Showalter. What caused him to throw his lot with the dwindling band of Assembly Secessionists will never be precisely understood. It is known that Mariposa County possessed a higher proportion of Southern-born settlers than any other locale in the state north of Los Angeles.*

On May 17, 1861, the Assembly took up a resolution calling on every Californian to ". . . honor unfailingly the Constitution and the Union in her hour of trial and need." Assembly rules required that any vote within the body be taken without a speech of explanation by the members. Until then the rule had been largely ignored, but on this occasion the leadership decided to enforce it. As those members who rose to vote against the resolution sought to explain themselves, they were abruptly cut off. Still, when Showalter rose to announce his "no" vote, he demanded a right to be heard. His motion was blocked by Charles Piercy.

Angered by the intrusion, Showalter retorted, "I have only to say that no one ever yet heard me object to any gentleman explaining his vote. It is a right which I have always maintained and I have nothing but contempt for any gentleman who does object."

Piercy rose and asked Showalter if there was anything in his statement he would like to retract. Showalter replied there was nothing to retract. Two attempts in two days to reach an accord were made by fellow assemblymen,

---

*The 1852 census of Mariposa County revealed that 49 percent of its residents were from Southern states. As the state census progressed northward the percentage of Southerners trails off markedly.

without success. Finally on the third day Showalter received a challenge from Piercy, delivered by Henry P. Watkins, State Senator of Yuba County.

He accepted, chose Thomas Hayes as his primary second, and rifles (make and caliber unknown) carrying 2½-inch slugs at forty paces. The site was the Fairfax House, built by former Speaker of the Assembly Charles Fairfax and his wife, Ada. The former assemblyman in fact had offered his bucolic premises in hopes of patching over the feud. But his attempts to heal the rift over refreshments at his dining table only prodded Piercy into demanding a twenty pace reduction in distance, a request that Showalter and Hayes refused to consider. With the failure of this last meeting, Showalter retired to his room and wrote out his will.

At 4:15 on the morning of May 24 he left the Fairfax House for a nearby glen surrounded by thickly branched live oaks, through which a creek ran. He wore a dark, wide-brimmed hat and a similarly shaded coat buttoned to the collar. Accompanying Showalter through the trees was Hayes and his two auxiliary seconds, Thomas Laspeyer of Stockton and A.J. Gregory of Mariposa. His physician was the same William Hammond who had attended Terry in his duel with Broderick.

By a different route through the trees Piercy was accompanied by Henry Watkins, his auxiliary second Samuel Smith, and the venerable Doctor Wake Briarly, acting both as an auxiliary and surgeon.

On the ground the two took their approximate places, as arm-in-arm Hayes and Watkins measured off the forty paces. Showalter won the single toss for position and call, and the two took their posts. Watkins then read off portions of the *code duello*, concluding, "Gentleman, if either antagonist violates the rule forbidding him to shoot before 'fire,' or after the word 'stop,' he lays himself liable to that provision of the code which declares that the offender shall be shot down summarily by the second of his opponent."

Moments later Showalter and Piercy stood facing each other, rifle stocks on hips, muzzles pointing upward at 60 degrees, left hands gripping barrels, right hands covering the trigger guards. As the sun's first rays touched the summit of Mount Tamalpais, turning the grass below bright green, Hayes called out, "Gentlemen, are you ready?"

"Ready," called both.

"Fire, one, two, three—stop!"

Both fired at "two" and missed, Showalter feeling a rush of air as Piercy's bullet narrowly missed his head.

"Load the weapons again," he shouted.

Minutes later the two stood waiting as Hayes again called, "Fire, one, two, three—stop!"

At "two," both guns roared simultaneously. Piercy started forward, threw his hands back and fell to the earth, shot through the mouth.

Showalter abruptly turned and asked Dr. Hammond to save his life. Despite his efforts and those of Dr. Briarly, the assemblyman died in three minutes. After praising Piercy's courage: "He was a brave man, a very brave man," Showalter left the ground and made his way to Mariposa where he was well received by his constituents.

But even in Mariposa he could find no peace. Though he had been the challenged party and shown himself much more amenable to a settlement than Piercy, the wrath of state officialdom was upon him. Buried with Piercy in May 1861 was California's Age of Chivalry. Showalter, the first duelist ever to face real time inside San Quentin Prison, abruptly left for Nevada.

A few months later he reappeared in El Monte, Southern California. In November 1861 the newspapers reported that he and a party of some twenty Texans had left California to join the Confederate Army. A Union patrol was sent in pursuit, and in the midst of the Mojave Desert overtook them. They surrendered, and were escorted to Fort Yuma where they were held prisoner until April 1862. The Union officer in charge of the fort, after extracting a dubious oath of allegiance, released them. Evidence suggests that the officer was bribed by Confederate sympathizers.

An arduous trek over Mexico's Sierra Madre followed before the party reached Texas. There, Showalter enlisted in the Confederate Army, fought at the battle of Sabine Pass under General John B. Magruder and ultimately attained the rank of lieutenant colonel. In 1864 he wrote to Major General Kirby Smith, offering to lead a force of Confederates across the Southwest to seize California. By then, however, the South was nearing collapse, and with no resources available for the effort, Smith turned him down.

The fall of the Confederacy left Showalter embittered, and in the company of David Terry and several others, he left the United States to begin a new life in Mexico. Despite a crippling fall from a horse en route, he reached Mazatlan where he bought a hotel and bar. But the move to Mexico's west coast only brought him more misery. Still afflicted by the injuries suffered in his fall, unhappy with life in Mazatlan, he began drinking heavily and brooding. On a February evening in 1866, while on a furniture smashing spree, his own bartender accused him of "not acting like a gentleman."

Showalter paused in his exertions to argue the point. When the bartender retorted "You are not acting like one," he drew a Bowie knife and applying its broad side, slapped his face. In turn, the bartender drew his gun and fired, shattering Showalter's right arm. Lockjaw set in, and three days later he died.

Epilogue

It is April 1869. Charles Fairfax lies dying in a room at Barnum's City Hotel in Baltimore, partly because of the sword wound he received ten years before at the hands of Harvey Lee. Reclining on his pillows, he listens to his old Pennsylvania sidekick from pre–Civil War days, Ned McGowan. Between weak fits of coughing and laughter, Fairfax pleads for the graying swashbuckler to tell him one more story of old California and how it was. And McGowan, as is his wont, launches into yet another recollection of an epoch unlike any other in America: a magic time of intrigue, of scandal in the air, riotous evenings at the Blue Wing Saloon, a time when young men wild with rage one day lay dying the next.

By then, McGowan, after having served in the Confederate Army during the Civil War, was assistant doorman to the U.S. House of Representatives. That he was able to obtain the post, despite his disloyalty to the Union, is but another tribute to his slick grace.

Shortly after Fairfax died, McGowan set out for Arizona where it is said he added more luster to his name. In 1878 he returned to his former stomping grounds—San Francisco. The old sinner was greeted not only by surviving cronies, but by many former vigilantes who had long since forgiven his antics of decades past. Only in his last years did he fall into poverty. He was then supported by the generosity of old friends—and old enemies, such as vigilante leader William Tell Coleman. He died on December 8, 1893, aged 80.

Duels were occasionally fought in California after 1861, but as Billy Mulligan found out several years later, the public regarded them largely as curiosities. No longer thought of as a paladin, the duelist at best was an oddity, a throwback to another age. At worst, he was a criminal, liable to an extensive term inside San Quentin.

Which brings to mind the question—what and who precisely was chivalry in the Golden State? In its most narrow sense, as presented by post–Civil War historians, the term meant Southerners who had migrated to California during the Gold Rush. But as the annals tell it, Chivalry with a capital "C" was a political movement embracing not only those from the South, but every state of the Union, including Massachusetts. In point of fact Chivalry was more than a political movement. It was a state of mind, a way of life that crossed political parties to embrace Whigs, Know-Nothings, and even a Republican or two.

Contrary to popular perception more than half of California's duelists were from Northern states, with New York bestowing at least as many as the state of Mississippi. The most triumphant duelists seemed to also have come from the North—Pennsylvania alone bequeathing William H. Carter, Will Hicks Graham, and Dan Showalter. Not only did Americans duel, so did foreign nationals: the English, the French, the Irish, the Germans, and Mexicans—though usually within their own groups.

Finally, the duel itself must be placed into another perspective. The toll taken over the years between 1847 and 1861 by knifings, shootouts, and ambushes was far greater than that lost through dueling. Worse, in contrast to the formal duel, these killings tended to be anything but "just and honorable" encounters.

James Casey's shooting of James King in 1856, the event that touched off the vigilante uprising, was typical of these slayings. With gun drawn the assailant would typically push toward the object of his fury and shout, "Are you armed?!" If the victim even reflexively moved his hand he was cut down. Often, as was in the case of King, even without a reflexive move, he was shot. Thus the code of honor, unlike the common shootout of its time, and the countless shootings of our time, did ensure—with some notable exceptions—that the duelist would face his opponent on terms that were approximately "just and honorable."

Notes

Poem

The poem by Ned McGowan appeared in the *San Francisco Evening Post*, August 3, 1878.

Chapter 1: Golden Era California

See Robert E. Cowan, "The Folsom-Leidesdorff Estate," *California Historical Society Quarterly*, June 1928, and H. Brett Melendy, "Who was John McDougal?" *Pacific Historical Review*, Volume 29. Another good sketch of McDougal can be found in Stewart, George R., *Committee of Vigilance: Revolution in San Francisco*, pp. 215–216, 228, 259–264. Also, *Alta California*, May 19, 1851, and the *San Francisco Examiner*, February 13, 1882.

Chapter 2: In the Beginning

Most of the information was gleaned from Robert Baldick,'s *The Duel: A History of Dueling*. Portions of "A Traveler" appeared on pp. 45–47.

Chapter 3: The Duel in America

Much of this chapter was again gleaned from Baldick, pp. 115–130. Also helpful was Major Ben Truman's *The Field of Honor*, pp. 374–377.

Chapter 4: The Duel Comes to California

Sources are Allen Nevins, *Fremont: Pathmarker of the West*, and Helen S. Giffen, *Man of Destiny, Pierson Barton Reading*. Important with regard to events at the California Constitutional Convention is the *San Francisco Evening Post*, May 16, 1896.

Chapter 5: The Year 1850

See J. Edward Johnson, *A History of the Supreme Court of California, 1850–1900*. Also, the *Alta California*, April 19, 1850, and September 16, 1858; in addition the *Sacramento Union*, February 14, 1854, the *San Francisco Evening Bulletin*, June, 11, 1856, and the *San Francisco Evening Post*, September 7, 1878.

Chapter 6: The Keystone Fire-Eater

See William Perkins, *Journal of Life at Sonora, 1849–52*, pp. 261, 280, 281. Perkins gives interesting insight into how pioneers from different parts of the country regarded one another. So do C.W. Haskins in *The Argonauts of California*, pp. 303–305, and George R. Stewart in his *Committee of Vigilance: Revolution in San Francisco*, p. 165.

Also read *The Argonaut*, June 30, 1877, the *San Francisco Chronicle*, August 13, 1895 and August 31, 1895. Important also is the *San Francisco Evening Bulletin*, November 14, 1896, and the *San Francisco Evening Post*, May 16, 1896, September 7, 1878, and August 31, 1878.

Chapter 7: The Duel at Coyote Hill

See the *San Francisco Call*, December 25, 1881, and the *Alta California*, October 19, 1884.

Chapter 8: Murder at Industry Bar

The *San Francisco Evening Post* of February 22, 1896, and May 19, 1896. Also the *Alta California*, July 4, 1880, and the *Nevada Journal*, November 3, 1851.

Chapter 9: Judge Terry's First Duel

See V. Covert Martin, *Stockton Album Through the Years*, p. 38, Carvel Collins's *Sam Ward in the Gold Rush*, 45–46, and Jeremiah Lynch, *A Senator for the Fifties*, 213–214. Also, *Alta California*, April 19, 1850, *San Joaquin Republican*, October 5, 1856, and most importantly the *San Francisco Evening Post*, January 18, 1896.

Chapter 10: Senator Broderick's First Duel

See James O'Meara, Broderick and Gwin. p 28, 106, and Paul W. Gates, "Carpet Baggers Join the Rush for California Land," *California Historical Society Quarterly*, June 1977, p. 101. Also, *Alta California*, January 11, 1851, *San Francisco Evening Post*, September 12, 14, 1878, January 4, 1896, and the *San Francisco Examiner*, February 20, 1881.

Chapter 11: Juanita Avenged

Swisher, pp. 52–53. *The San Francisco Evening Post*, September 7, 1878, September 12, 1878, and November 2, 1895.

Chapter 12: California's Dueling Bard of Avon

See Edward Kemble, *A History of California Newspapers, 1846–1858*, p. 182, Truman, 331, the *Alta California*, May 9, 1852, and September 12, 1854, the *Butte Enterprise Record*, November 12, 1953, and *San Francisco Evening Post*, December 14, 1895.

Chapter 13: Gentleman John

Albert Z. Carr, *The World and William Walker*, p. 57. See also James O'Meara, "Editors of Early California," *Overland Monthly*, November 1889, pp. 489–492, 494–496, and the *San Francisco Evening Post*, August 3, 1878, and September 2, 1878.

Chapter 14: The Duel at Rancho del Paso

George C. Barnes, *Denver the Man*, pp. 1–22, 48–55; Oscar T. Shuck, *The Bench and Bar in California*, p. 230, and John F. Wilhelm, "Shootout at Oak Grove," *Golden Notes, Volume 29*, p. 3, 4, 11. The *Sacramento Union*, April 27, 1883, August 13, 1892, and *Trinity Journal*, May 21, 1858, provide additional background.

Chapter 15: The Captain and the Auctioneer

See *Alta California*, August 13, 1852, the *San Francisco Evening Post*, July 17, 1878, July 27, 1878, and *Themis*, August 17, 1889, 1–3.

Chapter 16: The Leggett-Morrison Duel

Themis, August 17, 1889, pp. 1–3. Also, the *San Francisco Evening Post*, April. 11, 1896.

Chapter 17: Groveling in Los Angeles

Horace Bell, *Reminiscences of a Ranger*, p. 75–77, and Shelby Foote, *The Civil War: A Narrative*, Volume I, p. 398, 399.

Chapter 18: Honorable Mention: 1852

William L. Roper, "Roy Bean fights a Duel," *Westways Magazine*, August 1954, p. 7, the *San Francisco Evening Post*, January 25, 1879, and May 19, 1896.

Chapter 19: The Senate Challenges the House

Lately, Thomas, *Between Two Empires; the Life Story of California's First Senator, William McKendree Gwin*, p. 28, 44, 47. Also, the *Sacramento Daily Bee*, October 17, 1885, and the *San Francisco Evening Post*, February 29, 1896.

For good background on Joseph W. McCorkle see Michele Shover, 'The Doctor, the Lawyer and the Political Chief in the 1850s of Butte County,' *The University Journal*, Winter 1982, California State University, Chico.

Chapter 20. The Dentist and the Grocer

Themis, August 17, 1889, pp. 1–3, the *San Francisco Daily Herald*, June 12, 1853, and the *San Francisco Evening Post*, April 4, 1896.

Chapter 21: The Surprise Acceptance

Chester A. Kennedy, "Editors of the Northern Mines," p. 144. See also *Alta California*, August 16, 1872, *Sacramento Union*, July 3, 1888, *San Francisco Evening Bulletin*, October 14, 1895, and *San Francisco Evening Post*, February 24, 1883.

Chapter 22: The Fatal Friendship

Alta California, August 9, 1853, *San Francisco Daily Herald*, August 8, 1853, *San Francisco Evening Post*, May 2, 1896, *San Francisco News Letter*, March 22, 1884, and the *Shasta Courier*, November 12, 1853.

Chapter 23: The Fool Alternate

Kenneth M. Johnson, *The Strange, Eventful Life of Parker H. French*, p. 27. Major Ben Truman, "An Early California Duel," *Grizzly Bear*, December, 1907, and O'Meara, p. 70. Also, *Alta California*, March 11, 1854, *Placer Herald*, March 11, 1854, *San Francisco Evening Post*, August 24, 1878, and December 21, 1895.

Chapter 24: Requiem by Moonlight

David A Williams, *David Broderick; A Political Portrait*, p. 87, O'Meara, p. 61, Truman, p. 419, and *San Francisco Evening Post*, March 14, and May 16, 1896.

Chapter 25: Our Founding Father's Nephew

John S. Hittell, *The History of San Francisco*, A..L. Bancroft Company, 1879, p. 313, and O'Meara, 80, 81. Also, *Alta California*, January 28, and March 24, 1854. There are other references to the feud dating from January through March 1854, among them the *Sacramento Union*, March 23, 1854, and *San Francisco Daily Herald*, March 22, 1854. The *San Francisco Examiner*, January 23, 1872, provides a detailed account.

Chapter 26: The Hubert-Hunt Duel

There are brief period notices in the newspapers, but the best account is in the *San Francisco Evening Post*, March 3, 1882.

Chapter 27: A Longshoreman's Affair

There are period reports of the duel in the *San Francisco Daily Herald*, May 25, 1854, and the *Shasta Courier*, May 31, 1854, but the *San Francisco Evening Post* of February. 8, 1896 gives the best account.

Chapter 28: California's Don Quixote

George H. Tinkham, *The History of San Joaquin County*, p. 199. See also the *Alta California*, September 22, 1854, the *San Francisco Daily Herald*, September 22, 1854, the *Santa Cruz Sentinal*, May 30, 1866, and most importantly the *San Francisco Evening Bulletin*, September 20, 1890. The Crabb disaster was extensively reported in many California newspapers during April, May and June of 1857.

Chapter 29: An Affair of the Heart

The single detailed account of this duel appeared in the *San Francisco Evening Post* of April 18, 1896.

Chapter 30: The Democracy versus the Know-Nothings

Several period newspapers note the Kewan-Woodleif duel, but the best accounts appear in the *Oakland Post-Enquirer*, January 25, 1926, the *San Francisco Evening Post*, November 9, 1895, and May 16, 1896.

Chapter 31: Galahad Shot Again

O'Meara's *Broderick and Gwin* is a good source for readers wanting to know more about the key figures in the decade long struggle for political supremacy. An inside player himself, O'Meara is even handed in his treatment of the subject. Many newspapers reported on the Democratic Convention, including the *Sacramento Daily Union*, July 19, 1854. The Carter-Walker duel is reported in the *Alta California*, March 16, 1855, and most thoroughly in the *San Francisco Evening Post*, September 14, 1879.

Chapter 32: The Evils of Temperance

William H. Downie, *Hunting for Gold*, p.154, 161; also, Oscar T. Shuck, *The Bench and Bar in California*, p. 237, 238, 239, and the *San Francisco Evening Post*, March 4, 1882.

Chapter 33: Crawfishing in San Jose

Kenneth M. Johnson, *The Strange, Eventful Life of Parker H. French*, p. 6, 11, 20, 30, 31. Other good sources on French's activities can be obtained from the *California Chronicle*, February 21, 1856, the *San Francisco Daily Herald*, June 21, 1856, and most of all, the *San Francisco Evening Post*, January 4, 1879.

Chapter 34: The Salted Claim

The only detailed source is the *San Francisco Evening Post*, May 9, 1896. See also *Nevada Journal*, November 6, 1855.

Chapter 35: The Grand Burlesque

O'Meara, p. 102, *Alta California*, October 19, 1855, and the *San Francisco Evening Post*, January 25, 1896.

Chapter 36: A Fighting Editor Takes a Stand

Hubert H. Bancroft, *Popular Tribunals*, 1888, p. 131, and Albert Shumate, *The Notorious I.C. Woods of the Adams Express*, pp. 47–56, and the *San Francisco Evening Post*, April 25, 1896.

Chapter 37: Year of Bedlam: 1856

Bancroft, *Popular Tribunals*, p. 157, 293, *Argonaut*, June 30, 1877, p. 1, *California Chronicle*, June 23, 1856, *San Francisco Morning Call*, May 7, 1882, *San Francisco Evening Bulletin*, June 14, 15, 16, 1856, *San Francisco Evening Post*, May 16, 1896, and the *Shasta Republican*, June 14, 1856.

Chapter 38. The Doctors' Duel

Most of the details for the Ryer-Langdon duel were found in the James Shebl Manuscript, titled "The Ryer-Langdon Duel." Other sources are the *Sacramento Daily Bee*, February 26, 1857, the *San Joaquin Republican*, February 25, 1857, the *Stockton Daily Argus*, February 23, 1857 and the *Stockton Daily Record*, November, 21, 1930.

Chapter 39. When Chivalry was in Bloom

Sources are the *San Francisco Evening Bulletin*, September 17, 1857, the *San Joaquin Republican*, September 16, 1857, the *Stockton Daily Argus*, September 16, 1857, and most importantly the *San Francisco Evening Post*, January 25, 1879, and May 16, 1896.

Chapter 40: The Duel at Angel Island

Shuck, p. 242. The *Alta California*, September 20, 1858, the *San Francisco Evening Post*, March 4, 1882, and November 30, 1895; also the *San Francisco Daily Examiner*, March 5, 1884, and the *Sacramento Daily Union*, February 12, 1858. A good profile of James Estill is in the *San Francisco Morning Call*, May 4, 1890.

Chapter 41: Honorable Mention: 1858

Marysville California Express, June 12, 1858, the *Alta California*, January 28, 1858, the *San Francisco Evening Post*; also see Roy Jenkins, *Saddlebags in the Siskiyous*, p. 76, the *Sacramento Daily Union*, September 26, 1858, and Bancroft's *Popular Tribunals*, pp. 608–609.

Chapter 42: Another Exciting Year

See the *San Francisco Evening Post*, August 31, 1879, the *San Andreas Independent*, December 5, 1857, and James Henry Nash's *James Woods Coffroth*, p. 11, 18, 20. Also, the *Sacramento Daily Bee*, June 18, 1859, the *Shasta Courier*, November 29, 1859, the *Sacramento Daily Union*, September 24, December 29, 1859, and the *Trinity Journal*, December 24, 1859.

Chapter 43: Duel of Infamy: Part One

Donald Hargis's "The Great Debate in California," *History Society of Southern California*, June, 1960, p. 152–157 is an excellent source for researching the feud between Broderick and Gwin. Frederick F. Low, formerly a governor and congressman, who knew Broderick personally, left behind a scathing portrait of him in a manuscript titled "Political Affairs in California," U.C. Berkeley. Arthur Quinn in his book *The Rivals: William Gwin and David Broderick, and the Birth of California*, sizes up the personally devastating effects of Broderick's political losses.

See too Russell Buchanan, *David S. Terry; the Dueling Judge*, 1956, p. 15, 102. Also, Theodore S. Hittell, *The History of San Francisco*, 307, Shuck, 260, 262, O'Meara, 163, 226, and Truman, 405–407. The *San Francisco Evening Post* article of October 5, 1878, is valuable. Most valuable is the groundbreaking work of James Shebl on the Ryer-Langdon Duel, which does much to place the Broderick-Terry duel in context.

Chapter 44: Duel of Infamy: Part Two

The most accurate appraisals of Broderick are in Hittell's work, pp 308–310; and in L. E. Fredman's "Broderick: A Reassessment," *Pacific Historical Review*. Other good sources on the duel are found in the works of Buchanan, p. 124, O'Meara, p. 226, 227; Shuck, 262, Thomas, 380, Truman, 400, 401, the *Sacramento Daily Union*, September 15, 1859, and the *San Francisco Call*, July 3, 1896.

Chapter 45: Duel at Moonlight Flat

See the *Calaveras Prospect*, April 13, 1880, the *San Andreas Independent*, September 17, 1859, *the San Diego Union*, October 10, 1968, the *San Francisco Examiner*, October 31, 1880, *San Francisco Evening Post*, March 21, 1896, and *Las Calaveras*, October 1966.

Chapter 46: Shootout in Visalia

Poems by Eulalie was published by Auburn Parlor #59, Native Sons of the Golden West pp, 3–14. See also *Sacramento Daily Union*, December. 26, 1854, the *Visalia Delta*, September 3 and October 18, 1860. More details of the gunfight were provided by Annie Mitchell, resident historian of Tulare County, in letter of 1 April 1988. For more on background of Morris see Bancroft, *Popular Tribunals*, 470, and C.A. Menefee, *Historical and Descriptive Sketch Book of Napa, Sonoma, Lake and Mendocino Counties*, p. 142.

Chapter 47: Sunrise on Mount Tam

San Francisco News Letter, May 22, 1884. Most important source is Clarence Clendenon,'s "Dan Showalter—California Secessionist," *California Historical Society Quarterly*, p. 311, 317, 319, 322, .323. Also, Aurora Hunt, *The Army of the Pacific*, p. 72, the *San Francisco Evening Post*, February 1, 1896, and the *San Joaquin Republican*, May 28, 1861.

Epilogue

See the *San Francisco Evening Post*, August 31, 1879, and the *San Francisco Examiner*, October 7, 1888. There were many extensive obituaries of McGowan including the *San Francisco Chronicle* of December 8, 1893. Billy Mulligan's last duel was reported in the *Alta California*, April 21, 26, 1864. Theodore S. Hittell and James O'Meara have a much clearer understanding of 1850s California politics than does Bancroft.

Bibliography

Books and Journals

Auburn Parlor Booklet #59, *Native Sons of the Golden West*, "Poems by Eulalie"

Baldick, Robert, *The Duel: A History of Dueling*, Clarkson B. Porter, Inc., 1965

Bancroft, Hubert H., *Popular Tribunals*, A.L. Bancroft Company, San Francisco, 1888

Barnes, George C., *Denver the Man*, Wilmington, Ohio, 1949

Bell, Horace, *Reminiscences of a Ranger*, W. Hebberd Company, Santa Barbara, 1927

Buchanan, Russell, *David S. Terry; the Dueling Judge*, Huntington Library, San Marino, 1956

Carr, Albert Z., *The World and William Walker*, Harper & Rowe, New York, 1963

Clendenon, Clarence, "Dan Showalter–California Secessionist," *California Historical Society Quarterly*, June 1981

Collins, Carvel, *Sam Ward in the Gold Rush*, Stanford University Press, 1948

Cowan, Robert E., "The Folsom-Leidesdorff Estate," *California Historical Society Quarterly*, June 1928

Downie, William H., *Hunting for Gold*, California Publishing Company, San Francisco, 1893

Foote, Shelby, *The Civil War: A Narrative*, Random House, New York, Volume I, 1958

Fredman, L.E., "Broderick: A Reassessment," *Pacific Historical Review*, February. 1961

Gates, Paul W., "Carpet Baggers Join the Rush for California Land," *California Historical Society Quarterly*, June, 1977

Giffen, Helen S., *Man of Destiny, Pierson Barton Reading*, Shasta Historical Society, Shasta, 1966

Hargis, Donald, "The Great Debate in California," *History Society of Southern California*, June, 1960

Haskins, C.W. *The Argonauts of California*, Fords, Howard & Hurlbert, San Francisco, 1890

Hittell, John S., *The History of San Francisco*, A.L. Bancroft Company, San Francisco, 1879

Hunt, Aurora, *The Army of the Pacific*, Arthur H. Clark Company, Glendale, 1951

Jenkins, J. Roy, *Saddlebags in the Siskiyous*

Johnson, J. Edward, *A History of the Supreme Court of California, 1850–1900*, Bender Moss, Sacramento, 1963

Johnson, Kenneth M., *The Strange Eventful Life of Parker H. French*, Glen Dawson, Los Angeles, 1958

Kemble, Edward, *A History of California Newspapers, 1846–1858*, edited by Helen Harding Bretner, 1962

Kennedy, Chester A., "Editors of the Northern Mines," Stanford Graduate Thesis, California Room, State Library, Sacramento

Lynch, Jeremiah, *A Senator for the Fifties*, A.A. Robertson Co., Los Angeles, 1911

Martin, V. Covert, *Stockton Album Through the Years*, College of the Pacific, Stockton, 1959

Melendy, H. Brett, "Who was John McDougal?" *Pacific Historical Review*, Volume 29

Menefee, C.A., *Historical and Descriptive Sketch Book of Napa, Sonoma, Lake and Mendocino Counties*, Reporter Publishing House, Sacramento, 1879

Nash, James Henry, *James Woods Coffroth*, San Francisco, 1926

Nevins, Allen, *Fremont: Pathmarker of the West*, Long, Green and Company, 1954

O'Meara, James, *Broderick and Gwin*, Bacon and Company, San Francisco, 1881

O'Meara, James "Editors of Early California," *Overland Monthly*, November 1889

Perkins, William, *Journal of Life at Sonora, 1849–52*, University California Press, Berkeley, 1964

Roper, William L., "Roy Bean fights a Duel," *Westways Magazine*, August 1954

Shebl, James, manuscript, "The Ryer-Langdon Duel," Master's degree thesis, at the University of the Pacific, Stockton

Michele Shover, 'The Doctor, the Lawyer and the Political Chief in the 1850s of Butte County,' *The University Journal*, Winter 1982, California State University, Chico

Shuck, Oscar T., *The Bench and Bar in California*, Occidental Publishing, San Francisco, 1889

Shumate, Albert, *The Notorious I..C. Woods of the Adams Express*, Arthur H. Clark Company, Glendale, 1986

Stewart, George R., *Committee of Vigilance: Revolution in San Francisco*, Houghton-Mifflin Company, New York, 1964

Swisher, Carl, Brent, *Stephen J. Field, Craftsman of the Law*, Brookings Institute, Washington, D.C. 1930

Thomas, Lately, *Between Two Empires; the Life Story of California's First Senator, William McKendree Gwin*, Houghton-Mifflin Company, New York, 1969

Tinkham, George H., *The History of San Joaquin County*, History Record Company, Stockton, 1923

Truman, Major Ben, *The Field of Honor*, Fords, Howard & Hurlburt, 1879

Wilhelm, John F., "Shootout at Oak Grove," *Golden Notes*, Volume 29, Sacramento Historical Society, Sacramento

Williams, David A., *David Broderick; A Political Portrait*, Huntington Library, San Marino, 1969

Newspapers
Alta California
Amador Ledger
Argonaut
Butte Enterprise Record
Butte Record
Calaveras Prospect
California Chronicle
Las Calaveras

Mariposa Gazette
Mariposa Star
Marysville California Express
Nevada Democrat
Nevada Journal
Oakland Post-Enquirer Placer Herald
Sacramento Daily Bee
Sacramento Union
San Andreas Independent
San Diego Union
San Francisco Chronicle
San Francisco Daily Examiner
San Francisco Daily Herald
San Francisco Evening Bulletin
San Francisco Evening Post
San Francisco Morning Call
San Francisco News Letter
San Joaquin Republican
Santa Cruz Sentinel
Shasta Courier
Shasta Republican
Sierra Citizen
Sonora Union-Democrat
Stockton Daily Argus
Stockton Daily Record
Themis
Trinity Journal
Visalia Delta

Other Documents
California Census, 1852
Mitchell, Annie, resident historian, Tulare County, letter of April 1, 1988

Illustration Credits

California Statue Supreme Court Justice Alexander Wells: Peter Bartczak

San Francisco County Sherriff Jack Hays: Peter Bartczak

Governor John McDougal: California Section, California State Library

San Francisco Daily Herald editor John Nugent: California Section, California State Library

Colonel Thomas Hayes: Peter Bartczak

Congressman and *Alta California* editor Edward Gilbert: California Section, California State Library

Alta California co-editors Edward Kemble and Edward Gilbert: California Section, California State Library

State Senator James W. Denver: Jesse Harrison Whitehurst

U.S. Senator William M. Gwin: California Section, California State Library

Judge Edward McGowan: Peter Bartczak

Governor John Bigler: California Section, California State Library

Governor John B. Weller: California Section, California State Library

Governor and U.S. Senator Milton Latham: *California Territorial Quarterly*, volume 85, p. 25

Stewart Menzies: Peter Bartczak

California State Senator Parker H. French: Engraving by S.F. Baker from ambrotype by Matthew Brady

William Walker: John Chester Buttre

California State Supreme Court Justice Hugh Campbell Murray: Peter Bartczak

Assemblyman George "Penn" Johnston: Peter Bartczak

California State Supreme Court Justice David Terry: California Section, California State Library

U.S. Senator David Broderick: Matthew Brady

Index

Ryer, Washington, 150-154, 182, 187
Ryerland, H. O., 100

Sacramento Baptist Church, 39, 126-128, 175
Sacramento Bee, 169
Sacramento Democratic Journal, 53-54
Sacramento Democratic State Journal, 43
Sacramento State Journal, 37, 103
Sacramento Tribune, 136
Sacramento Union, 5, 118, 179
San Francisco City Council, 50
San Francisco Daily Herald, 21-22, 47-50, 52, 76, 106
San Francisco Evening Bulletin, 144, 146-147
San Francisco Examiner, 108, 170
San Francisco Herald, 1, 55
San Francisco Pharo, 171
San Francisco Picayune, 1, 52
San Francisco Spectator, 171-172
San Francisco Times, 108
San Francisco Times and Transcript, 106-108
San Francisco Union, 3
San Francisco Vigilance Committee, 2-3, 28, 34, 39, 51, 57, 82, 143, 148-149, 178, 179

San Francisco Vigilantes, 108
San Francisco Whig, 45, 50
San Joaquin County Race Track, 155
San Joaquin Republican, 151
San Quentin Prison, 24, 167, 202
San Souci House, 51, 128
Sanchez, Jose Maria, 135
Saulnier, J. R., 96
Scannel, David, 117, 146
Scott, Alfred G., 94-96, 98, 111, 124
Scott, Walter, 47
Seabough, Samuel, 193
Seguin, Brandt, 87
Selover, Abia A., 102-103
Shafer, Frank, 156
Shakespeare, William, 43, 46
Shannon, John, 194-196
Sheridan, 157
Showalter, Dan, 189, 198-200, 203
Sierra Citizen, 130-131
(Deputy Sheriff) Simmons, 124
Sinclair, Catherine, 110-111
Siskiyou County Hospital, 172
(Captain) Skerrett, 123-124
Slavery, 165-167, 178-180, 182-183
Slocum, 139
Smith, Austin E., 140, 143
Smith, Caleb, 37, 39, 140-143
Smith, Edward "Ned," 132-133

Smith, J. A., 192
Smith, Kirby, 201
Smith, Peter, 94, 98, 111, 144
Smith, Samuel, 200
Smith, William X. "Extra Billy," 37
Snyder, Jacob, 144
Society of Natural History, 151
Somers, Charles, 96
Sons of Temperance League, 130-132
Speare, William S., 40-42
Spence, John, 156
Sportsman's Flat, 41
State Marine Hospital, 83, 98-99
Stevenson, John, 1, 14, 20, 32, 52
Stewart, Frank, 69-71
Stidger, Oliver P., 47, 89-93, 111, 174
Stiles, C. W., 46
Stockton, Robert, 17
Stockton Insane Asylum, 59, 151, 153
Stockton Daily Argus, 4, 116, 152
Stoneman, George, 156
Strong, John, 149
Stovall, James, 166
Sullivan, Eugene L., 167
Sullivan, Yankee, 28, 48, 146
Swartwout, John, 10
Swasey, William S., 33

Taylor, Andrew Jackson "Natchez," 50, 69, 95, 112, 114, 167, 172-173, 186
Teel, Louis, 58
Tefft, Henry A., 15-16, 37
Tejon Indian Reservation, 116-117

223

About the Author

Christopher Burchfield has been writing about Gold Rush history for more than three decades with articles published in numerous magazines and newspapers, including *The Californians*, *California Mining Journal*, *The California Territorial*, *California Highway Patrol*, and *Old West* and *True West* magazines. Christopher and his wife Genendal live in Chico, California.

New Books on the West

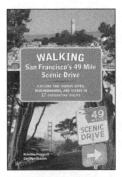

$16.95
($21.95 Canada)

Walking San Francisco's 49 Mile Scenic Drive

Explore the Famous Sites, Neighborhoods, and Vistas in 17 Enchanting Walks

by Kristine Poggioli and Carolyn Eidson

Walking San Francisco's 49 Mile Scenic Drive takes you the length of the famous 49 Mile Drive in 17 bite-size walks, complete with turn-by-turn instructions, maps, and historical facts—a perfect guidebook for today's urban enthusiast who values walkable neighborhoods, hyperlocal culture, and the pleasure of walking..

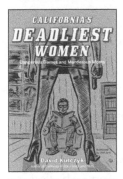

$14.95
($18.95 Canada)

California's Deadliest Women

Dangerous Dames and Murderous Moms

by David Kulczyk

A masterpiece of pure trashy tabloid fun, **California's Deadliest Women** is the definitive guide to the murderesses of the Golden State, a horrifying compendium of women driven to kill by jealousy, greed, desperation, or their own inner demons. From Brynn Hartman, who killed her husband, comedian Phil Hartman, to chemist Larissa Schuster, who dissolved her husband in acid, these 28 killers show the fairer sex can be as deadly as any man.

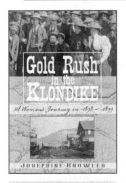

$22.95
($28.95 Canada)

Gold Rush in the Klondike

A Woman's Journey in 1898–1899

by Josephine Knowles

Never before published, **Gold Rush in the Klondike** is Josephine Knowles' personal memoir of day-to-day life in the height of the Klondike Gold Rush. A Victorian gentlewoman of refinement, Knowles endured cold, disease, and malnutrition, and won the friendship and trust of the miners for her stoicism, courage, and compassion. Knowles presents terrifying struggles against a hostile environment, picturesque descriptions of an untouched Arctic wilderness and keen observations of men and women on the frontier.

Secrets of California History

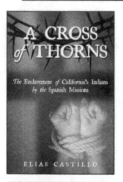

Wild West California

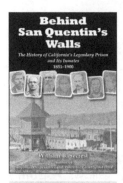

$18.95
($19.95 Canada)

Behind San Quentin's Walls

The History of California's Legendary Prison and Its Inmates, 1851–1900

by William B. Secrest

Behind San Quentin's Walls uncovers San Quentin's unlikely beginnings as a real estate scheme, its sorry early record of mismanagement, and its essential role in taming lawless Gold Rush California. Filled with exciting true stories of gunfights, brawls, prison riots, daring escapes, and intrepid manhunts, **Behind San Quentin's Walls** is a must-read for every fan of Western history.

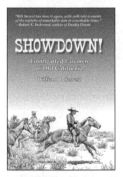

$15.95
($17.95 Canada)

Showdown!

Lionhearted Lawmen of Old California

by William B. Secrest,

In the 1850s and 1860s, San Francisco and Los Angeles were deadly frontier towns where a lawman's nerves and trigger finger were the only line between murder and justice, or life and death. In **Showdown!**, you'll meet six forgotten California lawmen who never made it into the dime novels, but settled their cases in a cloud of gunsmoke to civilize an untamed state. Lavishly illustrated with period photos, these true tales vividly describe a time long gone.

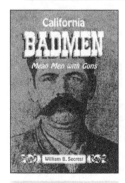

$15.95
($17.95 Canada)

California Badmen

Mean Men with Guns

by William B. Secrest

In **California Badmen** you will find little-known desperadoes and gunmen who couldn't stay out of trouble if they tried. Here are true stories of men who spit in the eye of the devil as they relentlessly pursued what was often a bloody destiny. Read **California Badmen** and ride the hills and dales of Old California, where you will meet some of the most unrepentant scoundrels ever born.

Available from bookstores, online bookstores, and
CravenStreetBooks.com, or by calling toll-free 1-800-345-4447.

California True Crime

$16.95
($18.95 Canada)

Folsom's 93
The Lives and Crimes of Folsom Prison's Executed Men
by April Moore

Illustrated with haunting prison photographs hidden from the public for nearly 70 years, *Folsom's 93* presents the full stories of all 93 men executed at Folsom from 1895 to 1937—their origins, their crimes, the investigations that brought them to justice, their trials, and their deaths at the gallows. *Folsom's 93* brings the crimes and punishments of a vanished era into sharp and realistic life.

$24.95
($27.95 Canada)

Hands Through Stone
How Clarence Ray Allen Masterminded Murder from Behind Folsom's Prison Walls
by James A. Ardaiz

A true crime story that reads like an intricate mystery novel, *Hands Through Stone* reveals the true story behind California's Fran's Market murders and their psychopathic mastermind, Clarence Ray Allen. Written by James Ardaiz, the prosecutor who built the case against Allen, *Hands Through Stone* gives an insider's view of a cold-blooded murderer and the tireless multi-year investigation that brought him to justice.

$14.95
($16.95 Canada)

California Fruits, Flakes and Nuts
True Tales of California Crazies, Crackpots, and Creeps
by David Kulczyk

A freewheeling catalog of misfits, eccentrics, creeps, criminals and failed dreamers, *California Fruits, Flakes and Nuts* relates the hilarious and heartbreaking lives of 48 bizarre personalities who exemplify California's well-deserved reputation for nonconformity. It's a side-splitting, shocking, and salacious salute to the people who made California the strangest place on earth.

Available from bookstores, online bookstores, and CravenStreetBooks.com, or by calling toll-free 1-800-345-4447.